PENGUIN BOOKS
SANG KANCIL

James Chai is a Malaysian writer, researcher, and political analyst. His work has been cited internationally by outlets such as *CNN*, *Bloomberg*, *Washington Post*, *NBC*, *Reuters*, *The Diplomat*, *Nikkei Asia*, *South China Morning Post*, *Business Times*, *The Straits Times*, *Phoenix Weekly*, *The Paper*, *Taiwan News*, and others. As a columnist for *Malaysiakini* and *Sin Chew Daily*, Malaysia's largest English and Mandarin news sites respectively, he has written over 250 articles on Malaysia. He is also a regular guest on TV and radio—internationally for media such as Channel News Asia, NPR, Al Jazeera, WION News India; and locally for Astro Awani, Astro AEC, and BFM. During his time as a Visiting Fellow at ISEAS-Yusof Ishak Institute, he published papers on Malaysian youths' political inclinations and the structure of political parties in Malaysia. He is also the author of two book chapters on Malaysia's fourteenth and fifteenth general elections for the same institution.

He holds a graduate degree from the University of Oxford (Best Student) and a first-class law degree from Queen Mary, University of London. He also graduated top of class at the Malaysian legal qualification exam. He became the first recipient of The Fan Yew Teng Grant for Independent Writing 2023 for this book.

James now lives in Kuala Lumpur with no cats (working on it) and no dogs. Above all, he believes that the most important thing in life is to do interesting things and hope they pay the bills.

'The conventional wisdom is that big social changes require large-scale confrontational—even violent—movements, led by charismatic heroes. Built around extraordinary stories of integrity, courage, and action by seven ordinary Malaysians, this book directly challenges the idea. In this eye-opening book, James Chai shows how apparently small actions based on common decency can have huge transformative consequences if they are pursued with bravery and in solidarity. This book will change the way we understand social transformation—and thus the way our societies are transformed—in the coming years.'
        —**Ha-Joon Chang, Professor at SOAS University of London, and author of *Economics: The User's Guide* and *Edible Economics—A Hungry Economist Explains the World***

'In this luminous book, James Chai records the stories of seven "ordinary" Malaysians who show what is possible when decency, courage, and kindness guide human action. Those whose remarkable stories are told range from a grandmother and former school teacher who became the face of one of Malaysia's largest protest movements to a middle-ranking public servant whose secret recording led to the charging of former prime Minister Najib Razak over the 1MDB scandal; from a group of Sikhs who fed and cared for thousands of people during one of Malaysia's worst floods to a Dayak engineer whose grassroots movement stopped the construction of a mega-dam on one of Sarawak's great rivers. But the book is much more than a set of stories, inspirational though these are. Importantly, Chai uses the stories to map a way forward for all of us who want to make a difference in this world but cannot see how to do it.

Sang Kancil is a powerful, beautiful book. It shows us that in an increasingly fraught and divided world, true leadership is often not to be found in our formal 'leaders' but rather in quiet, humble folk who are driven by a simple sense of what is right. Chai reminds us that the finest elements of humanity are all around us if only we look in the right places. His vivid, compelling narration of these stories will have you thinking about them—and pondering their lessons—long after you lay the book down. *Sang Kancil* is compulsory reading for anyone who yearns to make the world a better place.'

—Christine Helliwell, Emeritus Professor at Australian National University and author of *Semut: The Untold Story of a Secret Australian Operation in WWII Borneo*, winner of the Australian Prime Minister's Literary Award

'James Chai's [book] begins with Malaysians' frustration with their political masters. He states, "The antidote to disillusionment is hope". This book starts from "hope"—this hope. The metaphor given is *Sang Kancil*, a small animal that has a big mind and can defeat an enormous enemy. Chai portrays several characters from our multiracial Malaysian society, who fight against the power that looms over them. The use of *Sang Kancil* (mousedeer) as a symbol of the underdog warrior is highly appropriate, and brings an element of folklore to these stories of ordinary Malaysians. All of them are the mousedeers—they are brave and understand how to resolve dilemmas.'

—Muhammad Haji Salleh, Judge's citation for The Fan Yew Teng Grant for Independent Writing 2023

'We all need heroes, and in Malaysia even more so. The past few years have been rough on the psyches of Malaysians, and *Sang Kancil* offers these superheroes (sans capes and masks) to the reader, teaching them absolute resolve and resilience. If you believe you can, you will, but if you don't, you won't.'

—Dina Zaman, bestselling author of *I Am Muslim*

'Rarest presentation of literature. Compilation of small voices making giant moves. A collection of oral history on how ordinary people can shape the world.'

—Faisal Tehrani, author of *1515* and winner of Malaysia's National Art Award

Words by James Chai
Illustrations by Ida Thien

Winner of The Fan Yew Teng Grant
for Independent Writing 2023

Sang Kancil

A Tale about How Ordinary Malaysians Defied the Odds

James Chai

PENGUIN BOOKS

An imprint of Penguin Random House

PENGUIN BOOKS

USA | Canada | UK | Ireland | Australia
New Zealand | India | South Africa | China | Southeast Asia

Penguin books is part of the Penguin Random House group of companies
whose addresses can be found at global.penguinrandomhouse.com

Published by Penguin Random House SEA Pte Ltd
9, Changi South Street 3, Level 08-01,
Singapore 486361

First published in Penguin books by Penguin Random House SEA 2023

ISBN 9789815127133

Typeset in Adobe Garamond Pro by MAP Systems, Bengaluru, India

www.penguin.sg

To the ordinary people who try, and Malaysia,
my favourite underdog in the world

'Our deepest fear is not that we are inadequate.
Our deepest fear is that we are powerful beyond measure.'
—Marianne Williamson[1]

---

[1] Often misattributed to a giant named Nelson Mandela.

Contents

How to Read this Book

One of my favourite books is Ha-Joon Chang's *Economics: The User's Guide*. Before starting the first chapter of the book, it has a section called 'How to Read this Book'. I found the honesty refreshing. Writers try to convince themselves that all readers are ideal readers who will flip through every page. But we know that is not true. Most readers, especially for non-fiction, do not go through every page. Non-fiction books are also not meant to be read in a linear way. The best you could hope for is that at least *some* insights are picked up rather than none. So, this is my attempt of imitating the master's method. After all, what good is a book if it is not at least partially read?

If you have only 10 minutes . . . I would encourage you to read the final chapter called 'What We Can Do'. This chapter encapsulates universal lessons that can be applied in our daily lives to make our country better. It is the 'so-what' of the book after spending a few hundred pages giving examples of what other inspiring Malaysian underdogs have done.

If you have only 30 minutes . . . I would encourage you to read the subtitle of each chapter and the final boxed section of 'Key Takeaways', as well as the final chapter. The key takeaways are supposed to show you *how* the underdogs have succeeded in their unique ways. This would give more context to the final chapter, hopefully persuading you to take action.

If you have only 1 hour . . . I would encourage you to browse the 'Contents' page and decide if there is one chapter that is worth reading in its entirety. Each chapter is written like creative non-fiction with the consideration of a theory that undergirds the event(s). Other than reading a good story, I hope that you can at least pick up a thing or two from reading an interesting chapter.

If you are intrigued and willing to put aside other important things to read this book in its entirety . . . I would be most delighted. I consider myself lucky to have found interesting stories for this book that cover different angles and converge to a central theme of underdogs' success. The most nerve-racking part of putting a book out is to hear from readers who have read and considered my work seriously. If this book made you think, I hope you can talk about it with your friends and family. When you see this book on your bookshelf again, I hope you are reminded of the power of the ordinary.

Chapter 1

Sang Kancil

Famous Mousedeer Folklore in Southeast Asia

Facing the romantic Seine River of Paris[1] is one of the oldest libraries in the world, called the Bibliothèque Nationale de France. Church books confiscated by hot-blooded revolutionaries and Napoleon's overseas loot in the eighteenth century formed the earliest collections at the library. Since then, the library has massively expanded to host up to twelve million documents—books, magazines, sheet music, prints, audio, and the oldest modern and medieval manuscripts in the world.

Among the manuscripts was a 120-page small booklet, measuring 15 cm by 12 cm, written in Arabic with legible lamp-black ink. The first page was missing, and the few pages after were ragged and fragile. A mosquito was trapped and suffocated between the pages; insects crawled and poked holes; betel juice and watermarks stained the thin and whitish handmade paper.

The booklet is a funny and fast-moving epic about one of the smallest creatures in the jungle who battled larger giants through a series of underdog tactics. This story, passed down orally as folklore, has lived in the minds of Malaysians for hundreds of years, the way Brer Rabbit did for southern Americans, Anansi the Spider for West Africans, and Reynard the Fox for Europeans. Any boy or girl in Malaysia could tell you stories about this. The manuscript was entitled *Hikayat Pelanduk*

---

[1] The Seine has featured in famous impressionist paintings by Monet and Renoir. Joan of Arc's ashes were also scattered in this river after her death.

Jenaka (*The Wily Mousedeer*), and later became popularly known as *Hikayat Sang Kancil*.

Its central character, Sang Kancil, was a mousedeer, weighing only a few kilograms and reaching below 30 cm. 'It is an animal about the size of a cat . . . It has the legs and the tail of a deer, and the face and the body of a mouse—but it is not really a mouse or a deer,' described one storyteller. It is the smallest deer in the world that eats only vegetables and prefers to lay under water to avoid the predatory assault of larger animals. It has wide eyes and a small stubby tail, with front legs shorter than the hind. It has no special gifts—in fact, it is timid and easily frightened. Yet, its miraculous victories and survival became one of Malaysia's favourite folklore that was passed down through generations.

Over the generations there have been many versions of this story. But the manuscript started like this, 'This is a tale from olden days . . .'

* * *

After a full lunch of vegetables and fruits, Kancil was thirsty. She went to the river for a drink. But she knew that many crocodiles were quietly waiting underwater to eat her.

'I wonder if the water's warm today . . . I'll put my leg in and find out,' said Kancil. She took a stick with her mouth and used it to reach the water.

Chomp! A crocodile grabbed the stick and pulled it into the water.

Kancil knew that she could only drink water in another river that didn't have crocodiles, but she would need to cross this river to get there. So, she had an idea.

'Crocodile!' said Kancil. 'I have been ordered by the King to take a census, so come to the top of the water and line up.'

Upon hearing the summons, the crocodiles lined up in a row from one end of the riverbank to the other. Kancil jumped on their backs and counted out loud. 'One, two, three, four, five . . .'

When Kancil reached the other end of the river, she cheekily yelled back, 'Crocodiles! I fooled you. Thank you for making me a bridge!'

The crocodiles grew angry and started growling in anger, but Kancil ran off swiftly.

When Kancil arrived at the other part of the jungle, she picked fruits from the trees to quench her thirst. Suddenly, the leaves around her started to ruffle, and a loud roar was heard behind her. Vertical brown and black stripes appeared and disappeared among the green leaves.

'Have you come out today to be my lunch?' asked the tiger rhetorically.

Kancil knew that it was too late to run. The hair behind her neck stood up in fear. Then she had an idea. She picked up a large leaf from the ground and covered up some water-buffalo faeces she had found. Then she took a large banana leaf and started fanning the faeces.

When the tiger saw Kancil up close, he asked, 'What are you doing, so that your hands move like that?'

Kancil did not answer but continued to fan the object.

The tiger's face turned red. 'Hey, Kancil! It seems you're a mute! You better run away now for you're in a bad situation. Why are you still here?'

'Hello, tiger. My, but you look old and tired today. You must be a very great fool if you can't tell what I'm doing. Well, I'll tell you. I'm fanning a feast that belongs to the King. I am entrusted to guard it for him,' replied Kancil.

'If what you say is true, why am I not entrusted to do it for the King instead? I am stronger than you, and my teeth are sharp. See?' said the tiger, showing his sharp white teeth. 'Let me have a taste of this royal feast!'

'The King doesn't allow anyone to come close to it,' said Kancil.

The tiger grew madder. *Rowr!*

'Kancil, if you don't be quiet and go away, I will split open your head. Who do you think you are, addressing me in such an impolite tone? Do you want me to chew you up?'

'Be patient, tiger,' said Kancil. 'Don't misunderstand me, for I'm speaking the truth. If you want to risk eating this feast, I won't stop you. But there is one condition: I must leave here first. You can eat it after I've gone away. That way, I will not see you eat this royal meal, and therefore, neither of us will be disobeying the King.'

'All right, you can go now!' said the tiger.

Kancil sprinted off as fast as she could. The tiger, with his greedy nature, devoured the meal in a mouthful.

'Yuck, ugh! That's not a royal meal!' the tiger shouted. In seconds, he started vomiting, becoming increasingly mad at Kancil who had forced him to eat faeces.

'If I meet you, I'll split your head open and eat your bones!' the tiger said, pacing as fast as he could to find Kancil. But Kancil had long disappeared to the darker parts of the woods, safe from being eaten by the tiger.

* * *

Besides the crocodiles and the tiger, Kancil was forced to confront a series of larger animals who wanted to eat her throughout the epic: Bears, ogres, goats, elephants, and an army of monkeys. At every turn, Kancil had to outthink her opponents so that she could compensate for her significant lack of physical advantage and survive.

In a jungle, physical strength is the most important survival toolkit. Lions and tigers rule the animal kingdom because they are physically superior. Kancil lacked significant physical strength; the only thing she had was her intellect. This supposed jungle weakness, however, transformed into her unique advantage, and on each occasion, it spared her an exit opportunity that she exploited with her light and nimble body to escape. Further, in all her ideas, Kancil used the opponents' weakness against them. In the crocodile episode, she used the crocodiles' unthinking and blind submission to authority to form a bridge for her to cross. In the tiger episode, she used the tiger's greed for a royal feast to trap him into eating water-buffalo faeces, buying herself time to run away into safety.

This book draws parallels with the century-old folklore that lives on in the minds of Malaysians. We will investigate two key organizing theories throughout this book. First, the value of being an underdog. While we are dear to underdog sports teams and storied protagonists, we almost never wish to be put in an underdog situation with little prospect of success. Being an underdog may be theoretically romantic, but we certainly do not think it is ideal or necessary to assume such a position. I want to challenge that notion and show that carrying ordinary traits without the semblance of giftedness and genius—and occasionally, even disadvantages—may work to our benefit if we know how to use them. What explains our resonance with underdogs? Is there a benefit in being underestimated? Is there an advantage in being overlooked and invisible to the power at the top?

Second, to recast light on power and what it means to be powerful. Our traditional assumptions of power, created and sustained through formal authority and tools of legitimacy, may not hold upon further investigation. A brutal government with a high concentration of power may deploy censorship and prosecution tools to silence its critics—but is there a breaking point where silencing tools are not only ineffective, but also counterproductive? Today, our perception of a charismatic, articulate, strongman leader who can save us from a country's mess persists throughout southeast Asia—but have these qualities created the most success, or have faceless, humble, quiet leaders made the biggest difference to history? In grassroots activism, we have traditionally assumed that to drive real change, we need movers and shakers from the highest rungs of power—but what if a collection of weak ties consisting of acquaintances is the secret formula for successful activism? What if the key to excel in what you do is to do what nobody does, including taking risks and running into conflict?

The seven stories that will be shared in this book are stories of individuals whose names rarely make the news, but who have shaped our society in fundamental and profound ways. By virtue of being underdogs, they have shied away from taking credit and drawing attention to themselves, resulting in their being overlooked and forgotten by most of us. This book is an attempt to memorialize their underdog success, and to remind ourselves of the possibility of creating outsized victories through small actions.

I will take you to the scene of Malaysia's largest protest through the eyes of one of the oldest participants who emerged as the face of inspiration. I will take you to Cambridge to see how a Malaysian doctor made pathbreaking findings in cancer research and became the first female awardee of the 'Nobel Prize for Cancer Research'. I will let you eavesdrop into a high-profile conversation between Malaysian officials in one of the largest white-collar scandals in the world. I will show you how one of the most memorable artworks in Malaysia got made by a punk designer and how it changed hearts and minds of millions. I will walk with you in a small indigenous village in Baram, Sarawak, and tell you how one retiree saved his childhood village from total destruction. I will swim with you in the muddy waters of one of the largest floods in modern Malaysia and remember how a group of gurdwara-going devotees saved the lives of thousands and gave them dignity. I will bring you to the battlefields of Afghanistan and show you how a man born in the suburban parts of Malaysia captured a few of humanity's most important photos.

Sang Kancil has always lived among Malaysians. Revered author Benedict Anderson once talked about how cultural artefacts like the Sang Kancil stories have the capability of being transplanted into the national consciousness and forming a national identity. Similar to Sang Kancil, these seven underdogs were put against the grave odds when they tried to challenge status quo. By taking ordinary steps in an unconventional way, they succeeded in overcoming the giant forces of authoritarian rule, patriarchy, corruption, censorship, corporate greed, natural disasters, and war.

We live in a time of deep polarization and grave disillusionment with political institutions. More and more, people do not believe that better days will come. Oddly, this encourages people to turn to popular strongmen who promise the sky and the moon. The story of Sang Kancil and the seven underdogs in this book are meant to remind us that we never needed to wait for a saviour to change the country for the better—the power was always within us. Extraordinary events always start from ordinary acts by ordinary people like you and me.

* * *

Running away from attacks, a prince panted unceasingly with his men and moved to rest under the shade of a Malacca tree. A few minutes later, Kancil hopped right out of the forest after being chased by a few animals, flinging them off her coattails. One of the prince's dogs thought that Kancil was about to attack its prince, and thus charged towards her.

Kancil, using her featherlight weight, spread her body and ducked, and the rapidly moving dog was thrown to the sea under its own weight.

The prince was startled and stood on his feet. 'This is a fine place!' he said, taking it as a predestined sign. 'Even the mousedeer here are full of courage!'

The prince, whose name was Paramesvara, asked his men to take note of the name of the tree and went on to found the first kingdom in the land that would eventually be known as Malaysia.

Key takeaways

- The Sang Kancil (mousedeer) folklore is about the story of underdogs.
- To succeed against giants, underdogs do not need extraordinary talents or genius. They only need to adopt ordinary acts consistently, collectively, and unconventionally.
- Giants are not as powerful as they first seem.

Part I

The Power of the Ordinary

Chapter 2

Aunty Bersih (Anne Ooi)

How a sixty-four-year-old Chinese aunty became the face of the largest protest in Malaysia and why we identify with underdogs

'They see themselves in this frail, elderly woman holding a flower protesting against an unjust government.'

1

Anne Ooi is always late, even to the biggest event of the year—the Bersih protest.[2] You see, she is a clean freak. In her 800-square-foot flat in Setapak, Kuala Lumpur, she needs to clean every corner before she leaves the home. She lives alone. Her four children, all born before Anne turned twenty-eight, are spread across two states and two countries. Even then, the sixty-four-year-old has a tendency to get so engrossed with house chores that she loses track of time.

'As far as my eyes can see, it must be clean,' she often says. 'God has given us so much. The least we could do is to take care of them—make sure they're clean.'

She has figured out an efficient way to make sure her flat is always clean. After each cup of room-temperature sweet tea (she has two cups at a time), she washes them immediately. She cuts her trousers to make them short and thin so they dry easily. She cuts her grey hair short so long strands won't clog the toilet drain. She sweeps the community stairs and pulls out the weeds from the common lawn every other day.

'She will always find something to do around the house,' her daughter, Elaine, told me. 'Once, after she'd dusted the bookshelf, she started arranging the books by title. And then, the next day by height. And then, the next day by colour.'

In her spotless home, she allows only one major cleaning exception: The Drawing Wall. Behind the three-seater sofa is a giant pink wall that was scribbled by the two granddaughters she helped raise.[3] When they were young, Anne would teach them to love the little wonders of the world. To hold their hands over her mouth to feel the shape of words, to squat and watch how a praying mantis moves, and to decorate The Drawing Wall with anything their hearts desired—stars, rainbows, cats,

---

[2] Bersih ('clean' in Malay) was a coalition of NGOs advocating for free and fair elections. Eventually the movement grew and advocated for various reforms with the primary aim of replacing the sixty-one-year-old Barisan Nasional government.

[3] Other granddaughters, like Kayla, also scribbled here.

'No Smoking' signs, Dora the Explorer, or a giant dinosaur blowing a flame that reads 'God Bless You'.[4]

Every time Anne's two granddaughters, Keeva and Tierna, saw her, they shrieked and jumped up and down with both their legs in the air, calling their grandmother 'Nana!' And off they went on unending adventures. In the morning, Anne would bring them to a giant trampoline at their neighbour's house and jump high into the air and shout out funny phrases and giggle together. In the afternoon, Anne would bring them to the river that had waterfalls flushing down from above. She would give her granddaughters colour pencils and ask them to draw what they saw while their feet soaked in the cold, clear water. Before the sun set, in front of a closed bank office, Anne would give her granddaughters ten seconds to hide as she closed her eyes and started catching them at hidden corners.

Keeva and Tierna never seemed to tire whenever Anne was around. The three of them would tie colourful clothes on the living room poles and sing and dance to their favourite songs.[5] When Elaine warned them against staying up too late, Keeva and Tierna would tiptoe to Anne's room and sleep beside Anne into the morning.

Things got out of hand one holiday break. Anne was hosting a dinner with her friends and family. Earlier in the day, Keeva was caught hiding behind the kitchen cabinet stuffing herself with chocolates. During dinner that night, Keeva was excited about the fizzy drinks and poured them into her mouth like a water fountain. Then her face started turning green. Vomit flew out of her mouth in horizontal projection. Everyone was shocked and stared at her. Only Anne rushed to pick her up. Keeva vomited again on Anne's clothes. Anne didn't deflect or avoid. She just brought her to the toilet and washed her up, all the while patting and comforting a crying Keeva.

'If anyone asks me what my Nana is like, I will say she is the most amazing person on earth,' Keeva and Tierna would say. A lot of Anne's

---

[4] Anne's son, Kevin, drew a lot of characters too, including Dora the Explorer because he thought Tierna looked like her.

[5] Anne said that as long as the song is upbeat and happy, that would be her favourite song.

characteristics have been passed on to the two girls. 'Without her, half of me is broken.'[6]

When they heard that their Nana was going to a dangerous protest alone, they were worried. Elaine called Anne to ask a repeated, though futile, question.

'Mom, are you sure you're going to the rally?' asked Elaine.

'Yes, why not?' replied Anne.

'Are you going to wear the yellow T-shirt there?' Elaine followed up. The yellow T-shirt had been banned by the government a few days before the rally to prevent people from attending the rally. This was part of the government's fear tactics to suppress dissent.

'Why can't I wear yellow?' Anne replied nonchalantly. Threats and intimidation didn't bother Anne too much. For her, expressing discontent against a corrupt government was important, especially with the gradually worsening state of affairs. She was not the kind of person who would just take things as they were.

On that humid July day of 2011, Anne put on her banned yellow T-shirt, together with black trousers, matching shoes, and a pouch around her waist. She put her Identification Card (IC), mobile phone, house keys, and a few spare ringgits into her pouch. When she took the bus from Setapak to the city centre, she was already late. What she didn't know was that she would not come back the same any more.

* * *

Two weeks before the actual protest on 9 July 2011, Ambiga Sreenevasan, the former Bar Council chairwoman and the protest organizer, received a death threat that was circulated to a few protest leaders:

> *Don't you have any sense? Why should you support that pariah [racially-charged expletives] Ambiga? She is a scorned infidel. Don't you know*

---

[6] Elaine told me: 'There's this ugly mangy-looking cat hand-me-down soft toy that my mother [Anne] picked up somewhere. She washed it and gave it to Keeva and Tierna. It has the most hideous face but they loved it. I still can't get rid of that toy today.'

that she is a tool of those political dogs who are out to destroy the Malays.
She claims she wants to clean up the Election Commission. Clean up her
father's head . . .

I am warning you. If this rally takes place, my people and I will
kill Ambiga and those around her one by one, including these stupid
politicians who are hand-in-hand with this scorned infidel . . . this is my
warning. You watch.

(Anonymous SMS message of death threat)

At another instance, a right-wing extremist group Perkasa printed
Ambiga Sreenevasan's photo in black and white—described as 'a
dangerous Hindu woman'—and stomped on it with their feet before
burning it up in flames as a warning for those holding the protest.

'[If] the Bersih rally is not cancelled . . . [they] would have to
stock food at home. Anything can happen on that day,' said its leader,
Ibrahim Ali, implying a willingness to incite a riot similar to the worst
racial riot in 1969.[7]

The police and the government did not rein in on these extremist
elements that could threaten the social fabric. Instead, they escalated
the conflict between the peaceful protestors and authorities. In the
lead-up to the protest, 2,136 police reports were filed against Bersih,
and 225 Bersih supporters were arrested and called in for hours of
questioning. The then prime minister warned against chaos and said
that if anything untoward happened, the blame would lay on Bersih's
shoulders; the home minister called the rally 'illegal'.

People started spotting police and riot control officers surrounding
the city centre in the days leading up to the protest. More and more
people decided to stay home. From Anne's apartment complex, only
two other residents were going. A taxi driver she once met at the bus
station told Anne that it was a waste of time to attend the rally. They
entered a quarrel with the taxi driver asking her to go back to China
(she was born in Malaysia).

---

[7] The riot of 13 May 1969 was a deadly incident between the ethnic Malay and Chinese
of Malaysia at the capital of Kuala Lumpur. The number of casualties is disputed, but it
is widely considered one of the worst racial conflicts that is a taboo to discuss in public
and private.

For people who were brave enough to go, they did not let anyone know. They had a covert plan for the day. Lay low and keep your yellow T-shirt in your bag. Travel with friends but not in large groups. Do not make eye contact with any enforcers on that day. Wear a comfortable pair of shoes. Bring IC, mobile phone, and a small bottle of water. And a bag of salt.

Anne knew that her family would be worried. She was not a politician or a minister. She was not the Attorney General or a Malaysian Anti-Corruption Commission officer. She was just a grey-haired, scrawny sixty-four-year-old, who was no taller than a postbox. The only thing she could do was to get on the streets and make her voice heard. Like how she helped the homeless at her flat, it was better for her to do something small than to sit idly while her country rotted.

'I cannot stand rubbish. The country today has become like a house full of dirty things. We need to clean our house, clear up the mess,' she said.

'I'm marching at the rally for my grandchildren and all our children. My energy is limited, but my spirit is willing. Hope always runs strong in every human heart; we hope until hope dies itself.'

2

For thirty-five years, Anne was a teacher at a Malaysian national secondary school. She taught English, geography, and arts for forty hours a week. But she often had to use these lessons to teach other subjects because many of the teachers at her school were not up to par.

'I used my English class to teach my students mathematics because the mathematics teachers didn't teach anything during those classes—they just let the students do anything they wanted,' said Anne.

She got into fights with the principals who perpetuated a system of mediocrity, which saw the quality of education fall steeply over the decades. When the workload couldn't catch up with teacher supply, Anne had to teach students outside her cohort—a Form 1 teacher teaching Form 3 students. To rub salt over the wound, she saw undeserving teachers promoted over her because of favouritism.

But she couldn't say much, because as a civil servant, she was taught to stay silent, either directly through warnings or indirectly through the threat of losing her pensions. The culture of fear pervaded the schools; nobody spoke about politics, nobody went against the authority.

As a teacher, Anne was feared and loved by the students. The moment she set foot in a classroom, it would turn silent. Twice the height of her class students, tidily dressed with hands tucked on her slender waist, Anne's loud voice would travel to the back of the class and echo to the front. To her, being on your best behaviour to learn was important; she demanded her students' full attention.

Her students remember Anne's handwriting the most. Her cursives on the blackboard were memorable—evenly spaced, consistently sized, gracefully slanted, with unique embellishments. Her first letter 'a' would be exactly the same as her twenty-sixth letter 'a'. Her hand writes like a refined typewriter—she calls this 'God's gift'.

Ong Khoon Chye was one of her students. Big, shy, and smart, Khoon Chye was always first in class, and he was Anne's class monitor.

'I really had a hard time understanding English at school,' recalled Ong. 'Imagine your whole life only knowing Chinese, and now every subject had to be changed to English and Malay . . . We would get confused with simple words like "accept" and "except" and Teacher Anne was really patient to make sure we got it.'

That year was a turning point for Khoon Chye. He awoke to the tragedy of his father, the main breadwinner of the family, passing away. To make ends meet, Khoon Chye started a part-time job during the day. At 6.30 a.m. every day, he went to a nearby *Kuey Teow* stall to help with preparing, cleaning, and serving. When the clock struck 11.30 a.m., he would rush back, grab a bite, take a quick shower, pack his bag, and go to school before 1.10 p.m. At night, he would complete his homework and start the next day again.

Anne noticed a change in Khoon Chye. His grades started falling, his homework became sloppy, and he would sometimes doze off in class.

One day, they met at a bus station after work.

'Come teach my four kids, and I'll pay you every month,' said Anne. Khoon Chye was good at mathematics so that was what he taught.

Though Anne's salary was meagre, she paid Khoon Chye RM60 every month (approximately RM200 in today's terms).[8] This helped Khoon Chye get by so he could pay attention to his studies without working at a hawker stall.

When they grew close, Anne would invite Khoon Chye to their family gatherings.[9] He cycled with the children around Penang Hill. Once, Elaine fell and hurt herself. Khoon Chye expected Anne to rush over, pick up her children, and fuss over the fall like most Chinese families he knew. But she didn't. Elaine picked herself up and continued cycling.

'I've never seen something like that before,' recalled Khoon Chye. 'The children could speak their mind, do what they wanted, and Anne would just allow it.'[10]

When others called Anne's children 'beautiful' or 'handsome', Anne would reply, 'No use! Handsome no use! Pretty no use!' Good looks, like wealth and power, are useless if you are not good inside. It didn't even matter whether her children did well in class or achieved great success in their career—a life lived in service of others as the hallmark of a good child for her.

No matter how hard she tried to provide the best for her students and children, the institutional ills of the country exacerbated longstanding corruption, discrimination, poverty, abuse of power, and systemic unfairness. Behind the giant posters of a smiling prime minister in the market, billboards, and bus stations accompanied by mega-infrastructures were persistent poverty and a repressed citizenry. The country her children and grandchildren would inherit in the 2010s was worse than the one she found in the 1950s.

Politicians took advantage of the lenient guise of the people. Without anyone realizing, elections became merely a formality to

---

[8] Khoon Chye also said that Anne's four children were smart and independent thinkers, which made the tuition unnecessary except being a vehicle to enable Anne to help Khoon Chye.
[9] Until today, almost fifty years later, Anne would still invite Khoon Chye to spend time with them during birthday and festival celebrations.
[10] This was mostly out of school. When it came to academics, Anne was still very strict—she was a school teacher after all.

endorse the same government again and again. Gerrymandering and malapportionment got so bad that it was theoretically possible to form a government with only 16.5 per cent of the popular votes.

The electoral frauds found in Malaysia were some of the weirdest in the world: The oldest voter in the world, born in 1897, was found alive on the electoral roll; 500,000 voters shared the same addresses; 2,000,000 voters had no address; one vote in the smallest constituency was worth a few times more in another large constituency; mysterious power outages occurred during vote counting; cash was traded for votes . . .

A coalition of NGOs called Bersih, led by Ambiga Sreenevasan, organized a yellow protest to fight for what was deemed a basic piece of democracy: Free and fair elections. Among other things, they were demanding the use of indelible ink to prevent fraud, and the cleaning up of the electoral roll to remove phantom voters.

Though this seemed reasonable enough, the then government and extremist groups did everything they could to make it the most dangerous protest in modern history.

3

When Anne first arrived at the centre of Kuala Lumpur, she saw a ghost town. The once-bustling district of 1.6 million people was empty. Shops and offices were closed. Buses and cars were redirected out. Barbed wires and roadblocks covered the major entry points. For almost a week before the protest, the police and the riot control officers surrounded the area with extraordinary security measures, in what was known as 'Operation Erase Bersih'. Some of the officers had camped out for a week without going home. The only sound you could hear was the fire alarm, ringing incessantly. 'Don't hang around here,' one police officer advised a passer-by. 'It's not safe here today.'

The major gathering points were closed. Anne was stopped by the police four times from entering the compound. Helicopters hovered over the city. 'Black crows were watching us,' said Anne. The light on the police's guns and batons reflected sharply on Anne.

Several policemen asked her why she was wearing the banned yellow T-shirt. She answered them the same way: 'Why can't I wear yellow?' and walked away as quickly as she could.

Anne spent the first hour finding a way into the protest. She walked from the General Hospital down to the alley of Chow Kit, a place she went regularly to spend time with the homeless, a place plagued by stereotypes of drugs, crime, and sex work. She then walked down the road named after the country's first King,[11] as the stores got more expensive and, for most Malaysians, out of reach. Kuala Lumpur was a city of contrast, where the tallest corporate towers looked over the poorest alleyways—a symbolic reminder of Malaysia's persistent inequality. Anne then passed the oldest mosque in Malaysia, Masjid Jamek, which had pink and white minarets described as 'blood and bandage'.

As she reached the Petaling Street area, she found a sizeable crowd gathering. This was the only entryway in the entire city that had been left unguarded by the police and riot control officers—by mistake. Until today, it remains a mystery how this small cluster of 500, holding each other arm-to-arm, forming a human wall, could walk across the protest street and balloon up to 10,000 people in less than half an hour.

At every junction, arrest escapees, late joiners, and lucky entrants joined this snowballing crowd. Against all odds, the walls of the tightly guarded authoritarian fortress collapsed within hours.

Surrounded by a crowd of all races, Anne was overjoyed. The struggle before only made the fruits of the assembly sweeter. Photographers and journalists took notice of her as one of the oldest senior citizens on the march. She was photogenic and animated—making her interesting to capture.

She would open her arms wide like wings and run forward like a bird. She would take a white chrysanthemum, wave it up, and look to the sky. She would raise her fist in the air when the crowd chanted. She would follow the crowd of 50,000 and make a heart-shaped hand sign to the police.

---

[11] Tuanku Abdul Rahman was the country's first King. His face also appears in the paper notes of the Malaysian ringgit.

'Oh, that magical, thrilling feeling of being one people,' Anne recounted. 'So exhilarating, so indescribable. We were feeling so good standing with each other.'

But there was a question on everyone's minds: Could she run when the police started arresting? Her casual black shoes were not made for running. Her pouch didn't have much equipment for defence. Her frail and pale body made you wonder if she could withstand a sudden police siege.

This didn't seem to bother her. Anne continued to walk around asking others, 'Why aren't you wearing yellow?', 'Why are you afraid of the police in your own land?'

Soon the crowd moved within 'handshake distance' of the police in riot gear. Words spread that the police were willing to negotiate to let the protestors through so that they get closer to the agreed destination—the historic Stadium Merdeka where the first prime minister declared 'Merdeka!' seven times. The crowd started chanting *terima kasih* (thank you) to the police for finally allowing their request for a peaceful protest.

But then things started to turn. The police took the negotiators with them. The riot control officers (or Federal Reserve Unit, FRU) were marching in motion, hitting their shields at every two stomps in a coordinated motion. This left the crowd confused: Was there still a negotiation? Could they still walk through? Were the police coming for them?

And then—bang!

* * *

Within two minutes of turning the corner towards the square, the riot police fired rounds of tear gas at the middle of the crowd. And then another, then another, and another—thicker and more concentrated at every fire. The initial bell and 'bop' sound of the gun's release still traumatized the protestors. A helicopter came down at very low levels and started to release more gas over the crowd. People started running into hiding, with cries of *tipu!* (lies) and screaming mixed in the scene.

'At first we were told they would let us pass through . . . we didn't expect to be hit,' Anne recalled. 'I yelled at them, "Are we your enemies?"'

Tear gas, first developed in 1928 by two American chemists,[12] consists of a mix of charcoal, dusts of 'Chinese snow' (used to make gunpowder), with other chemical substances and magnesium carbonate (found in fire extinguishers) to keep it from turning into a bomb. It produces lachrymators that irritate your lungs, nose, and ears and make you cough, choke, or temporarily blind. Several people had complete and permanent loss of vision in one or both eyes after being hit by tear gas in the 2019–20 Chilean protests.

It causes pain so great that it was suggested for it to be called 'pain gas' instead. Imagine something 1,000 times more potent than Japanese wasabi. At high concentrations, this could be deadly. That's why in 1993, tear gas was specifically banned from international warfare. But somehow it was still allowed in the Bersih protest.

This was how some protestors described how the tear gas felt:

A: It crawls on your skin like ant bites, and then your skin starts to feel like it's peeling and itching, before turning into great burn.

B: At first, it smells slightly pleasant, even sweet. You think it isn't as bad as it's reputed to be. But you're in for a surprise. Take another whiff, and it hits you. The sharp spicy gas seizes your throat, stubbornly clinging on to it for dear life, and you can't get the burning sensation out, no matter how hard you cough. It chips little bits of your throat right out, suffocating you. It's worse if you're trapped in a cloud of it, not knowing up from down and left from right.

The gas stabs into your eyes, overflowing them with tears. You feel as if your eyes are burning, as if someone dropped Tabasco sauce into them. It's not just 'tears'. It attacks you. It burns you. And all this, for a single whiff.

---

[12] Also called 'CS gas', taking the last names of the inventor chemists Ben Corson and Roger Stoughton.

C: I was coughing really hard. It was getting harder to breathe. The
only thing that was flashing in my mind was death. The voice inside
my head was getting louder and louder, 'God, I'm going to die.'

The crowd was trapped. Police started chasing protestors, beating them
down with their batons and tying them with makeshift handcuffs. The
large FRU trucks used water cannons to flush out streams of water at
extremely high velocities. The only safe place was the hospital. People
started covering their eyes and noses with their T-shirts and towels,
smearing toothpaste and water over their eyes. They were passing
saltwater, and vinegar, and lemon to suck and spit out. The road was
filled with pools of blue-green tinted water and a foul-scented air
evaporated visibly from the ground.

Anne was the only one left behind. She couldn't run or hide like
the younger protestors. This was the problem of being old. She turned
her back to the police and FRU and took the tear gas in—four rounds
and more. She poured the water over herself from head to toe and
closed her eyes tightly.

'My back stung, everything was warm, I felt like I was burning,'
recalled Anne.

This was her first protest. She had nothing with her. No goggles,
no masks, no protection, no salt . . . Nothing. She couldn't stop
coughing and she didn't know what to do to make the pain stop. She
rubbed her eyes with her arms and shielded herself; tears dripped from
her eyes. Her left hand clutched the white chrysanthemum flower
and the near-empty plastic water bottle, taking in the pain as one foot
followed the other.

Hugo Teng, a freelance photographer, ran ahead, and turned to see
Anne walking alone.

She could hardly move forward any more. The pain was unbearable.
But the police were rushing from behind with a line of weapons. Unable
to hold any longer, Anne screamed loudly and repeatedly, 'Help! Help!'
The grey clouds started to open, and rain poured from the sky.

It was at this small moment that Hugo took out his phone, steadied
his hands, and snapped.

* * *

As soon as he got home, photographer Hugo Teng edited and uploaded the photos he took—mostly from his digital camera, but a few from his phone, typically the ones that had a shorter preparation time. One photo, blurrier than he would have preferred, stood out above others.

Photo by Hugo Teng

An old, frail, and skinny woman in yellow T-shirt and black trousers, probably in her sixties, was drenched from head to toe. The inner corners of her eyebrows were drawn inwards, the corner of her lips tilted down, her eyes shut tightly as if she wanted to turn away from what was behind her. Her background was filled with a sea of 'black crows'—police and riot controls dressed in full gear, all of them faceless and formless. There were two large FRU trucks larger than anyone in the photo. All of them are coming toward the old woman. No one else was on her side. The puddles of water behind her gave you a hint of what has happened, and what was to come. She was no match for them—you know she will be defeated.

But if you look closely at the old woman again, you will notice something amazing. In her hands were a water bottle and also a stalk of white chrysanthemum flowers—a universal symbol of peace and love. She never let it go. Her left leg took a step forward, and her right arm swung to follow. She was still moving forward.

This photo spread like wildfire that night of the protest. A few blogs started comparing her photo to the best protest photos in the *TIME* Magazine. Likes and comments piled up to the thousands. Video tributes, poems, posters, and a few Facebook fan pages sprung up. A fan page quickly racked up nearly 25,000 followers with thousands of protestors showing their support in each post, for their new heroine.

They started calling her the 'Aunty Bersih, the Lady of Liberty'.

4

In October 2016, a group of Thai pet show organizers, at the real estate concrete jungle of Muang Thong Thani, decided to hold a rematch of the oldest race in history. You've probably heard of this race before. It was last held in 620 BCE, between a tortoise and a hare.

The race was first written in the Aesop fable collection to teach younger children moral lessons through gripping animal stories. It goes like this:

> One day, a boastful hare challenged the tortoise to a race. Given its natural abilities to run, the hare sped ahead so quickly that the tortoise was thrown far behind. The hare then decided to take a nap; he was confident he could still win. But the tortoise took careful steps, and before the hare woke up, the impossible happened—the tortoise won. The moral lesson was 'slow and steady wins the race.'

The Thai organizers wanted to stage a real-life rematch. It was a bold and risky experiment. It would either prove an age-old fable or destroy millions of childhood imaginations.

Two dark blue lanes. The animals were released at the same time (the organizers did try to release tortoise slightly ahead for fear that the tortoise would lose too badly). The tortoise, carrying a weighty shell, pushed forward one step after another and led the race. The hare, upon release, hopped a few light steps and was already neck to neck. Then the grey-bodied hare took a few more hops forward and was just three steps to the finish line. The crowd squirmed.

And then, just like the Aesop table, the hare stopped. It started looking at the crowd. No more hops. The tortoise, on the other hand, continued to trudge along, with the same speed as the start. Before long, the tortoise pulled a step ahead again. The crowd was on the edge of their seats. The hare turned back. Its owner came forward to ask it to finish the race by tapping on the floor. At this moment, the audience started cheering the tortoise on, clapping to encourage it to finish the race. Photographers ran ahead to record the moment.

As soon as the tortoise's tail passed the finish line, we had a winner. At the time of writing, this video on YouTube had amassed forty-seven million views. Why wouldn't it? It was our favourite story—an underdog story.

Underdogs are people who are expected to lose. Joseph Vandello, a psychology professor at the University of South Florida, found our love for underdogs strange. In psychology, the classic understanding is that people love to identify with the winner because it gives them self-esteem, in the same way we adore people with expensive cars, big houses, and high status.

But our favourite fables were all about liking people who are *un*likely to win. Filipino children learn about the Monkey and the Turtle—a slow turtle protagonist being taken advantage of by a quick-thinking monkey. Korean children read about Kongji and Patzzi, ugly stepsisters mistreated by cruel stepmothers. In Russia, the popular Ivan the Fool was poor and simple-minded.

Joseph Vandello wanted to test this with his university students. So, he recruited fifty-seven undergraduate students to do a lab test in exchange for course credits. In one of his experiments, he chose two unfamiliar basketball teams for the students to pick, one that had won all previous matches, the other that had lost all:

CSKA Moscow
Won all 15 previous matches

Maccabi Tel Aviv
Lost all 15 previous matches

Then the professor asked the students to pick which team they would prefer to see win. Unsurprisingly, nearly 71 per cent of the students picked Maccabi Tel Aviv—the team that had lost all their previous matches.

Later, he asked each of them to watch a fifteen-minute basketball match between these two teams. They then had to rate how they felt about both teams: Who had more talent? Who tried harder? Who was the hustler? The students agreed that the top dog, CSKA Moscow, had more talent. But most of them thought that the underdog, Maccabi Tel Aviv, put in more effort. It seemed like they *tried* harder. It almost didn't matter whether Maccabi Tel Aviv would go on to win this game or more games in the future. We like the hustlers—the ones who try even though they don't succeed, even though they are underdogs who will never succeed.

But Joseph Vandello was not satisfied with this answer. In another experiment of a similar setting, he introduced one variation. What if students knew that CSKA Moscow was paid three times less than the players from Maccabi Tel Aviv? 88.1 per cent of the students switched to CSKA Moscow. Somehow, that simple variation changed how we looked at underdogs. Joseph Vandello explained that this proved that our preference for underdogs was tied to a primal instinct of fairness. We want those who have less to win so that the world obtains balance.

In many ways, we see ourselves in the underdogs. We want a world that is fair to us and others. We dislike bullies who take advantage of others. So even if the bullies are more talented, we hope they lose.

That is why we loved Anne's photo. Her son-in-law, Philip, explained it best:

> I think it's the weakness of Anne they see. People realize there is a David and Goliath situation. You got this frail, elderly woman who is holding a flower—a universal symbol of peace. What's so dangerous about a flower? She's victimized by an unjust, brutal, authoritarian government that is deeply corrupt. People associate themselves with the photo because they too feel weak and unable to fight against the government and bring about change. They see themselves in Anne— they think, 'We are Anne.' This, more than anything, gives them hope.

The contrast between the sea of black FRU and police and the bright-yellow Aunty Bersih was stark. The 9 July 2011 protest was the most violent protest in Malaysian history. 1,667 protestors (167 of them women) were arrested that day, including Ambiga Sreenevasan and other event organizers. There was even one death. Baharudin Ahmad, a former soldier and taxi driver, collapsed when the police were firing tear gas near the shopping mall of Avenue K, where people crawled over the metal grille into the building. He was fifty-eight when he died—only seven years younger than Anne. And there Anne was, alone and overwhelmed.

When we listen to the story of David and Goliath, we are always hoping David has a shot. When we first heard about the Tortoise and the Hare, we wished there was something to block the hare's way so the tortoise had a chance of winning the race. In the Sang Kancil story, we wished that Sang Kancil's wit was enough to drive out the other terrifying animals and render Sang Kancil safe again. We hope that this world is fair to everyone, even though we know it might not be. There is a primal sense of fairness we yearn.

Malaysians online felt the same. One said: 'Every time I looked at this [Lady of Liberty] photo, I could feel the hurt that Aunty Bersih was feeling. I couldn't help but tear up. We are so touched and proud to have you, Aunty Bersih.'

Another wrote: 'I looked at the photo and I asked myself, if I was in the scene, would I stand up like she did and walk through the water cannons and tear gas? Whether I would take the risk of being arrested and put into the lock-up? I am a coward. [Aunty Bersih] you are braver than me. I despise myself. I admire this brave woman.'

Zalina Abdullah, a middle-aged Malay woman, wrote in a blog comment: 'I am much younger than she, and she has made me ashamed of myself as a Malaysian. I was a Malaysian who was always afraid, but those brave people at Bersih 2.0 have opened my eyes on 9 July 2011. I am still afraid, but I will join any rally for clean elections in future. I cannot let my fellow Malaysians fight the battle for democracy by themselves. I will support the call for clean and fair elections from now on.'

They saw themselves in a frail, old, but spirited woman named Anne Ooi—because of one photo.

5

The day after the protest, Anne woke up later than usual. The tear gas and chemical water left her exhausted and wretched. She took the bus to her daughter Elaine's place to see her grandchildren. When she arrived at Elaine's place, there wasn't the usual exuberance.

'What happened to you?' Elaine asked, her face worried sick. 'I was trying to call you all day.'

Anne checked her mobile phone that she rarely used and saw that it had broken after falling on the ground during the protest. Her other children, too, had tried to call her to no avail. Her son and daughter-in-law in Penang were lost for words when they found out what happened to her, and they started crying. Another son was mad that she took such a big risk and asked her to not do it again. Anne became annoyed. Who told them what happened, she thought.

Then Elaine's phone started ringing. It was Al Jazeera—they wanted to interview Anne about her experience in the protest.

'Me?' Anne exclaimed.

Other media houses like CNN, Malaysiakini, The Malaysian Insider, Free Malaysia Today, and more reached out to Elaine, either through mobile or on Facebook. The attention became so overwhelming they had to shut off and change their social media accounts.

'At [that moment], I just wanted to kill them [photographer, journalists, fans] all. Why did you do this to me?' Anne recalled. 'I didn't give you permission [to take my photo] . . . I couldn't accept it. It was overwhelming for me.

'I wasn't sure how I was going to live my life. So, I hid. I just don't want to see anybody any more. I'm just a small person.'

Anne's granddaughters, Keeva and Tierna, had also seen the Lady of Liberty photo and other videos spread widely online. They couldn't fully comprehend what happened but they were angry. Once, Tierna even shouted at a random police officer for what they had done to their grandmother.

In their eyes, Anne was not just a fun and eccentric grandmother who taught them how to swim, dance, and jump the trampoline. She was also a compassionate grandmother who taught them kindness.

Anne would often buy huge loaves of bread from the market below the granddaughters' place. 'Are you making bread for us?' the granddaughters would ask. 'We're going out!' Anne would reply.

Then she would bring the two munchkins to a poor neighbourhood and start distributing the bread to the homeless—locals or refugees. She would squat and speak to the homeless, sometimes with a cup of tea in her hand. On the way back home, Anne would point to cyclists on the road and remind her granddaughters they should make way for them because 'they are not the ones with big, fancy cars.' She would tell them about her favourite mall, Avenue K in Kuala Lumpur, where she went not for shopping, but to meet her blind guitarist friend, Albert Ho. He would be busking with famous tunes by Elvis Presley and Sam Hui, and Anne would dance in front of him with untrained moves.

'If I dance, more people will crowd and pay attention, so more people would give him money,' she explained.

Most of all, she also taught her granddaughters her most famous act of charity: To leave money at random places. She would leave a few ringgits on the stairs, on the sidewalk, and between the fences so people would find them. 'Wouldn't you be happy if you found them?'

Anne couldn't stand seeing her granddaughters worried about her safety at the protest. She took them to the sofa and rolled them together in her arms to see her photos and videos of the protest. Gently she patted them and whispered to their ears, 'It is okay, it is okay' until they felt better. She rocked their bodies back and forth, and finally, they broke a laugh.

* * *

There was something I didn't tell you about the day Anne was tear-gassed. As the police were running to arrest the protestors, they actually left Anne untouched. Knowing she couldn't run any more, Anne surrendered herself to the police, thinking they would handcuff her. Instead, the police told her, 'Aunty, just go.' They didn't touch her.

'She felt insignificant, like she was of no importance and worthless,' her daughter, Elaine, recounted her feelings. Anne actually *wanted* to be arrested by the police, but they didn't want to do it.

After some time, she realized she had something rare and valuable to a protest movement—she had the immunity of old age.

Anne saw a man squirming and twisting on the ground, trying to catch a breath of fresh air, but his hands were tied to a handcuff. Another protestor had blood dripping from his head as the police used a makeshift handcuff (made of strings) to arrest him. She followed the arrested protestors to the staging area, where they were ready to be dragged onto a police van and sent for intense questioning.

Across the street, she saw tens of them squatted on the ground, with their hands behind their backs. Most of them young; faces weary and defeated, fearful of the unknown. For most of them, this was the first time being arrested. If the police were already violent, imagine how they could be when put in a confined room alone. Tear-gassed, beaten, arrested, thrown into the lockup for a peaceful protest against a corrupt regime—this was the country they would inherit. A black eye, a bloody nose, and a court case in your name.

'An old woman like me had lived a full life. I'm not scared because I have nothing else to lose,' Anne said. 'But the young people still have a future ahead of them. They have everything to lose.'

She thought of her grandchildren, who would inherit a country where the powerful trample on the weak. It would be so hard for them to understand because it was the opposite of what she tried to teach them. Help the weak, not step on them. The pain of the tear gas and water cannons slowly dissolved in her head. Something moved inside of her; she needed to do something.

Anne held up the white chrysanthemum flowers at the arrested protestors and took a long bow.

6

The protest next time was different. Anne, now known as Aunty Bersih, brought a bigger pouch around her waist. In it, she had salt and vinegar in case of another round of tear gas. She also brought a pen and some extra cash in case she got called to the police station for questioning. Around her neck was also a talisman to assure her family that with the power of God, she shall be okay.[13]

She now attended every rally—Bersih (clean elections), Kita Lawan (fight corruption), Tangkap Najib (catch the prime minister, Najib), Bantah 1050 (minimum wage), May Day (labour rights), GST Rally (new taxation), candlelight vigils—and engaged in all resistance methods. Whether it was a large-scale march, sit-in, handing of memorandum, holding a signboard at the roadside for honks . . . She would do it. Once an amateur in street protest, she started to advise others how to do sleep-ins by bringing her own mat.

'I learned this from the homeless—they taught me!' she said.

When someone recognized her in a mall or on a train, she no longer deflected the attention or went into hiding. She would happily take a photo with her fans and ask them, 'Are you afraid of being handcuffed or put in jail?' It would be strange for them to say yes in front of an old woman thrice their age.

At the protests, Aunty Bersih would go around checking on people—to see if they were okay, if they were afraid. She would help participants find toilets in restaurants while asking the restaurant owners to lower the food prices. Once, she saw a young woman crying for reasons unknown, so she helped her take refuge at a nearby shelter. People at a protest would look for her and call out 'Aunty Bersih! Aunty Bersih!' as she walked past as their source of comfort. *If Aunty Bersih is not afraid, maybe I shouldn't be too.*

More and more people who were once afraid started emulating Anne. These were what some of them said online:[14]

'She was the one who **influenced me** to go to the Bersih rallies. You are my idol, Aunty Bersih. Let the whole nation go for the Bersih rallies to come.'

---

[13] Anne's children were furious that they always had to find out about her arrests only through the news rather than directly through her.

[14] Emphasis is this author's own.

'Don't let the tears and strength go to waste. We **shall continue** to push for reforms!'

'We have to work together and fight for our rights, in order to have a better country to live in. Hope every one of us knows how to **vote** on the coming election day.'

Remember what Zalina Abdullah commented in the blog post after seeing Aunty Bersih's Lady of Liberty photo?

I am much younger than she, and she has made me ashamed of myself as a Malaysian. I was a Malaysian who was **always afraid**, but those brave people at Bersih 2.0 have opened my eyes on 9 July 2011. I am **still afraid, but I will join** any rally for clean elections in future. I cannot let my fellow Malaysians fight the battle for democracy by themselves. I will support the call for clean and fair elections from now on.[15]

Always afraid, still afraid—but I will join. That was the impact of Aunty Bersih.

* * *

Since her first Bersih protest, Anne subscribed to an effective but dangerous belief. She knew that the police would not arrest someone like her because of her age; they would rather go for the boisterous and rebellious youths. This was more effective in suppressing dissent because upon reaching the police station, the young rebels' face would typically turn white. Their safety, family, and future were in jeopardy. It served as a strong deterrent against other young rebels as well. To stop a protest, go for the young ones.

Anne wanted to flip that around to secure the safety of protestors. Every time the police started to arrest protestors; she would ask the police to handcuff her instead.

---

[15] Emphasis is this author's own.

In March 2015, a worker's party planned a GST sit-in protest at the Customs Office. Implementing new taxation would disproportionately burden the poor in an already-bad economy. The purpose of the sit-in was to send a memorandum to the Director General of the Customs Office and address their questions.

When the Director General refused to answer, the eighty-person crowd got angry. The police asked them to leave. When they repeatedly refused, the police arrested them and pulled them to the back of a police van.

Anne saw a protestor pushed to the ground, with both hands handcuffed to his back.

She turned to the police and said, 'I am doing this for everyone's children. If you think that is wrong, then by all means, cuff me . . . All I want is to ensure a better tomorrow for our children.'

If you were the police, would you handcuff her?

If you don't, you tolerate the protest and the right to dissent, encouraging others to do the same. This would be bad if you were part of an authoritarian regime. If you do handcuff this old woman, however, it would look horrible. People would react badly to the picture of Anne at the back of a Black Maria van, in the same way they reacted to the Lady of Liberty photo at the Bersih rally in 2011. This would make people angry, encouraging more to retaliate against the regime. This is also bad for the regime. But that was what they did— they arrested her.

Anne would do this again and again. Holding out her wrists to policemen, challenging them to arrest her.

'Why are you making me wait? I've been to jail three times. I want to go for one more time.'[16]

Putting an old woman into a lockup was already bad enough for the optics of the regime. An old woman sleeping on the cold, hard cement floor, being left without food and drinks was worse. Most people would be terrified by this, but not Anne—she treated it like a mini-party.

This was what her son, Kevin, said:

---

[16] Anne's family was not sure when and what her first two arrests were for, neither could Anne verify since she has lost memory of many things, including this.

She was probably the first-ever detainee to request cleaning supplies from the police officers so that she could clean her cell. She couldn't stand that the cell was dirty. Then she organized an impromptu singalong with other arrested protestors to make them less scared. Because once you sing, you become less afraid. When she came out of the police station, she asked others to go in. She said things like, 'There is nothing to be scared of!' She's so old, she could say anything she wanted.

Anne used her old age as a tool of rebellion. She taught Malaysians to not be afraid, by creating that psychological safety in protestors' minds. Once she treaded where nobody else had, it opened a new territory. The next time, others might not be scared of lock-ups any more—they might even sing.

'Walk proudly! Don't run like cowards! Do not turn your backs [on the police], face them!' Anne said in front of a candlelight vigil crowd of 100 outside the Kuala Lumpur Central Lockup in Jinjang in 2013. Remanded behind the lock-up walls were activists who were taken in for speaking at a forum about Malaysia's infamous race riot. 'If they want to handcuff you, put your hands out. Go inside to Hotel Jinjang!'

Then she pulls out something from her large waist pouch.

'I have prepared a toothbrush for my night at the lock-up!' she said to a laughing crowd. She lowered her voice and continued, 'If you did not kill anyone, if you did not steal, if you did no wrong, you have nothing to be afraid of!'

She accepted her role as 'Aunty Bersih, the activist'. Being manhandled, arrested, and thrown into lock-ups was part of the deal. One time, she was kicked up the police van so hard that her back suffered persistent pain for the next few months. But she never mentioned it to anyone until her family found that she was limping.[17]

'I don't remember it. It's just not a big deal to me,' she said, with a shrug.

---

[17] Anne's family had learned that Anne couldn't be controlled. Once she even brought a homeless man with tuberculosis (TB) home. She let him shower, have a meal, and nap on the bed. The children were shocked and told Anne that TB was contagious, and he should be sent to the hospital instead. So, they rushed to send him off.

7

I still had a few questions unanswered. Was she ever afraid in the jail cell? Did she achieve what she wanted? Was it worth trading a comfortable retirement life for police arrests and court cases?

I went to see Anne at her home twelve years after the Lady of Liberty photo was first taken. Her flat at Setapak was modest. Kids ran around the compound, playing chase. Stacks of clothes and beads were left at the side of the walk-up stairs (I later found out it was Anne's doing), leading to a long alleyway. Neighbours used different clothes to cover their white-coated grilles: Towels, cardboards, party flags, Malaysian flags. Anne's unit was at the quiet end of the alley, sheltered and protected from the midday heat. In her house, there was no TV, computer, or radio. Used clothes were cleaned and made into carpets. Nothing hung on the wall except a small cross. If you wiped your finger on her cabinet, you wouldn't find a speck of dust. The toilet felt like it was cleaned every hour. The balcony was a tiny garden of her favourite flowers.

I bought her a bag of fruits and healthy snacks as a thank-you gift.

'Have you given to your family?' Anne quizzed me.

'Yes.'

'Your neighbours?' she continued.

'Yes.'

'Your friends?'

'Yes.'

'Good,' she said. She planned to give the box away to her neighbours after I left.

Everything seemed the same, except for her. Since her stroke in 2021, she was much thinner (she now eats ten times a day at a handful each time, 'like a bird'), weaker ('my legs couldn't walk straight any more'), and quieter (she's lost a large part of her memory).

She adjusted the pillow behind my seat and asked me if I was comfortable. She took a plastic chair and sat in the middle of the living room. With the fan turning above us in the still 3 p.m. afternoon, I started interviewing her.

It didn't go well. To all questions I asked, she only mumbled 'I can't remember.' I went through the different events—before, during, and after the Bersih rally in 2011, but her answers were the same. She started looking away into the abyss as if she was embarrassed and resigned by how little she could recall.

'Keep talking. Maybe I'll recall if you keep talking,' said Anne.

The next twenty minutes were me talking about this great woman everyone called Aunty Bersih. There was no interview—it was just a young adult telling stories to help the older woman recall things she did in the past. I told her about the ghost town, the tear gas, the photo, the interviews, the fan pages, the arrests, the lock-ups . . . Then I opened my notebook to read out a poem that a citizen named Allan Goh wrote for her:

'Your frail look belies your strength, despite being gassed, sprayed
Your faith is firmly entrenched, you dared the hardship
Of marching for a true cause, even though harassed
Even though at a great cost
You inspire all, to stand solid for our right
In spite of foul threats, from sycophants of the might
Through your example, you have set the righteous tone
Others will follow, you will never walk alone.'

Without a word, she lifted her small frame from the chair and gave me a hug. Her body was thin and fragile, trembling at a few places. I held on to her arms and carried her gently back to her chair.

The only things she remembered clearly were the distant past of her childhood or the recent memories of gardening, cleaning, charity, and her doting grandchildren.

I showed her some photos of Aunty Bersih to jog her memory. She became embarrassed and left the room and popped back in again with two cups of tea in her hands.

'I didn't know your phone had so many pictures of me,' she said.

'It's from the internet. Let me show you some videos,' I replied.

I showed her a five-minute-twenty-seven-second video called 'Malaysian Lady of Liberty 2.0' edited by Bannai Rao. The video started with her marching in the Bersih rally, leading to a scene of her rubbing her eyes from the tear gas fired at her, drenched in chemical water the next. At the halfway mark, Aunty Bersih started scolding the police, who were firing tear gas into Hospital Tung Shin, where protestors went for shelter. She was fierce, fiery, and most of all, fearless.

Anne curled up holding her legs to her chest like a child watching the video. She pointed to her arms and whispered, 'Goosebumps.' And for the very first time, I saw her eyes slowly light up.

* * *

Harvard professor Erica Chenoweth is a rockstar academic whose name is known among activists and protestors. Erica Chenoweth has stopped replying to emails because every day, hundreds of activists would email to ask for tips and advice to defeat their terrible dictators. Born tough with a fascination for military might, the professor embarked on a grand—and personal—mission to prove if revolutions succeeded through the barrel of a gun or buds of roses. For five years, Erica Chenoweth and her colleague studied all 323 attempted revolutions that took place between 1900 to 2006. What they discovered changed how we understood protests forever.

If you used weapons and great military men to bring down a dictator, your chance of success was only 25 per cent. But if you used non-violent means like protest, sit-ins, boycotts, and strikes, your success rate shot up to 54 per cent—doubling the success rate of violent means. There is more. If we consider only protests that took place between 2000 to 2006, their success rate was 70 per cent compared to violent means that had a meagre 10 per cent success rate.

This may seem counterintuitive at first. The images of battlefield heroes and genius commanders overthrowing ruthless dictators were what stuck with us. Turns out, the ordinary acts of turning up to a protest, doing extremely mundane things like chanting, singing, marching, and running away from water cannons and pepper spray were the best ways of overthrowing a dictator.

Erica Chenoweth argues that this makes sense. Non-violent methods create a virtuous cycle of large numbers. Turning up for a

protest had a lower barrier of entry compared to training as a soldier
or picking up a weapon. As more people join a protest, it also creates a
natural psychological safety that would encourage the fence-sitters, even
children, grandmas, and the disabled to join. When there are enough
people, loyalty shifts and defection happens against the dictator. More
and more until it cracks—that's when the dictator falls.

In fact, the professor even came up with a magic number to
overthrow a dictator.

Peak Popular Participation	Success Rate
At least 3.5%	88.89%
1–3.5%	60.98%
0.25–1%	45.65%
0.06–0.25%	45.25%
0.015–0.06%	24.24%
0.0035–0.015%	9.09%
Less than 0.0035%	4.17%

Peak Popular Participation refers to the highest number of people
who have turned out for a mass non-violent event. Typically, this refers
to a protest since it's most easily measured. Movements that get less than
1 per cent of the population in a single protest struggle to overthrow
a dictator because there is less than an even chance of success. There
simply isn't enough buy-in to the cause to spark a widespread resistance
and key defections. If you succeed in getting more than 1 per cent of
the population to take the streets, you are on your way to a revolution.
If you get at least 3.5 per cent to turn out, you are virtually guaranteed
of an overthrow.

For the longest time, Bersih struggled to get enough people
on the street. In Bersih 2.0, where Anne Ooi was tear-gassed, only
50,000 people turned up. This represented only 0.17 per cent of the
population of thirty million Malaysians, and unsurprisingly, this was

insufficient to overthrow the government. At Bersih 3.0 in 2012, the number of protestors dramatically increased to 250,000 people, which was 0.83 per cent of the population, pushing it up a bracket of success to a 45.65 per cent chance. But this was still insufficient. Unsurprisingly, the government stayed on in 2013, though a two-thirds majority was denied for the first time.

The Bersih organizers held a fourth large-scale protest on 31 August 2015 to commemorate the country's 58th Merdeka Day. That night, the national anthem played throughout Kuala Lumpur to the thundering chorus of 500,000 Malaysians. Tears ran down protestors' cheeks as they feared passing down a country worse than how they found it.

What they didn't know, of course, was that Malaysia finally breached the 50:50 mark on that fateful night. From that day, Malaysia had a 61 per cent chance of overthrowing its government that was accused of the world's largest financial scandal. Twenty-one months later, ordinary Malaysian voters overcame mass gerrymandering and electoral manipulations to overthrow the longest-ruling coalition in the world and marked its first-ever democratic change—without weapons, riots, or a single drop of blood.

Epilogue

In a line over the windowpane, six-legged insects with large heads and elbowed antennae marched at an agile speed. A sixty-year-old Anne held Keeva and Tierna's hands and bent over to get their eyes level with the marching insects. Anne put a forefinger on her lips and mouthed the words 'Be quiet.'

Three pairs of hazel eyes took in the brightness of the sun, blinking cautiously to not scare the insects.

'Hey, look . . . these are ants!' Anne whispered to them. 'There, there . . . that one with a shell over its body is called a snail.'

This windowpane was where the three of them would take in the little wonders of the world. It was where they learned how to hold a ladybug in their hands and put it into a safe haven container. It was where they saw a giant praying mantis, an animal Tierna thought was

Anne's spirit animal. Before the break of dawn, it was here they rushed to see the sunrise, and to wonder at the unique leaves that stretched from the trees.

They giggled together in excitement. And then, they slowly retreated to lie against the wall. Keeva, barely more than a year old, blurted her first word as a toddler: 'Ant!'[18]

Key takeaways

- We identify with underdogs because of our innate yearning for fairness and balance.
- There is a unique power in old age, especially in activism. When you have nothing to lose, you become untouchable.
- To overthrow an authoritarian regime, at least 1 per cent of the population must turn out for a public protest. If 3.5 per cent turn out, the overthrow is close to certain.

---

[18] Anne Ooi has six grandchildren: Daniel, Zachary, Erica, Kayla, Keeva, and Tierna.

Chapter 3

Dr Serena Nik-Zainal

How a mother of two became the first woman to win the 'Nobel Prize for Cancer Research' and how being underestimated may be a good thing

'The thing about you is that you don't give a damn about what others think.'

1

Dr Serena Nik-Zainal's clinic is unlike any other. The most mysterious cases come through this door. Instead of the regular seven-minute speed consultation with general practitioners, patients get forty-five minutes with Dr Serena. Patients come in wondering about their missing fingers, enlarged toes, stunted height, fading memory, sun-damaged skin, non-stop bleeding . . .

'I never give good news,' said Dr Serena. 'It's always bad news.'

She runs the clinic for rare diseases. If no one can figure out what is happening to a patient, and they suspect a genetic cause, they get referred to Dr Serena.

'My job is to catch things early so that patients have the best care,' she said.

Most of the time, there was no cure for rare diseases like Down Syndrome, Hemophilia (easy bruising), Huntington's Disease (dementia), Turner Syndrome (short stature), and cancer. It was the draw of the lot. The best that patients and their families could hope for was to manage well enough with the doctors and avoid the worst-case scenarios.

A forty-five-minute consultation was not a purely medical process. It was also Dr Serena's attempt to listen to the patients' pains about a genetic disease that had no cure. 'I ask about their family, background, insecurity, money, what upsets them, a new wheelchair . . . I need to understand the whole picture as best I can so that I could guide the patients through the journey.'

There was one part of Dr Serena's job that was most heartbreaking: Prenatal screening tests.

'A couple would have a baby boy who couldn't breathe well from the day he was born. His inhale and exhale would be noisy, and the baby would cry weakly. The baby's muscles would then become increasingly weak, and the chest muscles would stop working. The baby would struggle to gasp for air, and then it would stop. It's one of the most awful things to see,' said Dr Serena.

The disease is called SMARD1 and the gene causing this is called IGHMBP2—it causes muscle atrophy in infants that stops their breathing. Dr Serena will take a sample from the baby to find out if there were mutations in the gene, and whether it was inherited from the mother or father, or both.

The human genome is packaged into twenty-three pairs of chromosomes, and every chromosome exists in twos. If you have a missing chromosome, such as the X chromosome, you have something called Turner Syndrome; if you have one extra chromosome 21, you have Down Syndrome. If a baby inherits one defective copy of IGHMBP2, the baby could still live a normal life if the other chromosomal copy is undefective. One normal copy can compensate for the other. But if the baby is unlucky and inherited two defective copies from the parents, then the baby has a clinical condition—which may not be compatible with life.

Parents with defective gene copies of the specific gene, in this case, IGHMBP2, may later seek genetic counselling regarding their chances of having another child with the same disease. They will be shown something like this before conceiving a child:

Gene copies	Chances of having the gene copies	Outcome to the baby
No defective gene copies	25%	Neither affected by SMARD1 nor a carrier
One defective gene copy	50%	A carrier of the mutation but healthy and unaffected by SMARD1
Two defective gene copies	25%	Affected by SMARD1

That means there is still a 75 per cent chance that the parents will have a child born normal. But there is also a 25 per cent chance that the baby might suffer from the disorder. Parents would want to do anything to avoid the deadly 25 per cent.

When couples try for another child, the mother would get a prenatal screening test at Dr Serena's clinic around the sixth week of pregnancy. Dr Serena refers the patient to a clinic, a needle is put into the patient's body, and the placenta is tested in a laboratory. When the results are out, the parents would find out the answer to the question: Is my baby in the 25 per cent who will not survive?

'It's awful to watch a child die like that. So, when the parents know the child is in the 25 per cent, they might opt to terminate the baby right away,' said Dr Serena. 'It's not a pleasant part of my job . . . I stopped doing it because it was too intense for me.'[19]

Patients with rare genetic diseases depended heavily on what Dr Serena told them. But genetics was a new field in the early 2000s. In the past few decades, most patients never knew what was causing their symptoms because doctors didn't have the tools to diagnose them. Scientists only found out that genes are made of DNA in 1952; the first full-length reading of the chromosomes only came in 1999. In ten tests that were run, only one would show the mutation doctors were looking for. The other times, doctors would have to tell the patients, 'We think you've got this syndrome, but I can't be 100 per cent sure.'

'I remember sitting in front of my patient, holding the chart, not knowing whether there was a gene causing the disease,' Dr Serena recalled. 'We could do the test, but we couldn't read it very well. Because it was so new, no one fully understood what they were seeing.'

Patients of rare diseases, already disillusioned and dejected, would wait patiently for Dr Serena, only to be told that she couldn't find out what caused the disease. Dr Serena could guess, but would that work?

'I was deeply frustrated. Telling patients that you're not sure was disempowering and unsatisfactory. We have all this technology, but we still couldn't understand the data we see,' said Dr Serena.

After almost three years of saying 'I'm not 100 per cent sure', Dr Serena decided to take matters into her own hands. 'I thought, "That's it, I had enough. I'm going to understand how this new technology works."' She put in an application to do her PhD at one of the most prestigious research institutes in the world, and she started with one of humanity's most complicated unsolved problems: Cancer.

---

[19] This also coincided with the time Dr Serena ventured into cancer research.

2

When Serena was first born in 1976, her mother felt she was the 'ugliest baby in the hospital.' Her elder brother, Halmey, was a beautiful, small baby when he was born. 'And there I was a fat, blobby thing,' Serena recalled.

Serena's mother, Daisy, was asking the nurse, 'Is this baby mine?' Then a nurse told her there was only one Chinese-looking baby born that night. So, it must be hers.

From a very young age, Serena knew that she grew up in a family of contrasts. Her father, Nik Zainal, was born to a quiet, religious, and dirt-poor Malay household in the small agrarian Kampung Banggol, Kota Bahru.[20] And Daisy came from a loud and expressive Baba Nyonya household in Melaka.[21] They both met during the racial riots of 13 May 1969, when they were stuck in the Kuala Lumpur General Hospital. Nik Zainal was finishing his shift as a government doctor and Daisy was just starting hers as a nurse.

The racial clash between the Malays and Chinese in the capital of Malaysia made it difficult for their families to bless their marriage. They didn't have a proper wedding—they eloped and got registered quietly.

Serena's family of four lived in a relatively rundown house compared to the other houses in the area. They weren't poor, but they were definitely not very comfortable in the earliest years.[22] Serena learned from a young age to keep herself occupied in the gardens and neighbourhood. She would ride her brother's bicycle and pretend it was a horse. Among her neighbourhood friends, she was known as Snake Girl because she would always find snakes in the bushes, and the children would all run in fear.

---

[20] 'Kelantan had lots of marriages within the family, within Nik's and Wan's. I found this so bizarre. So whenever there were efforts in our family in Kelantan to marry cousins, I would just hold my breath. "Is this okay?" I'd ask.'

[21] Daisy's family loved to dance. All family members were expected to break some moves when the music played.

[22] Dr Serena recalled her parents' car had a hole inside, making the tar road visible while driving.

Once, she saw tadpoles inside a small puddle on the roadside. Cars from Lorong Gurney would turn into the Jalan San Ah Wing housing area, and their cars would press into the grass. Over time, a dip was formed and after the rain, there would be a small puddle. Frogs went there to lay eggs.

'I would come out every day to see the eggs. Tadpoles would wiggle their way out of their bubbles and stick below the water surface,' Serena remembered. 'Then they'd start swimming and start eating the algae in the water with their gulping mouths. I was ecstatic when they finally grew out their little legs, because I knew they were going to turn into frogs at any moment.

'But when I came back from school one day, all of them were dead. They grew into frogs and started hopping onto the road. But the puddle was in the middle of the junction— cars drove over them. What was left was this huge pile of dead frogs.'

She continued, 'This was my first lesson: Life was short. One day I see the frogs, and the next day they are dead. It was also my first lesson in biology. Even today, I get excited looking at a cell through a microscope. The outdoors was my first laboratory.'

* * *

Serena's father, Dr Nik Zainal, was a strict and stressed man. Dr Nik Zainal was only thirty days old when his father died. His mother, who was only nineteen years old then, lost her only source of income and was left to fend for her four children. The feisty, 4'10" woman, who only spoke in the Kelantanese dialect, moved her family back to her fathers' and married a religious preacher as his fourth wife. The husband did not treat them well, and after a few years, she escaped with her children. Dr Nik Zainal's mother would later outlive three other husbands. Despite living in abject poverty and being looked down on by her community, Dr Nik Zainal's mother emphasized education.

Serena recalled, 'My grandfather's last words were "you must educate the children, no matter what," so my grandmother felt strongly about reading, writing, and going to school. All her children eventually made it to some level of tertiary or vocational education.'

Dr Nik Zainal was forced to compete harder than the rest because of what he didn't have. One of the houses he grew up in was an old wooden house that had non-flushing toilets. Near the house were paddy fields from which huge brown rats (Tikus Mondok) would come, run along the beams of the house, and terrorize the kids. A few months in the year, the monsoon would come. Waters would rise to waist level or more, and villagers would have to move around by boat. Defying all hardships, Dr Nik Zainal emerged as one of the smartest Malay students and enter the elite boarding school of Malay College Kuala Kangsar (MCKK).

The man was one-of-a-kind. He built the country's first cardiological unit in 1977 from a tiny storeroom to the National Heart Institute today. In his forties, he led the Malaysian dream team to Sydney, Australia, to learn how to perform open-heart surgery. Before they returned, Dr Nik Zainal told the press that 'We hope to perform fifty operations between April and December [in 1982].' In typical Dr Nik Zainal fashion, they overachieved and performed 232 operations, of which 127 were open-heart surgeries, including the first-ever coronary artery bypass on a thirty-nine-year-old Treasury staff member. His colleague, Dr Rozali Wathooth, called him 'simply irreplaceable'.

Without a father figure in his life, Dr Nik Zainal's secret to success was a relentless drive to success. Serena recalled this about her father,

> He had a reputation of being a very fierce man. Talk to anyone in that generation and they'll say that he had a foul temper, that people around were just scared of him. He felt like he needed to work incredibly hard and have an incredibly high expectation on himself and everyone around him. He used to walk into the intensive ward and scold doctors and nurses who he felt wasn't good enough. He felt like he had no other way but to yell to get them *up there*. I guess when you have no other compass—no father, no one who has been through the process to tell you—everything had to be self-driven.

Serena and her brother felt her father's high expectations. 'It was a scary household. He would yell and scold—this was normal in the house,' she recalled.

For Dr Nik Zainal, it was 100 per cent about academic achievements. He would expect all A's, top of the class, a scholarship, do medicine at a prestigious college—that was *up there*. Doing well in extracurricular like debating, music, sports was good, but nothing was more important than your studies. Let alone birthday parties. That was a waste of time—a distraction.

'For many years, my relationship with my father was transactional. It was keeping my head low, keep away from being shot, deliver quietly, and try not to rock the boat,' Serena recalled. 'I've learned to be smiley and stay out of trouble.'

But her elder brother, Halmey, was a hard act to follow. He was first in class, top of the school every year in the six years of his primary education. Like his father, he made it into MCKK and was set for a medical education. Serena, on the other hand, was playful and always busy with something other than studies.

The world came crashing during the primary school leavers' test, UPSR, at Standard 6.[23]

'I didn't get 5A's [straight A's]. Everybody got 5A's in those days, and people were asking me, "How the hell did you not get 5A's?"' said Serena.

A crying twelve-year-old Serena wiped off her tears.

Her father took her aside, and with his forefinger in front of her face, told her, 'Serena, this is the biggest academic disaster of your life!'

Without 5A's, Serena couldn't go to boarding school, which was seen as the ultimate social status and a stepping stone for greater things. Premier all-girls boarding schools like Kolej Tunku Kurshiah (Malay Girls College, or TKC) and Sekolah Seri Puteri (also SSP), which boast alumni like the royalty, ministers, and industry leaders, were now closed to her.

---

[23] Ujian Pencapaian Sekolah Rendah (UPSR) was also known as the Primary School Achievement Test. All students have to pass this exam during their sixth year to graduate from primary education.

'I was so upset. I was already disappointed with myself for not getting 5A's,' said Serena. 'To have your father tell you about this is worse. I was mortified. I was only twelve—I couldn't understand it.'

She went on to study at the oldest school in Kuala Lumpur, the Bukit Bintang Girls' School (BBGS). Here, she made friends from all spectrums of society regardless of skin colour. She learned about personal responsibility, and pushing herself to be the best; she also cleaned toilets. 'It really kept us grounded.'

During this time, she was chosen to join a character-building program called the Bakaugruv Project, where students lived in little villages among the mangrove swamps.

'I loved it because it took me away from home. The whole [Bakaugruv] experience was very physical. You had to climb over ropes and balance yourself. But almost everyone would fall deep into the mud. You had to pick yourself back up fast and put it behind you, not ruminate over it, and try not to be bitter.'

Three years later, the PMR exam results were released, and Serena was one of the few straight A's scorers in her school.[24] This was her second shot at the premier boarding schools.

'I decided I didn't want to go. I mean, why would I change this amazing environment at BBGS? I valued the mix, the people, the culture, the character it built in me. It pushed me to work in a different way. Boarding schools were a bit more spoon-fed . . .' she said.

When Serena told her father about her decision, he was surprised. Why would anyone pass out on an opportunity like that—to be *up there*?

'Life deals you with a set of cards you cannot choose. Sometimes that's your parents. I've learned that you don't always have to accept everything told to you. Surely it is okay to ask, "Is this something I want?"'

She simply smiled to her father and said 'thank you' before walking back to her bedroom.

---

[24] PMR, or Penilaian Menengah Rendah, refers to the Lower Secondary Assessment Malaysian students had to take, typically when they are fifteen years old. It had been abolished since 2014.

3

Serena was on track to be every Asian mother's dream. She went through five difficult years at Cambridge University's medical degree at Newhall College—a 'stern, austere, cold, ugly building' that was 'amazing, warm within'. The director taught her that she could excel being herself and she didn't need to be anyone else. This was during 1995 when gender equality hadn't become the mainstream lexicon. She was seen and heard by friends and lecturers alike. She was on track to becoming a National Health Service (NHS) consultant based in the United Kingdom.[25]

'A lot of people kind of had an idea of the specialist they wanted to be, but I really didn't,' she said. 'I tried so many different things . . . but it was all just okay. I didn't *love* any of it. Even cardiology [my father's specialty] didn't ignite anything in me.'

As a junior doctor, it was easy to lose sight of the patients you serve. After all, you had to see a patient every seven to ten minutes. Each patient was simply another number. Thousands in the queue; the NHS backlog was well known. Attending to every patient's medical and emotional needs simply became impossible.

Everything changed in 2003 when she was pregnant for the first time. Marrying her husband, Eoin O'Brien, a Caucasian Irish-Catholic physician from Northern Ireland, was already an uphill battle with Serena's mother who disapproved of the union in the earliest stages, although later, she was more than accepting of the couple.[26] Now

---

[25] An NHS consultant is a senior doctor in the public healthcare services in the United Kingdom, which are set up for everyone without charge. The starting salary of a consultant is typically £84,559 per annum.

[26] 'I didn't know what my mother's opposition was,' Serena recalled. 'Was it religion? Was it race? I told my mother, "You're not exactly Malay, and you weren't a Muslim before."' When her mother, Daisy, first met with her then-boyfriend, Eoin, she pretended to not know English and spoke only Malay and only to Serena. Eventually, Eoin agreed to convert to Islam in Regents Park Mosque in London and changed his name on the IC to "Isa". Once married, Daisy became good friends with Eoin at an instant—she returned as the big-hearted and warm person again.

Serena was about to face another big challenge at the tender age of twenty-seven.

When she was in the twentieth week of pregnancy, Serena felt there was something amiss, but she wasn't sure. She attended her twenty-week scan, a checking scan that is offered to all women to make sure that all is right. Unfortunately, it wasn't. Tears rushed down her cheeks as she sat on the chair. No matter how equipped the couple was, they could never truly prepare for a moment like this.

The doctor told them the most devastating news. She had a missed miscarriage.

'Suddenly I was the patient, not the doctor. I had zero control. I was a person who has never been in that position before, and I was scared. I'm not just a symptom or a number. I'm not just a box to be ticked,' she said.

'From that day, I told myself I want to do something meaningful. I wasn't going to be another doctor who just ticks boxes and goes home.'

* * *

Billions of dollars, thousands of scientists, many decades later, there is still no cure for cancer. One reason is that there isn't just one cancer to be cured; there are hundreds. One drug that worked for one cancer patient may not work for the other, even when the other person has the exact same type of cancer. Most of the time, cancer is more complex than we understand through a microscope.

All of us have a unique set of genes in our bodies. The genes are made up of DNA, which are just four types of building blocks called nucleotides: Adenine (A), Cytosine (C), Guanine (G), and Thymine (T). If you could unroll your DNA, you'd see these nucleotides in a strip—something like this:

ATCGATCGATCGATCG

This strip makes you who you are. The instruction of ATCGATCG could say 'make his eyes brown' and your eyes will be brown. Another instruction of ATCG could say 'make his hair thick' and your hair will be thick. What if one day the instruction for your thick hair was computed as ATTC (wrong code) instead of ATCG (right code)?

Thankfully, your body is miraculous. It has real-time editing and correcting function, via the DNA-repair machinery, that helps you repair that error and revert back to normal. The error is called a mutation. But what if more and more of these errors happen? Worse, what if the wrong instructions happened on the DNA-repair machinery?

One mutation may be tolerable. But five or six mutations that hit important genes, could cause a cell to become cancerous. Mutation is like a slick and mischievous dark venom. It changes its form so fast that it is hard to track. It could communicate with the healthy cells to supply its blood. It could even climb on top of an immune system and shut down its function. When mutations keep giving the wrong instructions to the body, a swollen tumour would grow.

Initially, it was so difficult to find these mutations that the plan was to use a knife to cut off the entire tumour of cancerous cells. This was called the resection method. It worked sometimes. But cancerous cells may grow back after some time. Then, some scientists suggested using extremely toxic methods to kill off cancerous cells in a targeted way: Radiation. Or chemotherapy that flows through the bloodstreams with the same purpose. The problem with these methods was that typically, the healthier cells die together with the unhealthy cancer cells, making the patient weaker than before.

The other problem was that if the toxic methods didn't kill off *all* the cancer cells, that made the surviving cancer cells even more resistant to future drugs, making the mutations an evolved, deadlier creature.

But if it was just a matter of errors in instructions by the mutations, why don't we just find out where the errors were and cure those? The problem with that is that it was tremendously difficult to find where the errors were. Our body has six billion DNA letters. And there could be thousands of possible combinations of a mutation. How will you find all of them, let alone kill them?

'Let's say you have 3,000 mutations among six billion letters of ATCG, it's pretty hard to find. You can't just use a pen and paper to figure it out. It would be impossible,' Serena explained. 'The only way was to use a computer with high-processing power. You need to take the normal genes, and compare them to cancer genes. Then you write a program to teach the computer to find the 3,000 mutations in a body.'

In the past, it would take months just to find one mutation. The Human Genome Project took over ten years, 1,000 scientists, and $2.7 billion to produce the first complete human genome, which acted as a history reference book for doctors and scientists.

'If you put the letters of a human genome into a telephone directory, it would take 220 telephone directories to cover everything. The whole process of reading out was so preposterous, so unreal.'

The process of reading out these letters was called 'sequencing'. When Serena first started in 2009, it took about three months to get the whole cancer genome—the mutations in the body. Today, with the help of computers with high processing powers and advanced analytical tools, the whole process takes only a day.

That means cancer research is no longer a 'lab-bench science that relies on test tubes and pipettes to study organisms', it is now dependent on computers and number crunchers.

And perhaps there was no better place to study these future-proof methods than the prestigious Wellcome Sanger Institute.

* * *

The first fifteen close-knit scientists who contributed to the most ambitious project in biology, the Human Genome Project, started in a rustic old factory building that was used to manufacture metal tubes. The paint was peeling, the floor was uneven, the area would be flooded sometimes—that didn't bother them. They were working on a project comparable to putting a man on the moon, or the invention of wheels. When the first draft of the genetic Book of Humankind was published, the Sanger Institute knew that they were touching history.

The Sanger Institute was the single-largest contributor to the complete set of genes of a human body, used as a gold standard for scientists of the future. Today, the Sanger Institute, located in the small village of Hinxton, seventeen minutes from Cambridge University, hosts more than 1,000 employees from seventy-seven countries. Inside the ceiling-to-floor glass building were power stations designed to handle the banks of computers lined up to read the human genome.

'Today, we can handle so much data that we are producing a couple of genomes every twenty-four hours,' the head of IT said.

Look out the windows, you'd see rows of woodland flowers, with butterflies, dragonflies, and damsel flying across the fifteen-acre Wetlands Nature Reserves. When the cold of winter comes, frost would grip the edges of the red-brick Hinxton Hall building, welcoming 24,000 visitors who will take in the idealism of science.[27]

Serena didn't have the confidence to apply to Wellcome Sanger Institute. The website, at that time, was old-fashioned. She wasn't sure if this was the place for her and whether she would fit in.

'If you want to study genetics with cutting-edge technology, you have to apply to Sanger Institute. You must be crazy not to!' Serena's father told her. Sanger's lab infrastructure, computational approaches, and robotics were second to none in the United Kingdom.

But then one day Serena met the late Leena Peltonen, the head of human genetics at Sanger. The Finnish geneticist was internationally regarded as one of the world's leading geneticists, often tipped as Finland's next Nobel Laureate. Among others, she led the teams that identified genetic mutations for schizophrenia, obesity, heart diseases, lactose intolerance, and MS disease. [28]

'I saw this Finnish professor with fabulous blonde hair, always in a suit and high heels . . .' recalled Serena. 'I've never seen a person from science who's so perfectly put together. So, I applied to work with her. It was totally naïve because I didn't know how competitive it was—but Professor Peltonen was sick at that time, and my CV landed up with Mike Stratton, Head of Cancer. He invited me up to the Sanger Institute for a visit and a chat (it was basically an interview) and then said, come and work in cancer. So, I did. Serendipity got me into cancer.'

---

[27] Most visitors who come to Sanger Institute will always mention the three giant stainless steel balls that are supposed to reflect back on the people walking past them.

[28] Leena Peltonen died at the early age of fifty-seven from bone cancer. Sanger's obituary read: 'Her disarming smile, her charisma, and the flash of colour as she moved across campus will provide lasting memories for her friends and colleagues . . .'

4

In 2009, Serena was a thirty-three-year-old mother of two doing a PhD at the Sanger Institute. She was surrounded by people who were tougher and a decade younger than her, eager to press forward, taking no prisoners. Her PhD topic was also one that nobody would choose to study.

The conventional wisdom at that time was that there were two kinds of mutations in a human cancer. Like a taxi, there was a driver and many passengers. Only the driver was thought to be important—drivers were the cause of cancer. Passengers were just funny mutations that meant nothing. It was generally believed that each cancer only has around one to five driver mutations. Kill off the driver, then we will kill off the cancer.

'If you look at the genome as a whole, there are thousands of mutations. If only one to five driver mutation are important, then what about the rest?' Serena asked.

A professor in charge of training clinicians in research sat Serena down in his office one day. Serena held a cup of coffee in her hands and sat her 5'2" stature on the chair with her feet dangling, swinging back and forth, not touching the ground.

'Serena, the whole world is studying driver mutations, and you are studying passengers, is that right?' the professor said.

She hesitated, took a sip of her coffee, and in a high-pitched cracked voice said, 'Yes.'

'Serena, you're wasting your time. Passenger mutations are just noise, mutational debris, just random events. Why are you foraging round the bin of mutational detritus?[29] You ought to be considering something more important, more consequential.'

When a normal cell becomes a cancer cell, a lot of physiological responses would have turned wrong along the way. They would have created some damage, and they could leave patterns. To Serena, those potential patterns were not random noise, they were clues to what went wrong—what was causing the cancer.

---

[29] Detritus is a polite way of saying 'trash'.

Serena uses the analogy of a beach to explain,[30]

If you look at a beach, things look pretty random. But if you look closer, you might be able to see footsteps, you can tell whether the footstep is a human's or an animal's footstep. Then you zoom out and look at more footsteps of the same kind. You can now tell whether it belongs to an adult or child, what the height was, how fast it was travelling, whether it was walking or running.

Then you zoom out even more and look at other footsteps on the beach. Maybe this time you can see a turtle dragging its feet and tail to the beach to lay eggs. And there is a longer line with monitor lizard's footsteps going in the same direction. Now you can observe the drama that unfolded before you. The lizard went to eat the turtle eggs! It is no longer just random events any more.

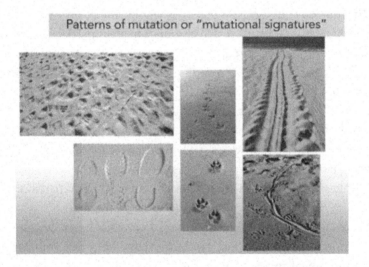

---

[30] A CNN Health report gave an alternative analogy of a murder crime scene: . . . [I]magine you're a forensic scientist dusting for fingerprints at a murder scene. You might strike it lucky and find a set of perfect prints on a windowpane or door handle that match a known killer in your database. But you're much more likely to uncover a mish-mash of fingerprints belonging to a whole range of folk—from the victim and potential suspects to innocent parties and police investigators—all laid on top of each other on all sorts of surfaces.

The footprints left behind are called mutational signatures. Imprints, patterns, clues. Essentially, Serena was arguing for a different way of seeing so that we get more insights into what was actually happening.

'I saw the power and the potential, and I couldn't understand why others couldn't see it,' said Serena. 'It's a bit like Christopher Columbus finding a new area—asking people to come over to the large piece of land. Except in this case, no one wanted to follow.

'I wasn't at all sure that it was going to work. I didn't really care. I just wanted to do what mattered to me, to learn. My aim wasn't to make it big—it was just to ask stupid questions and learn as much as possible.'

The next four years were gruelling for Serena. She slept three to four hours a day. Woke up at 5.00 a.m. to make breakfast and send her children to childcare, before entering the laboratory at 8.00 a.m. Then she would work till 5.00 or 5.30 p.m. without break, sometimes not even for toilet or food. Then she would rush back to prepare dinner for her family, and continue working from 8.00 p.m. till 1.00–2.00 a.m.

For her research, she was also required to deal with a huge amount of data. She had to learn coding from scratch to speed up her analysis. It was a stressful and competitive environment, and there wasn't a lot of camaraderie.

In 2012, Serena published a thesis that looked into the passenger mutations—also called mutational signatures—in breast cancer patients. It was a big deal. Most people would spend the entire PhD years on one gene or protein. Serena did twenty-one whole cancer genomes of breast cancer patients. Gathering thousands of mutation data, she showed that, even though breast cancers were traditionally classified into three categories, the idea of passenger mutations showed that it was even more individual and unique from one another than we assumed. Currently, although 70 per cent of breast cancer cases are cured, still around 30 per cent of breast cancer patients will not have good outcomes. Taking a holistic approach, by accounting for passenger mutations, we can see what else might be causing the cancer so that we could prescribe a different or additional treatment to these patients.

Her thesis ends with this passage,

> This study harnesses the full scale of whole-genome sequencing
> technology providing insights into hitherto unrecognized mutational
> signatures present in breast cancer genomes. **It is the first of its kind**
> and demonstrates the wealth of biological information that is **hidden**
> within these large datasets.[31]

Serena's thesis was widely celebrated. It was cited thousands of
times and published in one of the Big Three scientific journals: *Cell*.[32]
It was a hallmark of prestige and quality—the Big Three only publishes
the best of the best in the field.

She called her mother, Daisy, to explain her achievements—the
twenty-one breast cancers, the patterns left behind, the signatures—
but Daisy somehow seemed unamused.

'Okay, now you have a PhD in pretty patterns . . . but Serena,
you're still not an NHS consultant! How does this benefit humankind,
Serena?' asked Daisy.

Annoyed at first, it made Serena stop and think. 'I could easily
become a navel-gazing scientist who just puts her head down and gets
published or I could push it to clinical use and change some lives. It's
funny how parents still drive you even in your adulthood,' said Serena,
with a chuckle.

* * *

Joshua Barnfather was born in the port city of Hull in December 1987,
the final months of the economic boom under the neoliberal leadership
of Margaret Thatcher and Ronald Reagan. Born with soft blond hair,
bright blue eyes, and puffy red cheeks, Joshua was a healthy baby boy.
He was a smiley child, and that made his family jubilant. But his parents
realized something strange whenever they brought Joshua outdoors.

---

[31] Emphasis is this author's own.
[32] The Big Three of scientific journals are *Cell, Nature,* and *Science.*

Every time they returned from the outdoors, Joshua's face, arms, and lips would be covered with small spots of freckles. Joshua's parents started rubbing it off and applied lotion on the baby's skin. But it got worse. They didn't know what to do to stop it.

A few months later, Joshua's parents brought the baby to a doctor to ask if the freckles were unusual. The doctor looked at Joshua's spots and told the parents something doctors only told a hundred other patients: 'Your baby is allergic to the sun.'

Joshua was diagnosed with a rare genetic condition called Xeroderma Pigmentosum (XP), where Joshua had to avoid all forms of sunlight for all parts of his skin. Sunlight generally causes UV light damage to our skin. Sometimes if the sun is too strong, it may even leave a sunburn mark. But our bodies have cells that will detect these damages and send instructions to repair them. Joshua's body doesn't do that.

Children who have XP go through a tough time coping with this disease. Without knowing, they develop redness and blistering on their skin that would sting for weeks. Since he was young, Joshua has never left the house without wearing multiple layers of long-sleeved clothing and a protective visor that leaves no skin exposed. On the football field and playgrounds, Joshua will have a plastic separating his face and other children.

In the past, many children with XP developed their first skin cancer by the age of ten. Now, XP patients are taught to look after themselves, on what to wear and where to avoid, and to install UV-protected windows at schools, cars, and their houses. Children with XP these days do not have to die at a young age; they can live into adulthood.

Joshua didn't let the disease get in the way of the things he wanted to pursue in life. Courteous, intelligent, and always sweet, he was fascinated with how artificial intelligence and robotics could alter the world. He started his PhD in nuclear engineering at the University of Manchester when he was only twenty-three, where he studied the 'Metrology-Assisted Robotic Feature Machining on Large Nuclear Power Plant Components', collaborating with Rolls-Royce Civil Nuclear. All were indoors, of course.

'Despite the best efforts of mine and my family, over the course of my life I have developed several skin cancers that have been successfully treated without life-threatening impact . . . until now,' said Joshua.

In February 2017, twenty-nine-year-old Joshua Barnfather developed a tumour around the tip of his left eyebrow. His oncologists ran a test and diagnosed it as cancer called angiosarcoma and prescribed him a series of standard medications in hopes the lump would subside.

The next eight to nine months were hell for Joshua. The tumour developed into a giant lymph node in the shape of a ball, and it started to spread—to his lungs, livers, bones, and skull. His lungs were deflating all the time because of the tumour. His right cheek has swollen to the size of half his face. He became unrecognizable. A few doctors said it was hard to even look at him. Week in, week out of the doctor's room became futile. Nothing was working.

Death started to come to Joshua's mind when he found out that the disease got to the outer linings of his heart. This was not the first time he felt this way.

'[We] realize that the standard treatment doesn't quite fit me . . .' recalled Joshua. If he wanted to survive, he needed someone who was willing to do something unconventional. He was referred to Dr Serena Nik-Zainal.

* * *

Since Dr Serena's PhD publication, she has been one of the few experts regularly referred to when doctors can't figure out the diagnosis and treatment using the conventional way. Dr Serena still spends 10 per cent of her time as a doctor to keep her scientific research grounded. For Joshua's case, she was asked to look at the problem holistically and see if she could spot anything that the oncologists missed.

She showed me this chart that she found:

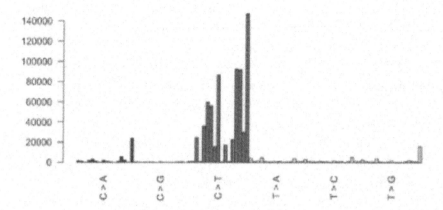

'A genomics analyst would just look at this and say this is a classic case of malignant melanoma—the most serious type of skin cancer that can happen to people under forty,' explained Dr Serena. 'But because Joshua has XP, it's normal for him to have this pattern of mutation. He's had it his entire life—that's not where to look. It's not the real cause of his metastatic cancer.'

Then she showed me another chart:

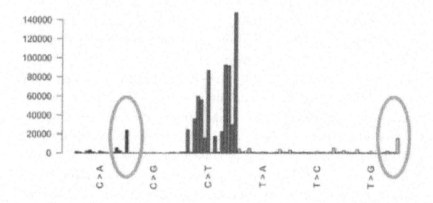

'What is really killing him—the mutations going through all of his organs, causing him tremendous suffering, almost costing his life—is actually this mutational signature, caused by defects in a protein called Polymerase Epsilon,' Dr Serena continued, referring to the two circled mutational data in the chart above.

'Polymerase Epsilon normally fixes DNA damage for most people, but in Joshua's cancer, it wasn't working, and it was producing this huge amount of mutations. When I found it, I said, "That's what's potentially killing him! It's that!"'

This was significant, because there may be one last therapy that Joshua could try: An immunotherapy called 'immune checkpoint inhibitors', with a drug called Pembrolizumab (pronounced pem-bro-lee-zoo-mab). Dr Serena knew that Pembrolizumab had cured patients with Polymerase Epsilon defects before—it was worth a shot.

Here's how it works. Joshua's body has cells called T-cells that can recognize and attack cancer cells. But there is a protein, called PD-1, that is stopping the T-cells from doing that. T-cells are the attacker and PD-1 is the inhibitor. Therefore, we need Pembrolizumab that will stop the inhibitor, PD-1, so that Joshua's T-cells could attack those cancer cells and save his life.

When Joshua heard this, he saw hope again. He was at the end of the list of options, and this seemed like his final chance.

'We[33] went to the oncologist and presented him with these findings and the possibility of using something like Pembrolizumab,' Dr Serena said. 'But the oncologist was hesitant. He said, "This is really experimental stuff, no?" But he's dying! Joshua doesn't have any other options—we've tried everything already. There was also another problem—it was an expensive drug. Because it wasn't an approved drug for this purpose, the NHS wouldn't fund this. We needed to look for funding elsewhere—it was £100,000 a year. That's a lot of money.'

They went to the local health authorities and made an Individual Funding Request application. It was rejected. Even though Dr Serena and her team were world experts on this, the local authorities still needed more evidence that it could work.

So, the medical team did more pathology experiments to prove it.

---

[33] 'We' refers to the medical team that had looked after Joshua's XP disease for many years, led by Dr Hiva Fassihi.

'The first time we did this pathology test called immuno-histochemistry for the PD-1 protein on his primary tumour, it returned negative. But we couldn't give up. I reasoned that what was killing him was the metastatic lesions. So, we pushed again, and this time got a slice from a metastatic lesion, and it returned positive. It worked! We now had additional evidence to support the idea that there was too much PD-1 in his cancer, and it could be a therapeutic target!' exclaimed Dr Serena.

They went back to apply to the local council for a second time. In less than twenty-four hours, they were rejected again. They weren't convinced that this experimental drug would work.

'It was absolutely depressing,' said Dr Serena. 'This man was literally dying!'

Joshua wasn't willing to squander his final chance at survival. Lying in the hospital bed, skinny from months of not eating well, he went online to a website called JustGiving and started his fundraising target. He posted,

I'm Joshua Barnfather. I'm 31 years old and I was born with a rare skin condition, Xeroderma Pigmentosum . . .

For my whole life, I've tried to avoid UV light. I've covered up during daylight hours, stayed indoors wherever possible and adjusted my life and environment to protect my skin and overall health.

Despite the best efforts of me and my family, over the course of my life I have developed several skin cancers that had been successfully treated without life-threatening impact; until now.

In February 2017, I was diagnosed with angiosarcoma, a cancer affecting the inner lining of the blood vessels.

I have had many unsuccessful attempts at face and lung surgery, chemotherapy, trial drugs and lymph node radiotherapy to tackle my cancer . . .

Because of my unique characteristics as a Xeroderma Pigmentosum patient, specialists believe that immunotherapy cancer treatment will be useful for me. However, this is not readily available on the NHS for my case and could cost around £100,000 per year, although there is a lot of uncertainty surrounding this.

Your generous contributions will help to fund this treatment and the associated care . . .

No matter how small, I am grateful for all contributions.

In twenty-four hours, thousands of pounds started pouring in. The Hull newspapers and Joshua's former high school started spreading his news and fundraised for him.[34] The mainstream newspaper, the *Daily Mail*, with a daily circulation of close to a million, made a story with a headline entitled, 'The businessman "allergic" to the SUN: 30-year-old battling a one-in-a-million condition has spent all his life avoiding daylight.' The BBC noticed his story and interviewed him.

'This man who is dying raised his own funds through crowdsourcing,' Dr Serena said. 'Through it all, he was so brave, smiling throughout without a word of complaint. Not a negative thing to say.'

Every few days, Joshua would share his updates with a 'Hi all' and ending with a smiley face to show his positivity throughout the process. Even as he was lying on the hospital bed with a tube circling his face, he still posted a picture of him giving a thumbs up thanking everyone. '[J]ust enjoying a night in hospital for a blood transfusion. Not doing too bad . . . You are really making a difference to my health. Thank you so much :)' he said. A few days later, he posted another photo of him in a brown T-shirt, face still swollen but managing a half-smile.

He said: 'I'm out of hospital now so I can begin my recovery in preparation for the Pembrolizumab treatment that we are all saving up for. It's been rough but we are all making good steps in the right direction everyday. Thanks all :)'

As he struggled through the days, he still tried to keep his head up and thanked the people for pushing the immunotherapy closer to reality—

---

[34] Joshua's former high school, Withersea High School, fundraised a total of £2,221 from sales of cakes and refreshments, cheques from staff and students, 'Mufti' day donations where students pay donation to wear non-school uniforms, as well as an eighteen-mile walk from Withersea to Hull along the old railway line.

Hi all, we are making excellent progress towards the goal. I can't thank you enough! Recently, it has been found that my condition has deteriorated a bit so this campaign is getting even more important to me. The cancer in my right lung has caused it to collapse so I'm having surgery this week to reinflate it . . . Looking forward to getting started :)

And then finally—

BIG NEWS!!! I've started immunotherapy and you all made it happen:) Docs soon decided I'd recovered enough to start immunotherapy! This meant I could pay with funds raised and get started . . . I can't thank you all enough.

After three cycles of Pembrolizumab, there was a significant reduction in the volume of disease. Then after the sixth cycle, he was already walking home 80 per cent recovered—smiling as always. His face shrunk back to its original form.

'The first time I saw pictures of Joshua, he was this man with a huge tumour on his face and about to die, and today, he's living a normal and healthy life,' Dr Serena recalled. 'To make a real impact on another human being . . . I felt this was a good enough reason for me to keep going and fighting. As my mom said, it's not enough to have pretty patterns on a computer screen—we must always ask, "How does this benefit humankind?"'

5

One of the most impactful psychological experiments started with a lie. Robert Rosenthal, then a thirty-five-year-old tenured professor at Harvard University, colluded with the principal of Spruce Elementary School, Lenore Jacobson, to lie to their teachers and students.

Among the teachers was a twenty-three-year-old Hispanic teacher, Beverly Cantello. Robert Rosenthal created a highfalutin sounding but inauthentic test called the 'Harvard Test of Inflected Acquisitions' and sent out a thousand copies to eighteen classrooms, including Beverly Cantello's class. The test, he said, was to see which students had the potential to excel. Then Robert Rosenthal pretended he leaked the 'results' of the test, where it says sixty-five out of 320 students were designated 'bloomers' (likely to do well).

Eight months later, he did an IQ test to the same group of students. He found that 255 non-bloomers had a four-point gain in their IQ. The sixty-five bloomers? Twelve points. One of the youngest students even had a whopping twenty-seven-point increase in IQ. What was more remarkable was that most of the bloomers were from lower-income Mexican families.

Only after the results were revealed did he and Lenore Jacobson tell the truth to the teachers.

'At first, I was offended. I thought, "How dare they?"' Beverly Cantello recalled, when she first found out about the lie.

But when the teachers saw the effect it had on students' performance, they couldn't stay mad any more.

'The bottom line is that if we expect certain behaviours of people, we treat them differently, and that treatment is likely to affect their behaviour,' said Robert Rosenthal. If you expect a student to be a bloomer, the student will believe he/she is a bloomer and perform better—even though the student isn't one. High expectations lead to high performance. The message to school was: Anyone can be great if the teachers told them so.

Robert Rosenthal called this the Pygmalion Effect. In Greek mythology, Pygmalion was a Cypriot sculptor who made an ivory model of a woman so perfect he fell in love with it. On a sacred festival, he made offerings to the sculpture and wished for a bride like her. That night, the sculpture turned warm and transformed into a woman who married him. Your expectations will soon be your reality—that is the power of a self-fulfilling prophecy.

The findings, published as 'Pygmalion in the Classroom', were groundbreaking. It made the front page of *The New York Times*. Robert was invited to the popular interview with Barbara Walters. It leapfrogged his name as one of 'The 100 Most Eminent Psychologists of the 20th Century'.[35] It remains one of the most widely cited psychology papers in the field today.

Amid the fanfare for his work, Robert Rosenthal thought about a darker side of the Pygmalion: What if you told students the opposite—that they are not meant for anything great, and their peers would overtake them? This could be the Golem Effect, he thought, named after clay-made robotlike statute brought to life to eradicate evil but that instead became a monster because of corrupting power. For years, nobody dared to carry out this real-life experiment with students for ethical reasons. What if the experiment had a powerful lingering effect where the students would feel worthless for the rest of their lives?

Even though experiments on the Golem Effect are limited, it is generally accepted that if you are told you're an underdog, you will likely perform poorly.

But Samir Nurmohamed, professor at the Wharton School of the University of Pennsylvania and an expert in underdog studies, challenged that. He thought the Golem Effect experiments were incomplete.

Before 2020, he recruited 327 participants for a mouse target task. It looked something like this:

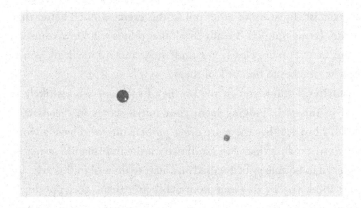

The rapidly moving circles in the video will turn larger one after another and will only burst when the participants click on them. The goal of this cognitive task was simple: Click as many moving circles as possible within five minutes. Every participant was given a fifteen-second practice round before they started.

But here's where it got interesting. After the practice round, all participants had to answer a list of questions while the reviewer was 'calculating' their practice-round scores to predict how well they will do. Before they started the actual task, they waited for thirty-two seconds before the reviewers' predictions were put on the screen.

Of course, this part is not actually real. The predictions were assigned at random into three groups: Underdog prediction, favourites prediction, and neutral prediction.

To make it believable, however, the reviewers' predictions were written informally with abbreviations, lowercase letters, and typos:

Underdogs: I do not think you fit the typical profile of someone who is likely to excel in this task. judging from your initial scores in the practice round, i can see that there are other participants who have a better shot at succeeding than you do. Based on the information available, you need to be able to be focused and alert to do well in this exercise. I just think other ppl fit this exercise much better than you do. In my opinion, I really think that others will blow you away in this task. You are clearly the underdog, and I dont think you've got what it takes to beat any of them.

Favourites: I think you fit the profile of someone who is likely to excel in this task. judging from your initial scores in the practice round, i can see that there are other participants who have a worse shot at succeeding than you do. Based on the information available, you need to be able to be focused and alert to do well in this exercise. I just think you fit this exercise much better than other ppl do. In my opinion, I really think that you will blow others away in this task. You are clearly the favorite, and I think you've got what it takes to beat all of them.

Neutral: Thanks for completing the practice round. You provided me what I needed to make a prediction. You can now proceed to the main task.

What did Samir Nurmohamed find? The reverse of Golem Effect. The underdogs, surprisingly, performed the best.

'What happens when we think that others expect us to fail? My research shows that these "underdog expectations" can actually motivate people to try to prove others . . . wrong,' he said in a *Harvard Business Review* article.

Howard Schultz, the former CEO and Chairman of Starbucks, attributed part of his success to this. He said, '[T]he entrepreneur in me was also fueled by feeling like an underdog . . . I was driven to prove that our company could achieve what others said was impossible.' The Grammy-winning musician, Jermaine Cole, called this underdog expectation his 'engine'. Aly Raisman, three-time Olympic gold-medallist, saw the comments of her being a 'Grandma', too old to perform, as the driving force behind her successful run at the 2016 Rio Olympics.

The same thing happened to Dr Serena when she first took up her PhD.

'At the beginning I was underestimated,' she said. 'People were looking at me and asking, "Who the hell is this thirty-something mom who goes home early?" I was the only one doing whole genome sequencing and passenger mutations, and the whole world was looking at driver mutations.'

Looking back now, it may have seemed like common sense that the passenger mutations that left footprints behind gave us clues on the causes of cancers and the personalized medicines we ought to develop. A healthy Joshua Barnfather doing robotics consultancy at Manchester with a smile makes us forget that he almost died because of the conventional thinking scientists held on to at that time.

From the outside, the science community is a group of dedicated professionals who put their heads down, waiting hard for the eureka discovery using cutting-edge technology, with the noble mission of making humanity better. In reality, however, inertia exists in adopting the latest technology and insights.

'Although the cost of doing a whole genome sequencing these days is equivalent to the price of a CT scan, many still prefer to do a lesser version of targeted sequencing, which doesn't give you an accurate picture of what is going on in the body of a cancer patient. Whole genome sequencing is like having a clear map, so you know the heights of the mountains and terrains. You don't want a sketchy map with only one or two genes and guess what is going on.

'Even when the cost part is settled, many doctors still fear the computational processes required to analyse data. I'm a doctor and I'm no great bio-informatician; I know my limits. But you need to do what's uncomfortable to push the envelope,' said Dr Serena.

Her questions about passenger mutations were considered 'stupid' at that time. She needed to actively block out the negative voices inside and outside of her head to maintain her focus. Statisticians thought her 'pretty graphs' were too simplistic. She was under the intense pressure of risking it all if it didn't work by the end of her PhD.

To challenge the conventional thinking, Dr Serena had to work much harder to prove what she was seeing was valuable. Three hours of sleep for three years straight. Not stopping for breaks, neither toilet nor food. Juggling two young children and a family. Learning to code from scratch. Twenty-one breast cancer samples.

All to prove something others considered noises, debris, detritus—trash. Something that saved Joshua's life. *I saw the power and the potential and I couldn't understand why others couldn't see it.*

But Dr Serena wasn't just underestimated because of the unpopular area she was researching. She was overlooked and mistreated for something much larger.

'I was actually thinking about leaving science altogether . . .' Dr Serena said. 'Behind all the success that people see, I was working under awful conditions. Joshua came at a crucial time—that moment saved me. I remember crying on my way to work every day. I told myself, "I don't want to do this for the rest of my life."'

6

The same year Serena published her PhD masterpiece, she was awarded the Wellcome Trust Intermediate Clinical Fellowship. A year later, she joined the Sanger Institute as a faculty member and continued to develop expertise in mutational signatures and seeing tumours differently.

'I was considered successful at the Sanger Institute in the traditional sense—I was publishing papers and producing scientific findings,' Dr Serena recalled. 'Behind that was a struggle every single day. It was like that since day one. But I just didn't have the courage to walk away because it was deemed so successful.

'My biggest mistake was that I continued to apply for funding, and I stayed.'

When Dr Serena first joined the Sanger Institute, she had already realized that she didn't fit in. It was a white, male, tough, alpha, masculine environment. Even though she was working on only three hours of sleep every day, Dr Serena still felt judged for leaving during early evening to prepare dinner for her children.

'A female post-doctoral fellow came to me one day and told me, "All the students here stay till 10:00 p.m. and that's what we're expected to do, and you always sworn off at 5:00 p.m. before the day turns dark."'

'I was taken aback by this because I thought, this is none of your business! I have two small kids, and I need to sort them out. Going home didn't mean that I stopped working in the evening. I was still learning to code and doing other work. It wasn't like I was slacking. But these snide remarks really made me feel judged as a mother, as an older scientist.'

Then it became more evident as she rose to the faculty member position. Among all faculty member, Dr Serena was the only non-white Asian female.

'I wasn't given lab space, I wasn't treated equally as the rest of the peers,' Dr Serena said. 'I wasn't put up for nominations. I also didn't have control of my funding—which was ridiculous for me. Every faculty member had control of their funding, which was put under their names.

'My funding sum was put under my boss's name. I thought, "Hang on, now that I'm a faculty member, my faculty funds should be under my name." It shouldn't be someone else's name. Because that means that whenever I need money from the funding pool, I have to ask someone's permission for it. Asking permission for something I am supposed to be in charge of?'

The academic team that she had been collaborating with on the mutational signatures work would schedule meetings at 5:00 p.m. on a weekend, without regard for common parent feeding time for a parent like Dr Serena. She would request that the meetings be put at another time, but the rest of the team would refuse. It was either that she attended or that the meeting was going to happen without her. These meetings would have major decisions made, and leaving Dr Serena out meant that she automatically didn't have a say.

During times when she attended, she tried to voice her disagreements, but oftentimes she would be without allies. She was treated differently, discriminated—almost ostracized in front of others sometimes. Some would feel awful for her, but they wouldn't say anything.

After these meetings, some would come up to Dr Serena and say things like, 'I'm so sorry for you, you shouldn't be treated like that, that was terrible!' But Dr Serena would tell them, 'Why didn't you say anything during the meeting! Don't tell me—I know what's going on. Tell him!'

'A lot of these little things happened all the time. It's very difficult to call out or stand up to it because these are little things. You feel like you're overreacting. But it wears you down because it happens every single day,' said Dr Serena.

The culture in any old and powerful establishment like the Sanger Institute favours the status quo—no one was encouraged to rock the boat. If you're unhappy with something, keep it to yourself. Don't be seen as challenging the conventional wisdom—don't be a troublemaker.

When people think of what scientists do, they think of a group of them in a laboratory, experimenting in their lab coats, solving the mysteries of the cosmos or the cure for cancer. Their shared idealism—almost romantic—drives their spirit in helping humanity take a step forward. But that was actually far from the truth.

Social psychologist Petra Boynton, who studied bullying in academia, said, 'It is an open secret in [academia]. You're hard-pressed to find a department that hasn't got a bully, and some places are a nest for them.'

In any year, approximately 25 per cent to 33 per cent of faculty members self-identify as being bullied; 40 per cent to 50 per cent say they have witnessed or heard of others being bullied. This is almost twice as high compared to other general workplaces.

Recent high-profile cases shed light on this overlooked phenomenon. A celebrated neuroscientist at the Max Planck Society, Tania Singer, who ironically was the world's pioneering expert on empathy, was accused of bullying, where any meeting with her had 'at least an even chance [the other person] would come out in tears.' One former lab member, Bethany Kok, said Tania Singer didn't accept her pregnancy, and that she screamed at her, calling her a slacker who was irresponsible and wasn't using good judgment. The same institution's astrophysicist, Guinevere Kauffmann, was also accused of bullying. Cancer genetics, neuroscience, palaeontology, and astrophysics were hotspots for allegations of this nature, where bosses would regularly abuse, belittle, unfairly criticize certain staff, creating an alienating and fearful environment.

Alison Antes, a workplace psychologist, said that bullying is the 'repeated and malicious mistreatment of someone that results in harm'. This could involve shouting, insulting, or intimidating the victims. Or it could be more indirect forms like 'spreading malicious rumours about another, undermining their work and opinions, or withholding information necessary for them to do their jobs.'

But why is it particularly bad in academia? And why do we know so little about it?

When a PhD student first joins the lab, they are at the bottom rung of a rigid hierarchy where the student is absolutely beholden to the supervisors for help, references, and opportunities. If your supervisor starts picking on you, gives you unrealistic workload and deadlines, and shouts at you for failing to deliver, your best bet is to keep your mouth shut and carry on. You look around you and you realize that's what everyone is doing. Confronting the supervisor would end your career.

Let's say you've succeeded and you're now on the next stage of your career. You're given a short-term contract, and the only way for you to secure a permanent position is to publish something great. You either publish or perish. The common whisper is that the brilliant people are often the biggest bullies. Nobody will touch them because they bring in big funding. They *can't help* their toxic behaviour, some may say. These environments are reinforced by silence, and over time, it becomes a pressure cooker where people feel like 'they're going to explode'.

'My colleagues wouldn't dare to rock the boat. God Almighty don't even mention anything about being female or Asian—it's just so taboo,' Dr Serena said. 'The establishment is something you protect at all cost. I tolerated it for very long . . . until I didn't any more.'

* * *

There came a point when, according to Dr Serena, she was no longer valued for what she brought to the table because she no longer 'toed the line and stayed in the box' and so there was no place for her there. Dr Serena recalled. 'I could see it coming. I didn't have a problem with it because I knew that I shouldn't stay in a place where I was no longer valued. So, I said, 'Fine, I'll go.' But that's when it started to get really painful.' According to Dr Serena, the Sanger Institute asked her to sign a settlement agreement, with a non-disclosure clause, that was highly unfavourable to her.

She said, 'the entire experience was dehumanizing for me—I felt I was treated like a lesser human being. I felt that if I wasn't female, small, and Asian they would have treated me differently. This whole thing about being aggressive on their terms. This was part of the alpha male stereotype. I was so angry—it made me even more vocal.'

Things reached a boiling point when, according to Dr Serena, Sanger sent lawyers to ask her to sign the settlement agreement or else they would sack her. This meant she would lose all her grants and her science. Nothing would belong to her any more.

Each time, Dr Serena would break down and cry at home due to the pressure. Everyone around her, including Dr Serena's lawyers, advised her to just sign it and start over. Many who left Sanger have signed settlement agreements. It was commonly held that the establishment was too powerful, and it wasn't worth the risk. Also, perhaps their terms were more favourable.

Finally on a Thursday afternoon, an emotionless Dr Serena went to the campus and slipped them a resignation letter.

She said, 'I thought, I'm not signing this. Here's my resignation letter, and I'll see you in court,' Dr Serena recalled. 'If you don't let me take everything that is mine, you'll be reading all about it in the newspapers. I didn't know if I was going to actually publicize it, of course. I'm not normally that confrontational. Even I surprised myself. But I was not going to be cowered so that's what I said.'

When she walked out of the campus, she did not sign a single piece of paper. This was an enormous risk. Sanger Institute was an establishment that nobody dared to cross. Cancer research was intense and competitive; people were not willing to risk Sanger for someone like Dr Serena. Sanger could give her a bad referral and nobody in cancer research or science would give Dr Serena a job.

'That could have happened easily—easily. I could really lose everything and without a job to go to.'

She walked off on Thursday, and on Friday morning, she was at Cambridge University, twenty minutes from the Sanger Institute. She brought her profile and the approved grants. She told them, 'I need a job. I just resigned from the Sanger Institute.'

They welcomed her immediately.

* * *

After Dr Serena had left, she met up with eleven others who left Sanger that year. It became apparent that more staff were leaving due to a series of mistreatments, and they knew they had to do something. Many remained anonymous to protect their careers; only three revealed their names to the public—one of them was Dr Serena Nik-Zainal. The twelve of them formed a whistleblowing group and reported several complaints that are not fully clear in the public domain, but included failure to follow due process in governance matters, bullying and harassment, and failure to deal with intellectual property and/or data matters appropriately.

A few months after Dr Serena had left, UK's *The Guardian* published this story with the headline, 'Bosses at leading UK science institute accused of bullying staff.'

A day before, Dr Serena's interview in a piece entitled 'The Duty to Speak Up' was published on one of the Big Three, *Nature*.

In the 899-word interview piece, she said,

> Highly successful environments are frequently dominated by alpha personalities who are more likely to be male . . . Frequently, powerful persons are the perpetrators, and societal pressure increases our ability to turn a blind eye.
>
> [I]t takes courage to speak up, and there can be consequences. The intensity of the reaction to my speaking up was severe. I missed out on a career step, a position in a high-profile grant, a nomination for something. I did not mourn those losses. Instead, I grieved for the overall message—I was valued for my contribution, but only if I remained silent.
>
> We need to speak up. All tyranny needs to gain a foothold is for good people to remain silent.

The story cooked up a storm. People outside academia were jolted by the scandal and public pressure built on the Sanger Institute to investigate. Within a month, *The Guardian* published another article that highlighted the shocking statistics of 300 academic staff who were bullied in the past year alone. One respondent compared his boss's managerial style to the 'classical tyrannical' behaviour of Henry VIII—everyone was treated with suspicion and seen as 'someone (sic) to be crushed.'

Another described her university as a 'Kafkaesque nightmare', where she was escorted from the workplace after making a bullying complaint, losing her job, family income, and her 'sanity'. Fourteen universities had used non-disclosure agreements to resolve bullying cases by asking staff to sign agreements in exchange for financial payouts.

Bullying had become ingrained in the culture of too many academic institutions, said the president of the Royal Society, the oldest scientific academy in continued existence.

After six months of investigations, the senior management of Sanger was cleared of all counts of allegations: Gender discrimination, wrongful exploitation of scientific work, misuse of grant monies, bullying. The director, Michael Stratton, issued an apology for 'failures in people management' and the 'unintended detrimental effects on individuals', but the investigation found that the way he managed staff was 'neither gender-specific nor amounts to harassment'.

'The whole investigation was a whitewash,' said Dr Serena. 'They didn't even interview some of us who lodged the complaints against the institute. There was no clearly independent, external investigation, no panel. It was only one investigator, and he was a lawyer hired by the Sanger Institute, who admitted to us he didn't have intellectual property experience!'

Being a key witness to the investigation, Dr Serena expected to be interviewed, but it never came. She emailed and called them to ask to be interviewed. Eventually the investigators agreed, reluctantly. In the final moment, however, they cancelled it, only to reorganize it after much discussions.

On the interview day, Dr Serena brought a senior colleague with her. The interviewer entered the room, and the first thing he said to Dr Serena was, 'We won't be asking you any questions, no discussions on bullying today.'

'So, for the rest of the interview, I was just sitting there, listening to the investigator interviewing my friend,' said Dr Serena. 'He didn't ask me a single question even though I was a key witness, he barely looked at me! It was clear to me at that point it was going to be a whitewash investigation.'

In contrast, the bullying investigations against top geneticist, Nazneen Rahman, done by the Institute of Cancer Research in 2018 had a full investigation panel, where they interviewed all twenty-two complainants and all twenty-three signed witnesses. In the end, Nazneen was suspended, losing a £3.5 million grant as part of the anti-bullying and anti-harassment policy of the funder.

For Sanger, the 626-page evidence was downplayed, including 13,000 samples intended to prove unethical use of data by Sanger, and the entire process was opaque. Two highly redacted versions of the reports were released: One to the lead complainant, another to four other complainants.

'THE REST OF US WERE RESTRICTED FROM SEEING EITHER!' Dr Serena lamented on Twitter.

In spite of the severely inadequate investigation process, the activism had an effect. More people from academia became comfortable questioning the establishment's behaviour. A year after the headline by *The Guardian*, another scandal from the Sanger Institute made the headlines.

'Genetics lab told to hand back African tribes' DNA,' read the headline of *The Sunday Times* of UK. Sanger Institute had been accused of taking 75,000 DNA samples from the indigenous tribes for commercialization without consent.

Stellenbosch University wrote to the Sanger Institute director in scathing words:

> This conduct raises serious legal and ethical consequences . . . [W]e
> have instructed the Wellcome Sanger Institute to cease any current
> or planned commercial activities related to the DNA and data in
> question, and to return the samples and data to the university.

Deepti Gurdasani, a former geneticist at the Sanger Institute, said that she raised this concern repeatedly, and she lost her job after she filed a complaint about this.

'It's great to see the silence around this being broken,' she said.

Things did not get easier for Dr Serena afterwards. While she was supported by colleagues, friends, and family who believed that bullying in academia ought to be confronted, many labelled her a 'troublemaker'. A few scientists avoided working with her because 'she tends to speak up.'

'You quickly figure out who's got a spine and who doesn't,' Dr Serena said, with a relenting laugh. 'If someone is really going to think less of me for speaking up, then I really can't care about working with that person anyway. People will think what they think—life is too short to care about what others think.

'One of my mentors once told me, "The thing about you, Serena, is that you don't give a damn what others think—you just say it." When I raise something, it's not to be difficult. It's to make things better. And sometimes people will get upset about it. But you know . . . it is what it is!' she said.

7

On the mild October autumn of 2019, Dr Serena Nik-Zainal flew to the University of Bern, a university founded in 1834 and the third largest in Switzerland. Light rain covered the grassy courtyard of the small campus; leaves loosened from tree branches and flew gently to the ground.

Dr Serena was dressed in a tangerine-red blouse with patterns of dancing blue petals and a thin bow at the centre of her chest. The ends of her sleeves were folded inwards. Her hair caressed her shoulders, in light-brown strings that matched her eyes. Round diamonds hung from her earlobes, two rings on each finger of her left hand. She walked into the august auditorium through a cascading staircase with checkered tiles to a dome crafted with allegories of the faculties.

Guests walked up to congratulate her. Dr Serena was the centre of attention that night—she was the first woman to win the prestigious Josef Steiner Award alone.

'I'm surprised to see that you're here all by yourself,' a few guests said to Dr Serena. 'Where is your family?'

Due to its rarefied quality of only awarding scientists every one to two years, the Josef Steiner Award is also called the 'Nobel Prize for Cancer Research'. Winners are called 'Laureates'. Every cancer researcher dreams of receiving this award, given how competitive the field is, and how difficult it is to solve one of humanity's biggest health problems.

'I honestly didn't realize it was such a big deal! The organizers told me a few months back and asked me to keep this under wraps. So, I did, and I just carried on with my life—research, clinic, conferences, being a mom. It totally went over my head.'

When the Malaysian newspapers blew up with her achievement, journalists and her BBGS girlfriends started calling to congratulate her.[36]

'I can't believe you didn't invite any of us, Serena . . .' said her mother on the phone. 'You went there alone!'

That night, Dr Serena received the award for her 'groundbreaking research' of holistic cancer genome profiling and mutational signatures, initially considered mere debris.

'Prizes like the Josef Steiner Award are aimed at midcareer or up-and-coming people (or teams) . . . usually for people who are not very senior in the field,' said Dr Serena, who was only forty-three when she received it. 'So, for my team, this is a wonderful boost and an enormous recognition.'

At the time of writing, Dr Serena works with a multidisciplinary team of twenty under a loose structure. These days, she wakes up slightly later than her gruelling PhD schedule. At 6.00 a.m. she stretches on her yoga mat, and she cycles to work with a smile, leaving the campus by 4.30 p.m. every day. The hours between 9.30 a.m. and 2.00 p.m. every day are most crucial for her team. That is a block dedicated to hardcore science. In other hours, her team can work anywhere at any time—as long as they get the work done.

'I have a diverse team, extremely so,' Dr Serena said. 'Not only diversity in things we can see (race, gender) but also in things we cannot see, like how you communicate and think. People in computation may think differently, and thus sometimes may say things that do not sound socially acceptable . . . I try to get people to acknowledge this spectrum of difference and still work together.

'But what I don't do is to make them versions of me. I want to develop them into the best versions of themselves. Above all, I try to make sure they feel safe in my team. A lot of bad behaviour comes from insecurity. If they're secure, they're more likely to collaborate and help each other. Pitting talents against each other may produce remarkable results but it creates bad people in the end.'

---

[36] Serena's BBGS WhatsApp group is one of the busiest groups she's in. They celebrated Serena's award with many 'Hoorays' as though 'they were the ones who won the prize.'

A few months before my interview with her, she was awarded another prestigious award: The Francis Crick Medal and Lecture 2022 for her 'enormous contribution to understanding the aetiology of cancers by her analyses of mutation signatures in cancer genomes.'[37]

'What do you do to release stress?' I asked.

'Kungfu!' said Dr Serena, who was coughing from Covid-19 the day of our interview. One of her favourite Kungfu moves was the roundhouse kick, a full force move that used the whole leg around the body to hit someone.

'What people don't know is that the key to deliver an effective roundhouse kick is actually the staying leg, not the kicking leg. The staying leg must keep the body's balance and turn with the kicking leg without falling over.

'If you think about it, a lot of Kungfu is about balance and how rooted you are to the ground. Much like life, isn't it?'

Epilogue

A year before the Covid-19 pandemic, Serena was invited to be the external international examiner by the Universiti Sains Malaysia Hospital in her grandmother's hometown, Kota Bharu, Kelantan.

'I said, great! Of course, I'd do it. I get to go to Kelantan again after so many years, and it's good to see how much it's changed. It has a university now!' said Serena.

When she arrived in Kelantan, the university staff welcomed her. The professors even drove her around town for food and sightseeing.

'Didn't you grow up here with your grandmother when you were young?' the professor asked. 'We should go find that house!'

'No one lives there any more though . . .' replied Serena. 'But sure-sure, let's find it.'

They drove to the address and found a dilapidated wooden home; the surrounding was unchanged for decades. Serena could still feel the

---

[37] The Francis Crick Medal and Lecture 2022 was awarded by the Royal Society.

strong winds, the waist-high waters during the monsoon, the itchy paddy fields air, the giant mouse racing below the ceiling.

Then she saw the house beside her grandmother's place that had five young girls she used to play with as a child.

She remembered that one of the girls had features similar to hers.

'I always think about her . . . We grew up and played together. We even looked alike. But I am now here in Cambridge and she barely left Kelantan. Our lives could easily have been swapped but for pure chance.

'Life deals you a set of cards. Where you grew up, who your parents are, what rare disease you have . . . it is completely chance. Of course, I worked hard and tried to do my best, but I cannot deny that privilege played a huge role in giving me what I have today.'

The parents of that family gave the five girls names that started with an 'S'—Suzana, Soraya . . . The girl who looked like her was called 'Nik Sarina'.

Key takeaways

- Being underestimated may not be a bad thing; it motivates you to try harder to succeed.
- Always make space for those who do not fit the standard mould.
- Luck plays a huge part in your success. Always count your privilege and give back as much as you can. Make the best use of the cards dealt to you.

Chapter 4

Nor Salwani Muhammad

How a middle-level government auditor exposed the
world's largest financial scandal and what it teaches
us about the power of being quiet and invisible

*'Even with the trembling voice, you realize, "Damn, this
fifty-something Malay aunty did all of this."'*

1

The High Court of Kuala Lumpur sits on a thirty-acre stretch of land as the second-largest court complex in Asia. Large pillars and granite stones hold the front entrance; the broad stairwells and elevated floors were designed to tower over you, making you feel small. In every courtroom, legal formalities of bowing in front of the judges as they enter, taking the oath on the witness stand, and the strict adherence to rules remind you that this is a serious venue—no one is above the law.

Until today, nobody remembered seeing Nor Salwani walking into the witness room. But even if you saw Nor Salwani outside of the court setting, you would probably still miss her. She is petite at around 160 cm, with an everyday light-framed pair of glasses, and a dark-coloured hijab; she is reserved and untalkative, occasionally frightful. She treads lightly on God's earth, appearing and disappearing without notice—a number in the crowd.

'She is your typical fifty-something Malay aunty working in the civil service—unmemorable,' journalist Emir Zainul, who covered court cases in Kuala Lumpur, told me. 'I could easily mistake her for any of my mother's friends.'

Nor Salwani Muhammad, a fifty-two-year-old middle-level government auditor, was the fifth witness in a long list of eighteen called by the prosecution to testify in court. When she walked in, journalists thought the same, *probably just an accountant to confirm some details.*

This was the only courtroom packed to the brim. The other courtrooms were almost devoid of audience beyond interested parties. High-profile court cases happened here once in a while but never with a former prime minister sitting at the dock. Supporters and reporters formed a beeline at the front entrance of the courtroom. Inside, every movement invited a reaction from the public gallery. A laugh of mockery, a murmur of confusion, a grumble of disbelief. There was even a bomb scare. The courtroom was a theatre.

Looking distraught and defeated, the fallen former prime minister, Najib Razak, was charged for abusing his power as a public officer, an offence under the Malaysian Anti-Corruption Commission Act 2009. If convicted, he could face a maximum of twenty years in jail.

At 1.40 p.m. on 20 November 2019, Nor Salwani took the witness stand to testify against the prime minister and his associate at the scandal-ridden company, 1Malaysia Development Berhad (1MDB).

'I, Nor Salwani binti Muhammad, do solemnly and sincerely swear that I shall speak the truth, the whole truth, and nothing but the truth,' she said.

But she might as well have said, 'I, Nor Salwani binti Muhammad, will today reveal the greatest bombshell you have ever heard of.'

2

Nor Salwani was twenty-four when she first became a government auditor. Like most government auditors, this was the first and only job in her career. For the next thirty years, Nor Salwani would climb up the National Audit Department (NAD) ranks at an expected pace, reaching a directorial level four months after she turned fifty. Her soon-to-be boss, Saadatul Nafisah, had just been transferred to the NAD headquarters at Kuala Lumpur when Nor Salwani first joined the service. Saadatul was thirty-six then and the opposite of Nor Salwani: Confident, eloquent, and poised to be leading a large organization. When she became the Director of Audit in the final parts of her civil service career, many thought she was exactly where she belonged. A 'lady boss' who comes with a stature, unintimidated and standing her ground when grilled by others. After retirement, Saadatul became a consultant to the Asian Development Bank and was appointed to the board of a subsidiary of the oldest conglomerate in Malaysia.

Nor Salwani and Saadatul would eventually report to the Auditor General, Ambrin Buang, a lanky and bespectacled gentleman, born in the thick of the Malayan Emergency of 1949. Ambrin spent a rich life in public service, working at the Ministry of Education, Ministry of Trade, National Institute of Public Administration, and the Malaysian Embassy; he was awarded the nation's second-highest title, 'Tan Sri', at the age of fifty-six. He has a gentle and unthreatening way of speaking, occasionally mincing the end of his sentences, reminding you of a grandfather. When he gets excited or furious about what he is talking, his voice jumps a few pitches.

When you visit the NAD's website, you would realize that the word 'integrity' appears many times. Every government auditor will mention a document they hold like a holy book—the Code of Ethics. In this thirteen-page document, the word 'integrity' is mentioned twelve times. In the nineteen-page description of the NAD's most recent planning document, 'integrity' appeared sixteen times.

To every newly recruited civil servant, Saadatul would always remind them, 'Work with honesty and integrity'. She continued this even after her retirement.

'Integrity' is often a tricky phrase to understand fully beyond a series of moral broad strokes. It is sometimes an umbrella stand-in for honesty, transparency, and trustworthiness. It is perhaps more interesting to comprehend integrity in a negative sense—what do you do when your integrity is threatened?

Besides leading a clean and uncontroversial personal life, the Code of Ethics at the NAD raises the concept of duty to report as part of integrity:

> *The auditor must inform the supervisor or superior if he/she is faced with integrity issues, like reporting worries or suspicion against a violation of integrity.*

If you have even the slightest of concern or suspicion—even if they are unconfirmed or turned out to be overly cautious—you are still encouraged to report it. The ultimate point of this Code is to ensure that the auditors err on the side of caution. The credibility and reputation of a government auditor rests on higher stakes than a private auditor. A government would rather you alert them early and frequently than to miss a signal—even if it turned out to be a false alarm.

This is necessary because an auditor's job is to be pre-emptive. They are the guardians of our beliefs. They tell us whether we could rely on something presented by government bodies or companies.

That was why the role of an auditor is held in great prestige. The Federal Constitution, the supreme law of the land, dedicates three articles to the roles and duties of the head of government auditors, i.e. Auditor General, a position appointed by the King. Ambrin explained the job of an auditor in this manner:

> Auditing can be considered a form of inspection, analysis, and evaluation that is continuous and systematic on the financial statements, record, operations, and administration of an organization to determine whether the general principles of accounting, management policies, rules, and procedures and followed.

A good analogy was explained by a chartered accountant based in New Delhi called Apurav Garg. The question asked, 'How do I explain to my eleven-year-old son [audit]?' He answered:

> When your kid comes home next time with some homework from school, ask him to complete it, with a promise of explaining the question he asked.
> Now, the following conversation could do the trick:
> You: Have you done your homework?
> Kid: Yes, Dad!
> Next day, the teacher finds two mistakes. She asks him to correct them.
> Now, on the basis of her reviews throughout the year, she forms an opinion about your child's performance and reports it to you.
> On the basis of [the] number of mistakes the teacher (an auditor) finds, he assesses the knowledge or intelligence of the child (in real life, that is the management's competency) and includes such an assessment in his report to the father (shareholders). He also reports the mistakes not corrected by the kid (management).

An auditor is not responsible for catching fraud. That is for the forensic accountants who will interview people in the organization to the get to the bottom of a suspicion. However, if something is highly unusual, then the auditor ought to flag this in the audit report as part of the auditor's opinion. Auditors are the early detectors. Using the teacher analogy above, if the kid has been delivering sub-par grades for History and one day delivered an 'A' from a paper with answers identical with his classmate's, you have reasons to suspect he cheated or plagiarized. You turn the kid in to the discipline teacher or even the police depending on the severity.

That is why an Auditor General has enormous power to request and inspect every document and explanation, to be given under oath, and to empower any party to investigate anyone related to the auditee organization.

In short, an auditor is always trying to find out whether what is presented is 'true and fair'. If an auditor says it is, that means you can trust it—that becomes your belief. If the auditor says no, then you become wary of the organization. Auditors are the guardians of our beliefs.

Bearing the burden of the nation's trust, Nor Salwani, Saadatul, and Ambrin will face the most arduous and problematic task of their career yet: To audit the highly controversial 1MDB, where the former prime minister sat as chairman. The word around was that this was a fraudulent scheme by a few unscrupulous and spendthrift party-goers—perhaps the largest in the world.

'At that time, there was information that 1MDB had made large borrowings and expenses and no one on the board [of 1MDB] were representatives from the Ministry of Finance,'[38] said Saadatul in her witness statement to the court.

The audit background of 1MDB was also extremely concerning, with three of the Big Four[39] accounting firms fired or terminated in the years before. Early in 2010, Ernst and Young were supposed to complete the audit for the 2010 annual reports. But when they raised questions about unspecified investments, they were fired. KPMG took the mantle for two years after that and signed off the previous auditor's

---

[38] 1MDB is a government-linked company and would thus be expected to have a representative from the government in the board.

[39] Big Four includes Deloitte, KPMG, Ernst and Young, and PwC.

audit report within three weeks, failing to take into account material disclosures of transactions in 1MDB's US$1 billion investment in a joint venture that were allegedly siphoned to a shell company called Good Star Limited.

But then things took a turn. It was said at the time that KPMG found out that Najib allegedly knew about the bogus investment by 1MDB in Brazen Sky Ltd, a British Virgin Islands company. KPMG did not conclude the 2013 financial reports because 1MDB's answers to their probing questions were not forthcoming. Najib kept calling the former 1MDB CEO Mohd Hazem Abdul Rahman on his mobile phone to ask for the accounts in 2013 to be closed. Mohd Hazem felt pressured, and thus suggested for KPMG to be dropped and be replaced with Deloitte. Two down.

Deloitte came in to sign off on KPMG's previous unsigned reports. However, in July 2016, US Attorney General Loretta Lynch announced that they would be filing to recover more than US$1 billion that was 'stolen from 1MDB', the largest ever by the department's Kleptocracy Asset Recovery Initiative. Royalties from *The Wolf of Wall Street*, Van Gogh, Monet, jet aircraft, Park Lane hotel in New York, high-end real estate in Los Angeles—all became items under investigations. A week after, Deloitte resigned and stated that their signed audit reports between 2011 to 2014 should no longer be relied on—a sign that something fishy was going on.

Due to intense public pressure, the Public Accounts Committee (PAC) of Parliament and the Cabinet turned to the country's foremost auditor, NAD, for a special audit,[40] which translates to 'tell us what is really going on.'

Everyone was asking: Is the NAD, like other government units, submissive to the control and command of the former prime minister, or independent and loyal to their enshrined value of 'integrity'?

Within a week of the request for a special audit, a team was put together. Ambrin knew that no one other than Saadatul could lead this as she was the Director of Audit of the NAD. To handle

---

[40] A special audit is an audit requested by special authorities like the Cabinet or Parliament that is not part of the NAD's planned audit. It has investigative intentions.

this gargantuan task, Saadatul selected twelve of the best and most trustable members of the NAD. Team members were further divided into smaller audit teams according to specific areas like Financial Analysis team, 1MDB Development team, and the Energy (Investments) team. The coordinator who oversaw all things big and small: Nor Salwani.

* * *

Frustrated. Disappointed. Cheated. Those were the words Ambrin used to describe how he felt throughout the 1MDB audit. What would have taken five months under normal circumstances took almost a year to complete due to the delays and an uncooperative 1MDB.

'[F]inancial statement for 1MDB was [given] only until March 2014, and other supporting documents sought by NAD including bank statements and management accounts were not given, despite various requests being made. This was the difficulty faced by the NAD in auditing 1MDB,' said Ambrin.

Typically, auditors would also have access to the auditee's computers or servers to cross-check certain information during the process. In this case, none was given.

This was despite the fact that it was the Auditor General's constitutional right to receive: 'records, books, vouchers, documents, cash, stamps, securities, stores or other property subject to [the Auditor General's] audit'.

Saadatul met the 1MDB CEO, Arul Kanda, personally and listed down the documents that were vital for audit verification. Without this, it was impossible to perform her duty as an auditor. Arul was no less obstructive than his predecessor, Shahrol Azral, who wrote letters preventing auditors from photocopying documents and requiring the prime minister's approval for any audit.

'I met [Arul] many times, but the information never came,' said Saadatul. 'We did not get 100 per cent [of the requested documents], only 60 per cent. It took a long time.'

The obstructions were getting increasingly serious because the NAD found many red flags in the 1MDB accounts that required urgent explanations.

In Ambrin's words to the court, this was what they found:

[O]ur findings were that 1MDB group's performance was unsatisfactory due to debt and cash flow problems only after six months into operations. Governance was very weak, almost without complying with the rules and Board's decisions, and major investments were made without due diligence or detailed evaluation. The business model of 1MDB depended on loans inside and outside the country, which proved burdensome to 1MDB. Its borrowings were higher than its revenue, and they didn't make a profit.

Saadatul gave another example of these inadequacies found in the 1MDB audit:

NAD found that the equity investments into the joint venture with PetroSaudi was not a move that had strategic planning because it was done in eight days without due diligence or detailed evaluation, and before the issues raised by the Board were addressed and resolved. The joint venture agreement also had many clauses that did not prioritize the interest of 1MDB.

As with every audit process, 1MDB was given a chance to provide feedback on the auditors' findings in an Exit Conference.[41] The NAD gave 1MDB two weeks to respond and attend. But characteristic of the audit process thus far, they received no reply.

In the weeks after, on 20 February 2016, Nor Salwani took the final report to the largest domestic security printer in Malaysia, Percetakan Keselamatan Nasional Sdn Bhd (or National Printing Security), for printing. Located in Jalan Chan Sow Lin of Kuala Lumpur, the printer was heavily securitized with limited people access and multiple physical checks. Nor Salwani needed to print sixty copies, each 354 pages long. She watermarked each copy in sequence, from '01' to '60'. The next day, the printed copies were sent to the Chief Government Security Office for storage of confidential government

---

[41] An Exit Conference is a formal meeting that takes place at the end of an audit between the head of departments and the auditors to discuss the latter's findings and recommendations.

assets like these. After a long audit process, this was the final step before tabling to the PAC on 24 February 2016. Najib and the Arul Kanda would be called to question.

Or so she thought.

Early in February 2016, Najib's principal private secretary, Shukry Salleh, called Ambrin. Shukry was a sixty-one-year-old civil service veteran with wavy middle-parted salt-and-pepper hair and stern eyes staring straight from his frameless glasses.

'[Najib] was afraid that nonsense may be written in the [audit] report,' Shukry recalled. The prime minister wanted to see what was being written before it was handed to the PAC. The 1MDB had become a crisis that needed to be 'handled'.

Never in the history of special audits had the auditee (1MDB here) been given a copy of the audit report before the final submission. After a visit to the prime minister's office, Ambrin informed Saadatul and Nor Salwani that there was a change of plans.

On 24 February 2016, the printed copies were not sent to Parliament's PAC as planned. Instead, there was a special meeting at the government chief secretary's office.

Nor Salwani and Saadatul didn't know what the meeting was about. It was an unusual request that broke the flow of the audit process. This meeting was held on the instruction of the prime minister. They wondered: What was going on?

3

The government chief secretary at that time was a sixty-one-year-old man named Ali Hamsa.[42] Like Shukry, Ali was a civil service veteran, who had spent thirty-five years in high-profile ministries and authored two books about public policy. He towered over others, making the thinning strands of hair on the top of his head less obvious and was comfortable in front of the crowds and the camera. During the height of the 1MDB scandal, he told the civil service to not 'bite the hand

---

[42] Ali Hamsa passed away on 21 April 2022 at the age of sixty-six.

that feeds you'. On another occasion, he warned civil servants against playing online games like Pokémon Go during work hours.

Ali's office was right next to the prime minister's office, at the centre of the administrative district of Putrajaya, surrounded by mighty landmarks such as the Putra Mosque, Moroccan Pavilion, Putra Perdana Park, and the largest man-made lake in Malaysia.

Nor Salwani arrived early at 8.30 a.m. to Ali's office on 24 February 2016. She brought along copies of the report as well as supporting documents to defend the NAD's findings. She could remember the details and location of every document like the back of her hand, each had been numbered and labelled. She chose a seat that gave her full vision of the meeting so she could record the minutes. Her boss, Saadatul, would be tasked with answering the questions. Recording minutes in a high-stakes meeting became a vital task. That was Nor Salwani's job. Saadatul came in shortly after, took her notes out and sat to the right of Nor Salwani. She took out her pencil case and placed it to the left side of her table. It was easier this way—she wrote with her left hand.

Minutes later, Ali's staff came in and asked every low-ranking officer to leave the room immediately. He repeated himself and ushered them out the door in a rush. *Leave!* Nor Salwani did not know what to do.

She needed to record the minutes to act as proof of every discussion with 1MDB but she was being chased out. The other officers quickly packed their documents and working papers into their bags and waited outside the room before the other powerful men came in. Nor Salwani didn't have time to tell anyone her concerns, nor did she have the standing to ask.

Nor Salwani was, after all, just a lowly ranked officer in the meeting on 24 February 2016.

* * *

Ambrin came late to the meeting. When he arrived, he already saw several high-ranked government servants. Other than Saadatul, there was Ali, Shukry, Arul Kanda (1MDB), and representatives from the Attorney General Chambers and the Treasury.

As Ambrin took his seat, Ali set the agenda for the meeting. He went through the talking points given to him by the prime minister's office, which contained points of contentions that must be 'resolved'. Without this, Ali would have been clueless; he only had a general idea of what would be discussed. He hadn't even read the audit report in contention.

When the meeting began, Ambrin and Saadatul already knew where this was headed. The government was trying to persuade the NAD to remove certain parts from their audit report.

'[T]he more we disclose [in the audit report], the more difficult for us to defend, especially the [prime minister]. His name will be tarnished. If his name is tarnished, then nationally, we are tarnished also, politically and economically,' Ali said. 'So that's why I thought we can go through some areas of concern since Ambrin has kindly agreed that we can bring Arul here, as the representative from 1MDB . . . so we can thrash out certain areas.'

He emphasized: 'We are looking more on the impact on the country and our leadership . . . you know, from that angle.'

Arul Kanda, the 1MDB CEO at that time, agreed and voiced his disapproval on matters raised in the audit report. He said they were not factual, merely hearsay. He insisted for these to be removed, and the report to be prepared in accordance with what he wanted. The 1MDB CEO would eventually confide in Ali to say that the NAD was 'difficult to deal with'.

While Ambrin and Saadatul were willing to go through those points with the powerful men in the room, at the back of their minds, they were furious.

'I found it insulting that the auditee (1MDB) was given the honour to review my report, page by page, paragraph by paragraph, so whatever opinion we expressed in the report will be removed,' recalled Ambrin.

Among the contentious passages was the existence of two financial statements of 1MDB. Ali called this 'a very dangerous material evidence'. This was the same issue that was raised when Ambrin met with the prime minister at his office a few days ago.

'One version of the financial statement sent to the Companies Commission stated that 1MDB had utilized the funds redeemed from its SPC[43] investment to repay 1MDB debts and for the working capital.

'Another version of the financial statement sent to the Finance Ministry, Deutsche Bank and AmBank stated that the funds redeemed from SPC investments were still in 1MDB's possession,' Ambrin said.

This was, indeed, dangerous material evidence because it related to where the US$1 billion currently was. Knowing where the huge sum was located was one of the most fundamental aspects of good accounting practices. Which version was correct—were the funds still there?

When Ambrin met with Najib, the former prime minister asked Ambrin to not include this, and that he would 'get to the bottom of this' with investigations. The same was echoed in the meeting as the powerful men agreed that an investigation would be conducted and thus the passage ought to be removed. Ali asked the representative from Ministry of Finance Incorporated to lodge the police report, to see if there was fraud or concealments of facts.

'He was the prime minister, I had no reason to not believe him . . . I viewed his requests as [something that must] be implemented without any prejudice,' Ambrin said. 'On that premise, I [agreed] to drop the issue of the two versions [of the 1MDB financial statements] from the [audit] report.

'A few days later, I asked my staff to check if any police report were lodged, and the answer was no . . . I felt cheated,' said Ambrin to the court, in a raised voice and with an intense hand gesture.

The meeting got increasingly heated when they got to the issue of a man named Jho Low, a thirty-four-year-old fugitive who had masterminded the massive fraud. Born to a wealthy family on Penang Island, his enrolment at Wharton Business School allowed him to be acquainted with the highest echelons of Malaysia, Kuwait, and Jordan. With a chubby baby face and a penchant for a lavish lifestyle, Jho

---

[43] SPC is an abbreviation for 'segregated portfolio company'.

Low, whose full name is Low Taek Jho, had never left his dream of rubbing shoulders with Hollywood's A-list celebrities. He was also a ferocious party-goer; sometimes spending more than US$3.6 million in one night.

His shadow role in 1MDB's transactions was important because he was the missing link to where the money went. 1MDB transferred up to US$1 billion to 1MDB PetroSaudi Ltd, of which subsequently US$700 million was redirected to Jho Low's Good Star Limited.

The NAD found that although Jho Low did not hold any official position or role at 1MDB, he was present at a Board meeting and called some of the shots. This was a red flag. Who was this person?

Najib's principal private secretary, Shukry, asked for this to be removed given the sensitivity of his name in the public spotlight and the risk of the information being spun by the opposition. At that time, the opposition parties felt that Jho Low was 1MDB's mastermind with an infamous history of flagrant dishonesty and deceit, so they urged the authorities to hunt him down. At the time of writing however, Jho Low was still nowhere to be found.

On Jho Low's role, there were two different versions of the minutes of meeting. The NAD initially found minutes of meeting showing that a Board of Directors meeting on 26 September 2009 had 'Low Taek Jho' as an attendee. But the NAD was not allowed to photocopy those minutes of meeting.

To verify this, Saadatul invited all the Board of Directors of 1MDB, including one Bakke Salleh to the NAD office for a verification interview. Bakke was a sixty-one-year-old eloquent and reputable businessman, who had led some of the largest conglomerates in Malaysia including Sime Darby, FELDA, and Petronas. He told Saadatul that Low Taek Jho was indeed in that 2009 meeting. Bakke even brought a copy of the minutes of meeting as proof of Low Taek Jho's attendance.

Saadatul went back to 1MDB to request the original copy of the minutes of meeting that Bakke showed her. But to no avail. When 1MDB finally sent the revised minutes to Saadatul, Low Taek Jho's name mysteriously disappeared. Which one was the right copy? Was Jho Low in attendance or not?

Throughout the meeting, there were a few more issues like that. Though the powerful men never directly asked for those sections to be removed, Ambrin and Saadatul knew that, by bringing the powerful men of government into the room and using the former prime minister's name, they were using a form of coercion. NAD needed to do 'abnormal things beyond the normal practice'—removing what the auditee, 1MDB, did not like. Using the teacher analogy, this was like a student telling the teacher how he wanted his papers marked.

When Ali said 'we are looking more on the impact on the country and our leadership', it meant that the audit report had to be amended to not make the prime minister look bad. Ali also used these threat-laced words such as *boleh la ni, AG boleh guna budi bicara untuk drop* (come on, this can be done, the Auditor General can use his discretion to drop this). He made it sound like it was their choice to make when they were stuck between a rock and a hard place. Arul Kanda's style was to 'force, but in a nice way'.

'This was coercion. If we do not drop [the matter], this issue will be raised again,' Saadatul said to the court.

'[T]he people [at the meeting] do not understand the role of the National Audit Department. We look at things based on facts and these facts must be verified by supporting documents,' said Ambrin.

'In this particular case [dropping the issues raised], there was no choice. I was under pressure to do the amendments, due to national interest,' he continued. 'It was difficult, it was almost like an instruction.'

To quell all kinds of refutation, Ali turned to Ambrin and reminded him, '[M]aybe you should manage your younger officers . . . we can see they are *rajin* (hardworking) . . . but for us, it is national interest, we want to take care of our leadership (Najib).'

That was all Ali and Shukry needed to say to compel action. Malaysia was a deeply hierarchical country where people rarely disrespected authority, especially in the civil service. In the Hofstede Power Distance Index, which measures how people feel about authority, Malaysia scored a perfect 100. That means 'people accept a hierarchical order in which everybody has a place and which needs no further justification' and the 'ideal boss is a benevolent autocrat'. And this was key: 'Challenges to the leadership are not well-received.'

Authorities do not need to directly impose; they already have the cultural forces helping them. They just need to be in a meeting with them and say soft autocratic words. *Boleh la ni, AG boleh guna budi bicara untuk drop.*

The former prime minister Najib's influence in government was also overwhelming at that point. A year before the meeting, the Attorney General and his deputy prime minister was sacked because they didn't follow the prime minister's wishes.

His former aide, Amhari Efendi Nazaruddin, described this invisible pressure at a trial:

> [The threats] may come from the previous [Najib] government, not necessarily from Najib but from his people or supporters . . . [Najib] still has enough clout in the country . . . he has the power to at least create instability . . . in my livelihood.

Journalist Emir Zainul said, 'The best example, perhaps, was the fear that Ali Hamsa showed when he was testifying against Najib in court years later. Before Ali answers any question by the lawyers, he would constantly look at Najib at the dock, as though he was still afraid, as though he was still seeking his approval. He looked very scared.'

The prosecutor had to reassure him by saying, 'Don't worry, you can speak freely. You are in the court of law.'

When you are in that suffocating environment, you surrender your control. Frustrated that all attempts at defending the NAD's findings were rendered futile, Ambrin started to sarcastically suggest dropping the summary sections where NAD knew about 1MDB's debt and cash flow problems, besides its weak governance and investment choices.

> **Ambrin:** Maybe we just drop the summary, keep all my feelings with me, [then] everybody [would be] happy.
> **Ali:** Maybe we can write a separate book on this.
> **Ambrin:** I will write a book and get it distributed after I die.

Before the meeting ended, Ali asked for the sixty copies of the printed audit reports to be shredded. 'In the end, there should not be two or three versions . . . only one version that has been agreed on should be there,' Ali said. He remembered Najib's advice to him: Do not print the 1MDB Audit Report until the prime minister has approved it.

After two hours and forty-five minutes, one by one the powerful men walked out of the meeting room. Ambrin was quiet and emotionless, mumbling something as he walked to the restroom. Nor Salwani sensed there was something wrong with him, as his footsteps became increasingly fragile.

Exhausted and defeated, Ambrin pressed the tap to wash his face. 'What is the purpose of the audit?' he mumbled.

Everything that you have just heard about the meeting on 24 February 2016 was supposed to be confidential. Nobody was supposed to know about this. Or so they wished.

4

Whenever chief prosecutor, the late Gopal Sri Ram, a seventy-six-year-old former Federal Court judge, walked into the courtroom, everyone would go silent and make way for him. He was, by far, the only lawyer who could instil fear and respect wherever he went. He remains the only person to ever be elevated from private legal practice directly to the Court of Appeal. Lawyers prepared extensively to face him because his legal knowledge was vast, having written 800 judgments over sixteen years as an appellate judge. 'I know the law because I wrote it,' he would often say, with extreme sureness and unapologetic directness, as he stared down at you. Now as lead counsel for the prosecutor, he carried the stature of a former top judge, walking into the court with a pair of aviator sunglasses tinted dark blue, a walking stick, and an aura that absorbed attention. He was many a defence team's worst nightmare; his loud and sharp questioning could even make a former prime minister's wife break down in court.[44] Defence teams had tried

---

[44] In a corruption trial against former prime minister's wife, Rosmah Mansor, the senior lawyer Gopal Sri Ram started his cross-examination by testing the credibility of Rosmah's court testimony and a statement to the anti-corruption agency she gave a few years ago.

to remove him as counsel many times but to no avail. Unquestionably brilliant and with a larger-than-life personality veering on narcissism, Gopal Sri Ram was a lawyer you hated to love and loved to hate.

With him in court was a senior deputy public prosecutor, Akram Gharib, a low-profile and cheerful lawyer, who conducted himself in fluent English and Malay in court. He was slim and well-kempt from head to toe—his tailored suit fitted perfectly; his hair was always in shape. Akram had spent his whole life at the Attorney General Chambers and developed a reputation for excellence, regularly being entrusted with difficult and complex cases.

In the warm afternoon of 20 November 2019, Akram approached the witness stand and asked Nor Salwani to read out her twenty-two-page witness statement to the court. Throughout the forty-three minutes of reading, her voice was 'resolute and steady'. She talked about her appointment as coordinator of the 1MDB audit taskforce, her bosses Ambrin and Saadatul, as well as the documents she encountered. The journalists were right that her evidence was merely confirmatory.

The next morning, at 11.15 a.m., things changed. The prosecution lawyer passed a pen drive to the court interpreter to be played in the court. The interpreter checked if the speakers were working clearly, and in a few minutes, the entire courtroom was hearing the two-hour-and-forty-five-minute recording of the 24 February 2016 meeting. The TV screen only displayed a default Windows Media Player interface, as everyone in the courtroom turned silent to hear what transpired in the meeting. Was there any attempt to change the audit report? Was there an abuse of power? Was there a crime?

Akram stopped the recording and asked Nor Salwani, *who recorded this?*

I recorded it with a voice recorder, she replied.

As Sri Ram tried to ask her to answer his question . . . Rosmah almost broke down and pleaded to the judge.
Sri Ram: I want you to keep your answer short, please answer the question?
Rosmah: Don't shout at me. I'm not used to people shouting at me.
After Justice Zaini gave her several moments to compose herself, the judge asked her to answer the question.

The entire courtroom gasped in shock. 'So, it was you!' a journalist exclaimed. Journalists were scrambling to write down what they saw and heard. The defence team started whispering to each other. Everyone was caught off guard. Up to that point, no one knew who had recorded the meeting. How did anyone get hold of a recording of a confidential meeting with the most powerful men in the country? It was Nor Salwani—a name most people hadn't heard of prior to this court session.

She explained:

> At first, I'm inside the meeting room, because it is normal for any exit conference [for] the secretariat or coordinator to join the meeting . . . So, I should take the minutes . . . But when the meeting was about to start, Ali's staff suddenly told all the lower-ranking officers to leave the room. They were very insistent, and everything became very chaotic. I was supposed to take down the minutes of the meeting for the National Audit Department, but they were asking me to leave the room. After I was asked hurriedly to leave the room . . . I noticed a pencil case on the table, and I slipped in the voice recorder . . . It was partially opened and left on the desk . . . I just slipped it in without anyone noticing. [After the meeting], I turned off the tape and I brought it back to my office.

If Nor Salwani had not recorded this meeting, it wouldn't have been known to the public that there were attempts by the most powerful men in the country to amend the audit report. A government that was controlled by select few influential men meant that the public only got to see sanitized versions of the document. Even the Parliament's PAC was only able to see the amended audit report without knowing they were amended under undue pressure. When the initial planned PAC meeting was cancelled, the public assumed that it was merely a delay on the part of NAD. They wouldn't have known that a meeting with 'abnormal things beyond normal practice' was taking place, and that the Auditor General was exhausted, helpless, and hopeless to the point of asking 'What is the purpose of the audit?'

The original audit report was 354 pages. The amended, sanitized version presented to the PAC was only 338 pages. That meant sixteen pages, with four areas, including the two different versions of the financial statements and minutes of meeting (one with Jho Low and another without), were removed.[45]

If anyone in that room found out that Nor Salwani had secretly recorded the high-stakes meeting, she would have been in trouble. The power of Najib's government, coupled with the power distance in the culture, meant that a low-profile and unknown civil servant like Nor Salwani would not be spared. If Najib could make even the chief secretary Ali Hamsa fearful of him even after he was no longer prime minister, the government then could really do anything to anyone.

It took enormous courage and unwavering integrity for Nor Salwani to do what she did. She took a gamble on her career and life to protect the interests of the country. Most civil servants would rather stay safe and follow instructions from the government of the day, even if it means enabling or endorsing corruption. They would rather toe the line and not risk their pension after having spent decades in one place.

Because of this vital piece of recording evidence, the Attorney General Chambers was able to bring forth a criminal charge for an offence that took place between 22–26 February 2016 at the Prime Minister's Department in Putrajaya, for the violation of Section 23 (1) of the Malaysian Anti-Corruption Commission Act 2009, which provided jail term up to twenty years and a fine no less than five times the amount of gratification. This was one of five prosecution cases brought against the former prime minister, a first in Malaysian history.

'It also made it the most straightforward, easy-to-understand trial,' said journalist Emir Zainul. 'The NAD wanted to do an audit on 1MDB. They got the final draft. But before the final draft went to the PAC [as it was supposed to], it went to Najib and other high-ranking civil servants first. And we know that such meeting did take

---

[45] The other salient sections removed relate to a bond-flipping exercise and Najib's meeting with the King.

place because there was a recording to prove it. You can say it was the most incriminating piece of evidence of the trial.'

The defence counsel wanted to know why she did it. 'You could have always informed the Chief Secretary [Ali Hamsa] . . . It is the Chief Secretary to the Government we are talking about here. You could have said you were going to record the proceedings.'

Nor Salwani only said, 'I was just a lowly officer.'

* * *

Secretly recording the 24 February 2016 meeting was not the only impressive thing Nor Salwani did. There were more—some of them in defiance of her boss, and all of them quietly.

This was what Nor Salwani did after she took the voice recorder back to the office:

> After I switched off the recording device, I returned to the office using a department vehicle and met with the other team members in a meeting room. We then listened to the recording to find out what transpired in the meeting. After listening to the recording, we were so shocked . . . upon hearing the request to omit some things from the report, including the existence of two [1MDB] financial statements. I then copied the audio onto a hard disc that belonged to the team. It was an official hard disc.

Nor Salwani shared it with her audit team so that everyone was kept aware. In the next few weeks, Nor Salwani further transferred the recording to another NAD external hard drive and a pen drive for additional safety to safeguard against a leak. The pen drive was sealed in an envelope and stored in the department's metal cabinet.

Within twenty days of the appointment of the new Auditor General, Madinah Mohamad, Nor Salwani confided in her about what she kept in secret. Slightly more than a week later, the audit team made a presentation to Madinah on what happened. When Najib's government had fallen, all the evidence was passed on to the relevant authorities, including the Malaysian Anti-Corruption Commission and the Council of Eminent Persons.[46] After learning about the ins and outs, Madinah would conclude that it was audit tampering by a high authority.

But there was still one missing piece. If it was true that there was a meeting to amend the original audit report, how do you prove that there was an original audit report before the amendments? After the 24 February 2016 meeting, Ambrin had instructed that all the original audit reports be shredded to avoid a leak. This was to comply with the Official Secrets Act which gazetted the 1MDB audit report as a classified document, and the Chief Government Security Office required this.

Anyone in violation could face up to seven years in prison.

But Nor Salwani did something different. She said:

I kept a copy of 1MDB Audit Report (watermark '09') to be handed to the new Auditor General. With a pure and sincere heart, I handed the report to enable the new Auditor General to gain a full picture on the audit findings that was conducted by the audit team. It served as a reference point, considering that the 1MDB Audit Report (watermark '01' to '06') that was handed to other parties [i.e., high-ranking civil servants and Najib] was not returned to the NAD for the purposes of shredding.

Not only did she secretly record, she recorded, shared, stored, copied, handed, and finally kept material evidence against her boss's knowledge and will.

Nor Salwani had chosen to defy in the interest of the truth, even though it came at enormous risks. There was no guarantee that the Najib government would fall, or that her team would not betray her, or that her new boss would not turn against her and put her in jeopardy. She did it anyway because it was the right thing to do.

---

[46] The Council of Eminent Persons was a special council set up to advise Mahathir Mohamad's government on the most important economic and financial issues.

'I used to think that a run-of-the-mill civil servant was a person who doesn't do much, wouldn't dare to defy orders. They were just there to get their pensions. That was the stereotype, and to my fault, I also thought that about her,' journalist Emir Zainul said, who saw Nor Salwani in court. 'Clearly, I was proven wrong—gladly so. I feel like I wouldn't have done what she did if I were in her position . . . But she did.'

In the end, this classified document '09' and the two-hour-forty-five-minute voice recording became the central pieces of evidence in the 1MDB audit tampering trial.

When the news broke, people started calling her a hero. The civil servants' motto was changed from 'I am just following orders' to 'I am just fulfilling my mandate as a civil servant'. One Reddit user suggested that Malaysia should have a new law that protects civil service whistleblowers and call it the 'Salwani Act'.

5

When you think of a leader, who do you think of? Probably Steve Jobs who revolutionized how we used technology, Winston Churchill who brought the West through the darkest days in World War II, or Martin Luther King who pursued extreme civil disobedience for a more equal world. Charismatic, confident, sociable, assertive, visionary, loud, and bold. We worship these qualities.

If you have extraverted qualities like them, you have a 25 per cent higher chance of being in a high-earning job. Your quietness and reservedness are viewed by 75 per cent of senior executives as a barrier—like something to be fixed. Perhaps by taking a course at Harvard Business School, or you could even take a pill called Paxil that helps 'cure' your social anxiety disorder. If you are an introvert, it is just because you haven't 'Unleashed Your Power Within', as Tony Robbins would think, and thus a US$895 four-day high-energy workshop was what you needed.

The problem is: Humans are notoriously bad at judging other people. A Princeton study showed that we only take 100 milliseconds to decide whether that person is trustworthy, competent, likeable, attractive, aggressive. All that in 0.1 seconds! For people who exhibit extraversion traits, we assume that they are smarter, healthier, have better judgment, and have higher morals. We give them a halo over their heads.

Our extraversion bias meant that it was hard to understand Nor Salwani as a stereotypical person of courage.

The defence counsel, Shafee Abdullah, knew this. Shafee was a sixty-seven-year-old lawyer who had represented some of the most controversial figures in the country—the prosecution against Anwar Ibrahim in the Sodomy II trial, the defence for Abdul Razak Baginda in the murder case of model-translator Altantuya, the corruption case of former Menteri Besar of Selangor Khir Toyo, former businessman Eric Chia's criminal breach of trust trial, and a series of 1MDB corruption cases. Often called an 'UMNO lawyer',[47] he was a trusted lawyer of Najib and commanded some of the highest litigation fees in the country. His firm, Shafee & Co, was located in the exclusive Bukit Tunku enclave. Not too far away was his RM9.5 million three-storey bungalow that is guarded by fierce and unrelenting Belgian Malinois. Shafee was sharply dressed in expensive clothes and well-groomed with combed-back white hair that evenly spread to a line around his face. He drove different luxury cars, had three wives, and one son who practiced with him.

'Whatever you hear about how good he is, it is probably true,' journalist Emir Zainul said after watching him in action. He wasn't afraid of letting others know. He would accept interviews by newspapers to talk about his achievements, with 'laudatory' remarks such as describing himself as a 'top lawyer at a high-profile firm'. After winning a controversial case against Anwar Ibrahim, Shafee went on roadshows to talk about it, never missing a boastful moment.

Shafee was seasoned in court, especially in cross-examinations.

'He has this technique where he would spend the first half of the cross-examination asking you seemingly irrelevant and petty—almost

---

[47] The United Malay National Organisation, also dubbed the 'Grand Old Party', is the longest-serving party in Malaysian history.

off-putting—questions. You would be confused and just answer without thinking,' Emir continued. 'But then he would start grilling you in the second half with pieces of answers you have given earlier, and now you are caught off guard and start appearing defensive. He was using you to build his plot. That's where Shafee could point out to the court that you are not a credible witness. That's what good lawyers like Shafee do.'[48]

Shafee took this opportunity when he faced the painfully ordinary and introverted Nor Salwani. He wanted to discredit her as a witness, and show that it wasn't courage, and she wasn't a hero; instead, she was just an unethical civil servant who made a mistake in recording the meeting and keeping the classified document.

> **Shafee:** Are you so unethical to the point of not informing Chief Secretary to the Government [Ali Hamsa] that, as a representative of NAD, you have to leave a recording device for the purpose of preparing the minutes?
>
> **Nor Salwani:** It was very chaotic then . . . everything was being rushed. I was just a lowly officer, and I did not have the opportunity to inform anyone.
>
> **Shafee:** You could have informed your own superior.
>
> **Nor Salwani:** No . . . I was being chased out.
>
> **Shafee:** Are you a *kalut* (panicky) kind of person?
>
> **Nor Salwani:** It was very chaotic then . . . I was being chased out.
>
> **Shafee:** It was only ethical for you to have obtained an approval first.

As Shafee was grilling her, she was visibly taken aback. A lawyer like Shafee would raise his voice and taunt you so that you say things you would later regret. Nor Salwani's voice started trembling. She seemed more intimidated than her bosses, Ambrin and Saadatul, on the stand. Compared to an extraverted lawyer like Shafee, Nor Salwani looked timid and small.

---

[48] In another 1MDB case, Shafee Abdullah stopped a witness who was explaining himself, and said 'Hold your horses . . . I want to peel this like an onion . . . layer by layer. At the end of it, I want to see whether you cry, or I cry . . . or we all cry.'

'I was looking at this timid Malay aunty, and Shafee overpowering her at the stand. You almost feel sorry for her,' said Emir.

'But as she's telling her story, you realize, "Damn, she really did all of this. She didn't have to do it. Her boss didn't do anything about it—and she went out of the way to make it happen. Even with the trembling and breaking voice, you can feel like she's trying to do the right thing. You just believe her."'

A year later, Shafee cross-examined her again, this time targeting her civilian honour, 'Datuk', that was awarded to her earlier that year. Shafee took a newspaper article congratulating Nor Salwani for the honour, and asked if her award was given to her because she kept the watermarked copy '09' of the 1MDB Audit Report. The purpose, once again, was to show a lack of credibility of Nor Salwani by drawing a motive of personal gain. Not courage, but unethical personal gain.

Nor Salwani had had a year to recompose herself. She had thought through her life's work at the NAD and the little acts of courage that had turned her life around. She was not used to fame; in fact, she detested it. 'I am just an ordinary person trying to do my part,' she would often say.

'The award was not just to appreciate me for keeping the evidence . . . I was nominated by the NAD for the Panglima Mahkota Wilayah (which carries the title Datuk) because I have served in the Ministry of Federal Territories and NAD for almost thirty years,' Nor Salwani replied.

She reminded the court: 'I am the head of the internal audit department and one of the pioneers in the internal audit unit in the Ministry of Federal Territories. I was working together with the current senior officials in the ministry during the initial stages of re-establishing the ministry.'

In a life of an introvert, who is quiet and unimpressive at first glance, she would have faced challenges in being given due recognition for her contribution. She was not a crowd favourite, more likely misunderstood than celebrated, and she wouldn't be noticed if she walked down the street. Nobody remembered her walking into the courtroom, or to the witness stand. But she did do all of that. In fact, her courage was immeasurable. She wasn't a nobody. She wasn't invisible. She wasn't just an accountant to confirm details.

Let it be known that her name is Nor Salwani.

Epilogue

If you want to study evil, you study the Holocaust. If you want to study goodness, you study a small French village called Le Chambon-sur-Lignon. As you walk down this small hideaway village in south-central France of only 2,470 people, you would feel like you've entered ten countries in one. Refugee children from war-torn countries learn the French syllabus. You could see a French woman holding three children who fled from Kosovo, a farmer from West Africa waiting for his crops, a Syrian family of four playing with a middle-aged French woman who comes from a family of rescuers.

Eighty-two years ago, this village became the only place that did not fall under the Nazi rule that infiltrated France. Instead, they defied orders and saved more refugees than the population of their village.

Marshal Philippe Pétain had been the chief of state of Vichy France. France had just lost to Nazi Germany, and Philippe was given full powers to govern from Vichy, France, as a dictatorship. He ran on a totalitarian ideology: School children saluted to the Nazi flag every morning, teachers signed loyalty oaths to the state, democracy was suspended, every move was watched, minorities hauled up to a camp to be sent to Auschwitz concentration camp.

The propaganda campaign was to ask the French people to surrender refugees to be deported. The outrageous lie was that, in Poland, Hitler planned to establish a homeland for them to live in peace. But everyone knew, Auschwitz meant gas chambers. Pastors Andre Trocme and Edouard Theis, who led the village, refused to obey.

They told the village in their sermon: 'We appeal to all . . . to refuse to cooperate with this violence. We shall resist whenever our adversaries demanded of us obedience . . . without fear, but also without pride and without hate.'

More and more refugees and minorities heard about the resistance of Le Chambon. When they asked for help, the villagers sat down with them and figured out how to rebuild a life. Food, shelter, and eventually faking identity cards for them. Children were the majority, the school enrolment shot up from 18 to 350.

In August 1942, George Lamirand, a minister in charge of youths, was sent to Le Chambon to set up youth camps, similar to the one set up by Hitler in Germany. He was told that the village was defiant. When he arrived, no one welcomed him. No one greeted him, no grand sign or well wishes; there was barely enough food. Trocme's daughter even 'accidentally' spilled soup on his uniform.

Then a group of students walked up to Lamirand and gave him a letter of protest to ask him to stop persecuting minorities.

> If our comrades, whose only fault is to be born in another religion, received the order to let themselves be deported, or even examined, they would disobey the order received, and we would try to hide them as best we could.

Lamirand turned to the police who looked straight in Trocme's eyes and warned him not to be defiant. Follow these orders or face severe punishments, he said. Trocme didn't budge.

Half a month later, the police raid started for a full three weeks in the village. In the end, they only found two to arrest, of which one was released shortly after.

When Nazi took over the French government, they hauled up the defiant troublemakers, Trocme and Theis, to a French internment camp; possessions confiscated, noses measured. At the same time, they raided the village of Le Chambon once again. Still, they could only find eight refugees.

The Nazi prison officials wanted to strike a deal. Sign the papers declaring that they accept Pétain's authority, and they would be free. Otherwise, death. But they once again said no.

'When we get home, we shall certainly continue to be opposed, and we shall certainly continue to disobey orders from the government. How could we sign this now?' Trocme said.

Finally, the authorities gave up and sent them home anyway. When Hitler was defeated in 1945, the 5,000 refugees who were saved by Le Chambon were finally safe. The population at that time was only 3,200 people—the people they saved outnumbered their own.

* * *

Researchers Francois Rochat and Andre Modigliani wanted to figure out what happened. Why did the village here take an enormous risk to disobey authorities to do good?

When they looked into the day-to-day account of what happened, they were surprised by what they found. Le Chambon's relative unimportance had given them time to rescue more minorities and develop a plan to keep them safe. The villagers started small, by sharing food and information. The authorities were hesitant to crack down the village, choosing to focus on the cities first, and this gave Le Chambon invaluable time to integrate refugees into schools and work; even creating false identity cards to avoid persecution.

Le Chambon was also a village trained in the power of invisibility. They were descendants of the original Protestants, and they broke away from the Catholic Church, making them persecuted groups. During the 'reign of terror', they were forced underground. They prayed in silence, they didn't draw attention, they learned to live in the forests. Throughout the years, they've done the same for other refugees, using the same tactic of invisibility.

So, when they helped refugees, they didn't talk openly about it— they were quiet and tactful. Neighbours kept quiet, even though they disagreed. It was a 'miracle in silence' (*le miracle de silence*). When you visited the village, everyone seemed to be going about their daily lives ordinarily—cooking, cleaning, schooling, working, selling. When the authorities came to raid, they would invite the Nazi soldiers to homemade soup to distract them with ordinary acts. And the authorities wouldn't find anyone. The more ordinary, the less suspicion—that was the power of invisibility.

Does this remind you of Nor Salwani?

When the powerful men rushed Nor Salwani out of the 24 February 2016 meeting, it was on the basis that she was a 'low-ranking officer'. Only Saadatul and Ambrin could stay. The quiet and reserved nature of Nor Salwani made her naturally invisible to loud, boisterous, and powerful men. Her emails and telephones were not constantly ringing like theirs. She did not appear in the news. They didn't know her role or position in the audit team. They probably didn't even know her name.

And that's why they didn't notice that she slipped in the voice recorder that turned out to be one of the most crucial pieces of evidence in a trial against Najib and 1MDB.

Nor Salwani occupied a position that is known as a 'middle manager' at the NAD. If you imagine an organizational hierarchy, she was right at the centre. At NAD, she was the Deputy Director of an audit arm. At the 1MDB audit taskforce, she was the coordinator with Saadatul and Ambrin above her. She was a seasoned middle manager.

Middle managers were often associated with the words 'invisible' or 'mediocre'. No one really takes note of them. They were perceived to be regressive and compliant. The assumption was that if you took care of the top management, then the middle managers would follow. Who cared too much about what the middle managers thought?

This was perhaps what Ali thought when he reminded Ambrin to 'manage your younger officers', who he mocked as being a little too hardworking. The subtext was: Ask the invisible middle managers to toe the line.

INSEAD Professor Quy Huy, who studied middle managers his entire career, found that there were benefits underneath the supposed invisibility. One was the informal networks they have that served as a support system for making radical decisions.

After Nor Salwani turned off the voice recorder, the first thing she did at the office was to share it with the rest of the 1MDB audit team—a group of middle managers, just like her. They shared their 'shock' at what had transpired and this provided Nor Salwani with the necessary support to go even further.

Like what happened in Le Chambon, when Najib, 1MDB executives, and high-ranking civil servants were busy putting out fire in other places, Nor Salwani took the opportunity to accumulate more evidence. She went to copy and transfer the recording into safer locations, and she secured the documents at the office where she could trust—the middle manager's abode. When there was an instruction to shred all the original reports, she kept one copy—watermark '09'. Having the backing of her team made her feel less alone, propelling an exponential rise in courage to defy.

When Nor Salwani was ready to hand over these documents, her team of invisible middle managers presented to the new Auditor General, Madinah, which led the latter to urge action on the authorities on the alleged audit tampering.

Even though Ambrin and Saadatul were more passionate about the oft-repeated value of 'integrity' at the NAD, they did not do what Nor Salwani did. They tried their best to resist in the meeting, but in the end, they were defeated by the giants because they were overly visible. That was the limit of power.

You wouldn't have expected that being invisible was so powerful.

* * *

We've answered *how* Nor Salwani did what she did. But *why*? Why did Nor Salwani do something so risky, something that could cost her career, and even, life?

In Rochat and Modigliani's paper, they found that the people of Le Chombon hated it when people called them heroes. Some people called the locals *les taiseux*—the taciturn ones—to mean that they don't talk much about their kindness. Don't mention it, they would insist.

The reason the people of Le Chambon helped minorities and refugees was not too different from the reason they treat people every day—just by following the ordinary rules of kindness. They were the same rules that a person would follow when they refused to impose electric shocks when they hear another person suffering.[49] The rules were so ordinary and simple:

1. Don't impose your will on others
2. Take responsibility for your actions
3. Refuse injurious instructions

Nor Salwani still struggled with the attention people give to her. Like many others covered in this book, they do not think they have done anything extraordinary or special. You could and would do it too if you were in my position, she would say.

The amendments of the audit reports violated ordinary rules of kindness in society because it used the power of the hierarchy to impose its will on others. Two versions of documents implied someone in the mix refused to take responsibility for their own actions. And the step of shredding the original copies was an injurious act that felt too much like burning incriminating evidence.

It didn't take a hero or a saint to recognize this. It only took a painfully ordinary woman who has her heart in the right place. Really, you would have done it too.

Epilogue II

At the time of writing, former prime minister Najib Razak is serving a twelve-year jail sentence for another 1MDB case, where RM42 million went into his private account. In a surprising turn of events, the High Court acquitted Najib Razak in the audit tampering trial on March 2023. The prosecution has decided to appeal.

---

[49] The Milgram Experiment was a famous obedience study by psychologist Stanley Milgram in the 1960s. Participants were told that they were administering electric shocks to a 'learner' with higher voltage each time. The test was to see how obedient participants were, even if it meant their actions would directly harm others.

Key takeaways

- There are benefits of being overlooked and invisible from power.
- Altruistic acts are motivated by the ordinary rules of kindness. Like the village of Le Chambon that saved more lives in World War II than their population.
- True heroes do not want to be called 'heroes'.

Part II

The Weakness of the Powerful

Chapter 5

Fahmi Reza

How a punk graphic artist created the most popular
political artwork and how state-sanctioned
censorship will inevitably fail

*'At a place where so many died without
reason—I realize I didn't die.'*

1

The most powerful artwork in Malaysia is not found in any art gallery.

It is found in the hands of ordinary Malaysians. In the first month of its release, the artwork spread to thirty cities worldwide, inspired hundreds of imitation pieces, and hundreds of thousands more printed copies. Finding the artwork at random corners of the street became a mystery game. On the electricity box, the side of a garbage bin, outside the toilet, on top of a pole, in the night market, between piles of *lemang*,[50] under water, on school uniforms, on old road signs, or the thousands of T-shirts, stickers, vignettes, phone covers, tote bags, and patches.

Once, the artist was stopped by a customs officer in Taipei City who asked him to open his bag for inspection. When the customs officer saw a bagful of T-shirts printed with the artwork, he looked at the artist, smiled and said, 'Move along.'

Another time, he went to a stationery shop in the sleepy city of Ipoh to buy red and black spray paint. The fifty-something store owner asked, 'Are you going to draw [the famous artwork] over the wall?' He said yes. 'Good, I follow your work,' she replied.

The artwork was made with simple brushstrokes of three colour bases: Red, white, and black. The lines are uneven, the tones are inconsistent, the words are pencil scribbles. To most, it looks foul and unpleasant.

The central figure was the then prime minister Najib Razak, in an official portrait, reduced to a pale and misty white, with dashes of salt-and-pepper at the edges of his features. The eyebrows were arched dramatically from his huge forehead like slimy worms. Two small triangles were extended from the centre of his thickly-eyeshadowed eyes to the middle of his cheeks. The tip and the lower sides of the nostrils were covered in red paint. And then the scariest part: The lips were painted with a curved-up blood-red slab to make a permanent, mutilated smile. Why is he smiling and frowning at the same time?

---

[50] *Lemang* is a glutinous rice mixed with coconut milk and salt, cooked in bamboo, eaten most typically during Aidilfitri.

Scribbled in pencil around the face were the words, '*Dalam negara yang penuh dengan korupsi, kita semua penghasut*' (In a country full of corruption, we are all seditious).

It was drawn by a forty-five-year-old who looks half his age. Always dressed in black from head to toe, the eloquent and fiery bilingual graphic designer holds the record of having the most artwork discussed in the courtroom. The tall and skinny punk rocker is also the author of a satirical colouring book that illustrated politicians biting on money, playing with a Toyota Vellfire, dressed as a cow, putting a tongue out, looking confused—arranged alphabetically from A to Z. Once, he gave the colouring book to another former prime minister Mahathir Mohamad and showed the artwork of him pointing two middle fingers to readers with the words 'Dictator' underneath. It left Mahathir speechless and grunting in disapproval.

The artist has been the subject of a death threat for a bounty of RM5,000.[51] He has been described as *kurang ajar*. Individually, the word 'kurang' means less and the word 'ajar' means teach. Together, the phrase is typically directed at impolite and distasteful acts, the ones that reflect poorly on the actor's upbringing, deserving shame. In a collectivist culture that is shy, indirect, and restrained like Malaysia, a kurang ajar person is considered an outcast who ought to be put in place. Giving the former prime minister a colouring book that mocked him is kurang ajar.

Twenty years of creation, fifteen police investigations, five charges, RM30,000 in fines, and a conviction later, this kurang ajar graphic designer remains fearless and defiant. There could only be one man who could withstand the nation's wrath and still carry on—that man is Fahmi Reza.

2

When Fahmi Reza was seven, his mother, Muselmah Zainudin, made one of the boldest decisions in her life. She divorced her husband and decided to raise her seven children—six boisterous boys and one girl—

---

[51] To which Fahmi Reza replied, 'Only RM5,000?'

on her own. Her job as a court interpreter was a full-body experience. She needed to be extremely punctual and be physically and mentally present to listen, process, analyse, and write what she heard in court. She couldn't miss a beat. After an exhausting day, Muselmah had to rush back to cook dinner for her children, who were cramped in their beige-walled three-bedroom government quarters at Cochrane Road. When her children became adults, she took early retirement to pursue what she always wanted: Explore the world. She would organize travels with her siblings, spend long hours at the museum, wonder about how her ancestors lived, and host hundreds of guests on the Couchsurfing platform to learn about different cultures.[52]

The price of being a single mother juggling between a full-time job and taking care of seven children was that the household lacked intimacy. They do not express feelings openly or have small talks like 'How was your day?'; they do not celebrate birthdays or have parties.

'I didn't see her as an absent mother. I saw her as providing absolute freedom,' said Fahmi. 'Lucky for her, we didn't do anything that got us into trouble when we were young.'

No smoking, no gangs, no fighting. Fahmi knew early on that the route to success required him to do well in his studies. He was a conforming student who wore a tie on regular days and a songkok on Fridays. He was punctual and well-loved by his teachers. Studies came easy to him. His elder brother recalled that he was a 'naturally gifted and smart' student who always ranked at the top of his class, even though he had little interest in any of them. To make his certificate look good for university applications, he went to a boarding school, joined the basketball team, and became a class monitor, librarian, and school prefect. People called him *murid contoh* (exemplary student).

Fahmi bought into the Happy Life path set out for him: Study hard, get good results, go to university, get a degree, get a good job, get married, buy a car and house, and have a family, and live a happy life.

---

[52] Muselmah Zainudin is the record-holder of the most guests hosted (718 guests, 71 countries) on Couchsurfing in Malaysia. Couchsurfing allows users to find locals for a homestay when they visit the country.

That was the only way he could get out of the stricken lower-middle-class life—it was the path to happiness.

In his teenage years, Fahmi found solace in his friendship with Ravin Raj and Cheng Chean, his classmates at Cochrane High School. They would hang out at each other's houses and listen to music. One day, Ravin went to Fahmi's house to listen to Nirvana and Vanilla Ice over the radio waves. Ravin had never seen ten cats under one roof before. As they were following the music, Ravin started scratching his arms and legs. Before long, his whole body was swollen.

'That was the first time I saw someone allergic to cats! He couldn't stop scratching himself,' Fahmi recalled, with the memory still tickling him. 'He never set foot in my house again after that.'

Friendships were sacred to Fahmi. Even today, he still keeps his friends' secrets. Once, his class teacher wanted to know why his classmate was always absent from school. It had been a few days in a row. So, the teacher summoned Fahmi, the class monitor, to go to his friend's house to see where he was.

It was an unusual task given by the teacher, but he needed to obey. He was uncomfortable; he didn't want to rat on a friend. So, he performed the task poorly on purpose.

'When I went to his house, I started pressing on the bell and hitting on his gate. But no one answered,' Fahmi recalled. 'Then I looked through the window, and there I saw—my friend. He held a big plastic bag in his hands and was sniffing heavy glue from it. He seemed lost in it. I just didn't want to call him out like that . . . So, I left and went back to school. I told the teacher that I couldn't find him and said he wasn't at home.'

Like tucking in his long sideburns to the back of his ears, this was his quiet disobedience.

That summer, Fahmi discovered a prized asset that would change his life—the Sony Walkman, a portable music cassette player.[53] He was obsessed with it.

---

[53] Fahmi also discovered skateboarding around the same time. He saved up enough money working at McDonald's to buy a skateboard with a grey-faced sketch and became the talk of the teenage misfits.

'I really like loud and angry-sounding music. The fast-paced beats, the shouting vocals. I can feel the angst, the frustration. It speaks to me,' Fahmi said.

Fahmi heard his first punk tune when he was fifteen and that passion had caught on like a lifelong bug. Every day, Fahmi would wait by the radio for his favourite tracks, press on 'record' and 'play' at the same time, and play them over and over again.

When his boarding school decided to ban Walkman from the campus, he was unhappy.

'It's a stupid rule. Why would they allow radio and not a Walkman? Both play music. There's no difference!'

Throughout his time as a student, Fahmi was confronted with the same problems. He knew that there were 'ridiculous' and 'stupid' rules imposed on them, but he was powerless to change them. Worse, he was constantly part of the authority line-up simply to improve his chances of getting a scholarship and a spot at a good university.

Fahmi decided to try something radical at boarding school. He smuggled his Walkman into campus by cutting a deep hole in the middle of a Malay dictionary to bring it in—like a prisoner smuggling a box of cigarettes. He became a prefect to avoid every dorm search. When the night turned quiet, he would open his hollowed-out dictionary, take out his Walkman, put on his earphones, and listen to his own mixtapes. In the sacred, uninterrupted escapes, Fahmi dared to dream big. He thought about his childhood dream of studying in the United States.

'When you go to the States . . . you're completely free,' Fahmi said. 'Coming from a lower-middle-income family, with many siblings, I knew that they couldn't afford to send me abroad [for studies]. I didn't think I'd have many opportunities to travel abroad too.'

Before Fahmi turned eighteen, he would receive the best news that would change his life. But it came at a price he wasn't ready to pay.

* * *

In 1995, Fahmi Reza became part of the first batch of scholars who received a scholarship from Telekom Malaysia to study in the United

States. Boasted as a meritorious scholarship to build the nation's future engineers, Fahmi was selected after scoring seven A's and two Cs in his SPM.[54] Fahmi was invited to a pre-departure briefing at the luxurious headquarters of the telecommunication company—he went there on a skateboard.

'When I walked into the room of 100-plus scholars, I only saw one or two non-Malays. Almost everyone was Malay,' Fahmi recalled. 'I realized that my close friends who were non-Malay didn't get anything. My results were okay. But why is it that someone who got better results was not accorded the same privilege just because of their race?'

He asked this to an officer in a roomful of Malay administrators and scholars. The answer he got was 'the country needed to create more Malay decision-makers in executive positions'. Fahmi was infuriated.

At that time, the Malaysian government under Mahathir Mohamad was pushing for more opportunities for the Bumiputera group[55] under the New Economic Policy (NEP)—a state-sanctioned affirmative action policy with a 'venerated, transformative, polarizing presence'. This included providing scholarships and university admission quotas to the Malays, which has caused great discontent in society. Every year, non-Malay students would make the news for scoring excellent results but failing to secure a government scholarship or a university course of their choice.

Cheng Chean, Fahmi's childhood best friend, remembered that there were almost no Chinese or Indian scholars in his school that year. 'We didn't even get the chance to apply because the scholarship criteria required us to be Bumiputeras, so we didn't even pass the first screening,' he said.

Fahmi, his best friends, and millions of Malaysians would be greeted to this harsh reality after high school: Post-school life in Malaysia is organized along racial lines. At primary school and the early parts of high school, you would have genuine friendships with people of

---

[54] SPM refers to *Sijil Pelajaran Malaysia*, or Malaysian Certificate of Education, a national examination taken by all fifth-form secondary school students in Malaysia.
[55] Loosely translated as 'son of the soil'.

different races. But once you have passed that, you would be separated by your skin colour.

'I didn't choose my friends based on 'Do you eat pork?' or 'What religion are you?' Back then, we were just friends who wanted to hang out and have a good time,' Fahmi recalled.

If you asked Cheng Chean who his top five closest friends were in high school, he could easily list people of different races without difficulty. But now, as an audit manager in a consulting firm, he could hardly name one Malay.

In Malaysia, most Malays, including Fahmi, would attempt to get into a boarding school before their final high school leavers' exam, and would then go on to pre-university, university, and employment that consisted largely of people of the same ethnic background as them. Malaysia remained a racially segregated country in almost every aspect—work, politics, culture, religion—perhaps too clean to an ill. This racial cleavage worsened through the decades, and the NEP programme, which has overstayed its schedule by more than thirty years, endures today.

More fundamentally, Fahmi didn't agree with all kinds of race-based policies. 'Any label that separates one race from another has no place in this country. Affirmative actions can exist, but they must exist based on needs and class, not based on race,' Fahmi said.

This made him unpopular among the scholars. Fahmi didn't reject the scholarship because he knew it wouldn't make a difference to the injustice of the system with just one case. He was, after all, only seventeen years old at that time.

'It made me uneasy at that time,' Fahmi said. 'I felt powerless. What can I do? I couldn't ask them to take mine away and give it to a non-Malay. But by taking it, I know that, in a way, I am responsible for perpetuating the injustice . . . and I became part of the system I hate.'

In June of 1995, Fahmi Reza took a one-way flight ticket to Nashville, United States, and left behind Cochrane Road, his family, his best friends, and the final piece of his childhood innocence.

3

Fahmi Reza studied Electrical Engineering at Vanderbilt University, but you wouldn't know this if you entered his dorm on campus. The half-length window overlooked tree branches that crawled across the view. Punk posters and self-made flyers decorated the wall; some hand-drawn, others stolen. A TV sat on top of two guitar amplifiers with paper cut-out letters of his favourite band, 'C R A S S', loosely pasted on it, beside a glorious Gibson Les Paul with a heritage cherry sunburst. Dozens of incomplete patches spread across the studying table. The bed was tidy, covered in a black duvet, and above it was a torn and layered jacket stitched with punk symbols—skulls, ransom note letters, studs.

You wouldn't find an Electrical Engineering textbook. The lyrical insights of punk music were infinitely more interesting than circuit boards, motors, plants, and ignition systems. Upon landing in the United States, the first place Fahmi went was to record stores, where he subscribed to a $1 per month CD-by-mail and signed up for as many gigs as possible.

Fahmi consumed punk music like he was preparing for an exam. He would listen to the songs on endless loops and recognize the band, harmony, and chord style within seconds of play. He devoured the discography of mainstream and underground bands and recounted their history with nuance. Unlike other punk fans who used the band's loud vocals as background noise to a mosh, Fahmi would flip through the album sleeves to read through page-long lyrics.

Among many, Fahmi's favourite punk band was Crass, a one-of-a-kind, fiercely idealistic British band nicknamed the 'Gandhis of rock'.[56] They wrote a song called 'Big A, Little A', which remains Fahmi's favourite; he keeps a vinyl copy in pristine condition until today.

'It's damn effective when I read the lyrics,' Fahmi said. 'It's about how we are being controlled at different levels of our lives. The whole

---

[56] Upon formation in 1977, the band vowed to disband by 1984 as an acknowledgement of George Orwell's *1984*.

song is sarcastic in tone—speaking in the voice of God, the Queen, and the government. In a short three minutes, it made me question things I never questioned before.'

The song starts with children's voices singing to the traditional British rhyme: 'Big A, little a, and bouncing B! / The cat's in the cupboard, and she can't C!'

Then it launches into shouting vocals to compensate for the loud background music in a classic punk three-chord structure:

External control are you gonna let them get you?
Do you wanna be a prisoner in the boundaries they set you?
You say you want to be yourself, by Christ do you think they'll let you?
They're out to get you get you get you get you get you get you get you

'The lesson of 'Big A, Little A' is similar to other classic punk songs. They're reminding you to not succumb to what society and the system expects of you,' said Fahmi. 'The most fulfilling life is one lived on your own terms, with autonomy, independence, and the freedom to decide.'

He continued, 'Before this, I was an unquestioning teenager who accepted what people of authority told me. What schools and parents taught me, what the government and media told me. Even the path set for me was unquestioned. With punk, I started to question everything. Why am I even pursuing this engineering course here that I have no interest to study?'

Instead of reading for his engineering degree, he read about the revolutions around the world. He became interested in the Paris Commune of 1871, the Spanish Civil War of the 1930s, and the May Uprising of 1968. In the protests, revolutions, and rebellions, he found power in the history of the people's struggles.

But one question stayed with him: Am I willing to give everything up to be an activist for the rest of my life?

Fahmi's engineering degree at one of America's best universities was still a passage to a stable and wealthy life. He could be what his childhood best friends envisioned him to be: A manager at a government-linked company, chauffeured in a luxury vehicle from a comfortable semi-detached home back and forth to a family of five. Since school, he had also been full of promise with a natural gift of comprehension; would it be a waste if he didn't put it to good, lucrative use in society? What would his teachers think of him?

By that time, most of his friends had resigned to the reality that they needed to work in the corporate world to earn a living. Fiery activism and chaotic punk are phases in life—they're not forever. Could Fahmi afford to be the only odd one out?

A life in punk and activism was also unattractive. Many of Fahmi's favourite bands like Crass, Sex Pistols, Dead Kennedys had to suffer constant police harassment and arrests, besides a lifetime of poverty without much material gain to keep them afloat. Being anti-establishment also meant that they had to spend their own money producing an album, designing the artworks without prior training, organizing their concerts, and distributing their music.

Why would he pick a downtrodden life that was stricken with police harassment and poverty—one that was worse than where he first started—when he had a much brighter alternative?

* * *

Fahmi was the only foreign Asian in a small, fringe punk community in Nashville, famous for a genre almost opposite to the loud, fast-paced, angry-sounding punk rock: Country music. But punk was democratic and inclusive—equality and non-discrimination were part of its beliefs—and the punk community embraced the skinny, dark-skinned, bespectacled Asian foreigner as their own. Punk became his family.

'If you go to a punk gig and you don't have a place to stay, you can just talk to anyone at the gig and crash their place for the night. There's this deep camaraderie, almost tribal connection, when you meet a fellow punk. If you listen to punk, you're automatically cool,' Fahmi said.

Punk's close community spirit allowed Fahmi to experiment with design. The DIY ethics of punk also meant that the designs had a low barrier of entry, consisting of easy-to-make and low-cost materials, so that anyone, even someone without prior art training like Fahmi, could create something that resembles its style.

To design artwork for a punk band, this is what you do:

1. Take a newspaper or magazine, cut out individual letters in different sizes and font typefaces, and form the words you need (Ransom Note Lettering).
2. Take a few images you want to use (bonus for skulls) and rip away or remove certain parts to create a damaged effect (De-collage).
3. Use a pencil or pen to scribble in elements you couldn't find.
4. Lastly, use a cheap brush to paint the rest of the corners in black using Chinese calligraphy ink and leave the rest out in white.

And then you print out hundreds and hundreds of copies.

'The copy machine at my university was on the ground floor of my dorm room. You only need to buy a printing card. So, I abused the machine to print out all my punk posters and flyers. Most punk flyers are black and white because it's more economical this way,' said Fahmi.

He started putting out posters and flyers for punk bands he liked at a nearby independent record shop called Lucy's Record Shop, a short-lived, privately owned shop that became a crowded hangout spot for underground punk and rock every Friday night.

There, he met a few friends who would eventually form a punk band called From Ashes Rise. Fahmi told them that their album covers were 'ugly'. When they were about to release their second EP, they challenged Fahmi to design their seven-inch vinyl album cover—giving Fahmi his first-ever professional design job.

Fahmi listened to every song on the album to figure out how his art could capture the main essence of the album. He thought the song 'Life and Death' encapsulated the central theme that other songs followed.

The word 'parasite' in the lyrics became the centrepiece of Fahmi's design. He drew a hairy, giant parasite leeching off the earth that was also a skull inspired by graphic designer Pushead. Fahmi wanted to convey the message of anti-globalization, which was a trending protest movement of that time. The band loved it, and Fahmi was paid in the form of twenty record copies.[57] Fahmi would design a few

---

[57] He later sold them to Malaysian punk kids for RM3 each.

more album covers and flyers, each giving him a higher satisfaction than the last.

Three years of university passed. On the flight home, Fahmi was thinking of ways to get out of the nine to five corporate job like the rest of the scholars.

'As a worker, you earn the company money, but you are treated like slaves,' Fahmi said. 'You are told what to wear or how to dress, what time to come in, what to do, how to act, and even when you are sick, you have to request for them to let you not work that day. It's a form of slavery!'

It reminded Fahmi of going to school—a place Fahmi once excelled as a *murid contoh*, but now saw as a rule-based, punitive environment that deprives one's freedom. His punk education transformed his worldview and gave him a certain sense of control to effect change. This time, he would not submit to the system.

He wanted to put his time into activism, a cause higher than himself. For the first time in his life, Fahmi would not follow the Happy Life path set out for him. Before he boarded his flight to Malaysia, he plugged into his Walkman for one last time,

Be exactly who you want to be, do what you want to do
I am he and she is she but you're the only you
No one else has got your eyes, can see the things you see
It's up to you to change your life and my life's up to me

4

The first time Fahmi Reza got brutally beaten up was when he was twenty-seven years old. After returning to Malaysia, he had attended forums, talks, and protest memorandum-writing gatherings to acquaint himself with the pressing issues facing Malaysians. One thing unsettled him from the start: Why were activism posters so ugly?

He volunteered to design posters, leaflets, and flyers for human rights organizations like Amnesty International and SUARAM. Every time a protest came, he would do it punk style—design with bold fonts and provocative imagery, print hundreds of them using a cheap black-and-white printer, and distribute them widely. But the NGOs couldn't afford to pay him—they couldn't even pay themselves. After many posters, they felt bad and started paying Fahmi RM50 per poster, which became his only source of income.

To survive in the activism scene, Fahmi Reza learned to survive with very little money. His austere lifestyle in the punk community had trained him to be as frugal as possible. He lived in the spare room of his mother's house, removing rental and some food costs. He bought only cheap RM2 clothes from the bundle store (black-coloured shirts lasted longer). He took only public transport. He went to RM1 public hospitals when he was sick. He only washed his hair with water, saving on shampoo costs. He didn't cut his hair. He didn't use any skincare products. He stopped buying his favourite punk CDs because they were too expensive. Once, he found out that his bank account had less than a hundred ringgit left. But that, somehow, still lasted him for a few months. He had learned the art of stretching the ringgit.

Living a minimal lifestyle allowed him to be independent and ethical. When his best friend, Cheng Chean, offered him a few graphic design jobs at medium-sized companies, Fahmi turned them down. It was part of the ethics in fighting against corporate greed. It was difficult living in poverty, but it was more difficult being a corporate sellout.

In February 2004, forty-six NGOs, including SUARAM, planned a protest in front of Bukit Aman police headquarters against the police force's abuse of power—something Fahmi called 'a problem that never went away'.

In the months preceding that protest, the news was filled with stories of police brutality, sudden deaths of detainees, and other systematic lack of accountability. People died in lockups without good reason, and no police had been charged up to that point.

The Royal Commission held in the same year raised severe concerns where 926 complaints were made regarding the general and specific inadequacy of the police force. The 600-page report concluded that there were 'extensive and consistent abuse of human rights in the implementation of the [Federal Constitution] and [Inspector General] standing orders by PDRM [police] personnel' and that the 'culture of impunity' needed to be removed.

'The protest was actually a protest in disguise,' Fahmi said. 'On paper, it was called a gathering to hand a memorandum to the police, but it was really a protest.'

NGOs needed to use these tactics because protest is dangerous in Malaysia. Massive police forces and riot controls would surround a protest, large or small, and whenever violence occurs, the state-controlled media will blame it on the protestors, regardless of who started them. This biased reporting would strengthen the police's hand for future crackdowns of so-called 'violent protestors'.

Fahmi read up on the guidelines distributed by the NGOs on what to do when you get arrested. It was common for the police to arrest and detain without reason. It was best to know your rights if things got out of hand.

One of the comrade rules was: Leave no one behind.

If a person gets arrested, the others have to surrender him- or herself so that there are witnesses if something untoward happens to the first detained person. Against an authoritarian regime that abused power, underdogs could only count on large numbers to defend their rights. The police could crackdown on one person, but it could not crackdown on a movement. That is the tactic of an underdog—the power of numbers.

By this time, Fahmi was known as the 'poster guy' in the activism scene. He was responsible for the giant posters, placards, and banners protestors hold. The poster he designed for this protest remained one of his favourites.

Inspired by JM Flagg's 1914 iconic army recruitment poster of Uncle Sam saying 'I want YOU!', Fahmi drew a giant, angry-looking cop staring right at you. The poster was coloured in the most economical black-and-white. The moustached cop had features that filled his face, with his mouth and nose just tilted slightly upwards, sneering at you. The peaked cap and starred police uniform gave him unquestionable authority over you.

He held up a double-action revolver, with a five-round cylinder, directly at you. The gun was held up so close to you it looked the size of the cop's head. His thick fingers pressed the revolver tight, with his forefinger surrounding the trigger, shooting anytime you move.

Then you realized the cop didn't have eyes. His ears didn't have canals. He was almost like a lifeless, soulless zombie, ignorant and insensitive to your humanity, ready to fire whenever he is ordered. You're reminded of the history of police brutality by the bold words underneath that say 'Police Abuse of Power'.

You froze. You raised your arms. You would do anything to make sure he doesn't fire.

This poster would almost cost Fahmi's life.

* * *

(The following two sections are Fahmi Reza's account of what happened.)

Fahmi was one of the earliest to arrive at the protest ground. He had promised his elder brother that he would rush over to his wedding at Tanjung Malim right after the protest.

Textured and messy, Fahmi's mod haircut was longer at the sideburns and the back, with slightly curly hair filling the fringe and the top of his head. He wore a black T-shirt that carried the Zombie Police image, thick-framed glasses and ripped black jeans, and a pair of sneakers.

He had attended a few protests in the past year but had never protested right in front of the police headquarters.

The protest started on time. Human rights activist P. Uthayakumar gave a speech about why they had gathered. Fahmi was still tying a makeshift banner on a tree.

Suddenly the police groups went to P. Uthayakumar and stopped his speech by force. This made the crowd mad, and they started pushing and shouting at each other to ask for the freedom to speak.

After tying the banner to a tree branch, Fahmi took a paper cutter from his pocket and cut off the string.

A plain-clothed policeman shouted in Fahmi's direction: 'Knife! Knife!' and went forward to twist his hands to stop what he was doing.

Two policemen went over to beat Fahmi into submission and tucked a pair of handcuffs tightly onto his wrists. Fahmi was shouting to be released, and the crowd rushed to pull him from the police. They continuously shouted: 'This is a peaceful protest! Let him go!'

As a group, the policemen beat him, pulled and tore his T-shirt, took his glasses, posters, paper cutter, and anything they found on him. When he fell to the ground, they kicked and stepped on him. And then the policemen, one in grey and another in white, dragged him across the tarred road, as Fahmi shouted and struggled to be released, and threw him to the back of a Black Maria truck to be sent to his jail cell.

Inside the Black Maria, he was drenched in sweat, and his breath grew shorter. He looked out the netted truck cell and saw no one; the protestors were out of sight and sound. The policemen started hurling insults at him, 'You're such a useless Malay who doesn't know his place!', 'Kurang ajar!' A policeman opened the truck door and came close to Fahmi. He lifted his right hand and gave Fahmi one hard slap on his face, and then another.

'Another policeman took the posters that I drew and shouted at me, "So this is your piece of work? Is this your piece of work?" And then he stuffed the posters directly to my face,' Fahmi recalled. He couldn't say or do anything in return because he was handcuffed and trapped in a police vehicle alone. The handcuffs were digging into his skin, and his arms were hurting, but the police refused to loosen them and pretended they didn't hear him.

With sixteen others, Fahmi was sent to the out-of-use 109-year-old Pudu Jail, a 394-metre former Chinese burial ground, which once housed criminals at the gallows before they were hung—some innocent, some guilty, some wildly notorious like Botak Chin.[58]

---

[58] Botak Chin was involved in many high-profile robberies and shootouts. To the police, he was almost impossible to catch because the locals, for fear or love, kept their mouths shut about his whereabouts. Some even believed he had superpowers that kept him invisible and

The police took the protestors' statements and released all of them.

'Except me, everyone left,' Fahmi said. 'I didn't know why. I didn't know what was going to happen to me.'

The police called Fahmi over and asked him to remove all clothing except for one article.

'Does underwear count as one?' Fahmi asked.

'Yes,' the policeman said.

'Is there a place to change?' Fahmi asked again.

'Just change here,' the policeman shouted in reply.

So Fahmi took off his torn T-shirt and jeans and pulled down his underwear before putting on his jeans as his only clothing.

'Give me your glasses,' the policeman said.

'I need my glasses,' Fahmi said as he was thinking about an excuse to keep it. He couldn't see without it otherwise, but the police wouldn't allow that reason. 'I would get migraines and dizziness if I don't have it on.' After a few arguments, he was able to keep his glasses.

Half-naked and bare-footed, Fahmi was pulled through several security doors along an alleyway to reach the jail cells at the back of the building. The place was dark, dusty, and dirty with cockroaches and mice running around, feeding off the surroundings. A pungent stench rose to the air, mixing the clogged-up drains, body odour, and a stale metallic smell that Fahmi still remembers today.

He saw day-holding drug criminals roaming in and out of their cells, waiting for their court hearing. If some were unlucky, they might be brought to the caning area behind the skeleton-shaped building structure. A few of them were wearing the orange-coloured prison cloth.

'Can I have one of those shirts?' Fahmi asked the officer holding him.

'Take those,' the officer said, pointing to a pile of used orange clothes that were stained with sweat and dirt. It didn't even look orange

---

escape unscathed. Locals also called him Robin Hood because he often gave to the poor what he looted from the rich. Contrary to popular belief, Botak Chin was not bald; in fact, he had a head full of hair. 'BOTAK' was an acronym for *Bantu Orang Tak Ada Kerja* (Help those who don't have a job). His psychiatrist called him a 'misguided genius' who believed that secret society could protect the weak. When he was at the gallows after a failed escape attempt, his final words were, '*Sudah sampai ah?*' (So we're here?)

any more. Fahmi took one for himself in case it got too cold, but he never wore it. 'It was too disgusting.'

The officers showed him his tiny jail cell, with a window the size of a shoebox as the only light source. The cement walls were ice-cold, with drawings by previous inmates, and a slightly elevated cement structure as a cold bed. The cell door was shut with a loud thump.

Fahmi could not stop thinking about the death-in-custody cases that he was protesting. Innocent detainees who were beaten up by the police, left alone, and who then died without anyone knowing. Those who died in custody are typically unknown, without friends and family or powerful politicians to protect; Fahmi knew he was a nobody. There were no other protestors who would be witnesses if something happened. This was precisely what he had been taught, and the worst was happening to him. The policemen at the Pudu Jail had virtually an unfettered authority over him in the tiny cell. Did the poster about the zombie police go too far in pissing the police off? They were targeting him because they were angry about what he did. The police would not go away easily without teaching Fahmi a lesson.

'At that moment I was all alone,' Fahmi said. 'I kept repeating to myself, "It is just twenty-four hours, it will be over soon" to calm myself down.'

He tried to shut his eyes to pretend this was all just a bad nightmare, and he would wake up somewhere else. But a thought could not escape him, 'This time, I could die.'

* * *

A loud bang at the jail cell jolted Fahmi up.

'Get up!' a fierce-looking police officer took a piece of paper and a pen and passed it to Fahmi. 'Sign this. Hurry!'

Fahmi looked at that paper. It was a form of consent to the confiscated items. He looked down the list and saw his phone, T-shirt, poster, wallet . . . and then the last one was 'knife' (*pisau*).

'What is this for?' Fahmi asked.

'Why do you ask so much? When we ask you to sign, just sign,' the police said.

'I don't know what this is. Could I ask my lawyers first and sign later?' Fahmi said, as his heart started pounding rapidly, his hands began to tremble. He looked at that list again—knife? Is it the same as paper cutter?

The police pointed a finger right at Fahmi's face. 'You listen to me! Are you challenging me? Are you not going to sign this piece of paper?'

Fahmi had heard about police planting evidence and forcing consent for a crime before. Was this one of those instances? Would signing this mean that Fahmi would be liable for the crime of possessing a dangerous weapon when he didn't? Or could this be merely procedural? If Fahmi didn't follow what the policeman wanted, would it make him angry enough to come in and beat him up? Who would help him? Who would know if something happens to him?

External control are you gonna let them get you?
Do you wanna be a prisoner in the boundaries they set you?

'I think it's best if I wait to ask my lawyer about this first . . .' Fahmi said.

'I'm giving you one final chance. Are you going to sign this or what?' the police shouted at him, with echoes resounding across the old building.

Fahmi's heart couldn't stop racing, sweat started flushing down his head. He was going to say yes. Then there was a force that came from nowhere, an act of last-minute courage, that made him shake his head.

'Good, good!' the police officer growled and snatched the paper form off Fahmi's hands and stormed off.

Minutes later, a few policemen came over and pulled open the door. 'You!' one pointed at Fahmi. 'Follow me.'

This is it, Fahmi thought to himself.

He followed them out of the sight of other cellmates, along the same alleyway, but this time to a room.

'Sit,' the police said.

'We are releasing you on bail.'

Fahmi was confused as he was relieved. Was it because he didn't sign the form? Was it because they couldn't find a reasonable charge other than peaceful protest? Was it because they came to their senses? These were questions that would follow Fahmi for the next few years.

He walked out in his torn clothes, seeing daylight for the first time in hours. He looked at his watch and ran back home and changed into a long-sleeved shirt and a new pair of jeans, before going to the nearest train station to Tanjung Malim. On the train, he used water to wipe off blood stains and rub off, futilely, the scuffs and bruises marked over him. He stretched his clothes to cover most of his arms and legs.

When he finally had a chance to breathe, he still could not believe what happened to him. 'I was at the police lock-up where many suspects died for no reason—and I didn't die.'

A simple poster, drawn in black and white, could invite such an aggressive reaction from the authorities. He was the first one to be handcuffed (within fifteen minutes of the protest), the only one to be beaten up, the only one to stay behind, the only one who was hit by the object he made. A simple—but awfully powerful—poster. Fahmi Reza wasn't just the 'poster guy'; he was an activist who could rattle the system.

When Fahmi finally arrived at his brother's wedding, it was already late evening. The place was dark with only a few glowing retro bulbs tied by fairy strings. His brother, still in his wedding suit, walked over to Fahmi and asked, 'What happened to you?'

'Nothing.'

5

The first time I met Fahmi Reza on Zoom, it was delayed by fifteen minutes.

'James, I need to take a call, give a few minutes,' he said.

The call was from the police in the main headquarters of Bukit Aman. Whenever he receives a phone call like that, the first question he would ask is, 'Which poster?' has gotten him into trouble. At the time of writing, he puts up at least one poster a day on issues of concern.

'At least they made an appointment this time,' he continued. 'The last time, twenty policemen busted my door for one satirical poster. It's ridiculous. I didn't open the door at that time because I was alone—anything could've happened. I called my lawyer in case anything bad happened to me.'

The second time I met Fahmi was a month later. This time it was worse. He almost had to cancel because he was just told to attend court for two charges for another set of posters, yet again.

The year before our meeting in 2022, he had nine investigations—making him the most wanted artist in the country. But this time, Fahmi was unperturbed. Instead, he started poking fun at these investigations and charges. He had created a loyalty card which he stamped every time he was called in for questioning. On his social media pages, he even made a 'Twenty Questions with Fahmi Reza', a parody of the trend by Vogue, where he talked about the common questions at a police investigation based on his experience.

Every time he stepped out of a police station, he would hold his target poster and take a photo with a 'V' sign in front of the station. Unmistakably his captions would say 'satire is not a crime' and *'jumpa lagi next time, apa2 roger'* (see you again next time, just call me if anything).

Fahmi's portrayal of these charges was laced with sarcasm and humour, sometimes almost comical. This was deliberate. On 8 February 2022—a day before his charge—he posted a mock exam paper that he let his followers guess the right answer.

'In 2021–2022, Fahmi Reza was investigated 10 times for his satire artworks. Among them, which artwork has caused him to be criminally charged in court?'

'Try answering this question,' Fahmi posted with choices of A, B, C, and D. '10 marks.'

'I know the effect of this charge is fear,' he told me. 'The message is "Look at Fahmi Reza, he is arrested for his artwork. You [others] won't get away with it. You will be arrested. You will be charged." So, I would use humour to diffuse that fear. Let's laugh at it.' You cannot laugh and be fearful at the same time.

To get to this point of absolute fearlessness, Fahmi followed a two-step process that seemed almost like a manual.

Step One: Let everyone know

To grow from a trauma, you need to talk about it. By talking about what happened, you slowly dissolve the pain of the incident; by talking about what was happening internally, you transform debilitating thoughts into strengths.

In classic Fahmi Reza fashion, he disclosed what happened at the police station in 2004 in a big way.

'The [police brutality] incident [in 2004] wasn't reported in the media. So, I took the torn cloth, my spare paper cutter, posters from the protest, and a flyer—and I turned it into an exhibition,' said Fahmi.

The art exhibition that hosted his work, five months after the police beatings, was Lostgens' Art Space. Ili Farhana organized an art festival called 'Notthatbalai', which acted as an alternative to Malaysia's mainstream Balai Seni Negara. It was a huge bungalow in Seputeh that turned into an art gallery that celebrated 'anomalies and adaptations'. Art exhibitions, music gigs, flea markets, movement-based performances, and theatrical drama and dances happened over five days.

On a makeshift display gallery, Fahmi hung and pasted his incident materials and labelled them. Against a mahogany background and four unequally distanced spotlights shining from below, there were six exhibits shown.

Exhibit 1 (top left), T-SHIRT: Fahmi Reza's Zombie Police poster T-shirt, ripped from the centre of his chest all the way to the bottom left of the T-shirt, with only a string loosely hanging out.

Exhibit 2 (top right), POSTER: Zombie Police poster, torn at its edges; the police still looking directly at you with his revolver. The power is not lost.

Exhibit 3 (bottom leftmost), FOTOGRAF: Fahmi Reza being dragged by the police on the road, with his legs folded, almost falling on the ground, only to be pulled up by two plain-clothed policemen.

Exhibit 4 (bottom middle-left), SURAT JAMIN (bail letter): Slightly folded, written and signed.

Exhibit 5 (bottom middle-right), PISAU (knife): A paper cutter.

Exhibit 6 (bottom rightmost), FLYER: A vertical flyer of a policeman holding a baton, looking at you, about to hit you in the head.

Most people who have had a close shave with death at the hands of the police would go silent after. That is the point of intimidation: To stop your smartass from creating another poster that mocks authority. Scaring you with insults, violence, and gruesome prison cells is effective. They make victims question themselves and engage in self-blame. When victims see daylight again, their only wish is to reverse their actions and disappear quietly from the world.

Fahmi did the opposite—he told the story in all its gore. He showed you the actual artefacts so that you could feel his trauma in a visceral way. He didn't downplay or sidestep it; he owned it and displayed it for all to see—his confiscated items, his scuffs and bruises, his innermost wound.

'Everybody [who saw his exhibit] could not believe that something like this happened to me. They kept asking, 'Did this really happen?' Because it was an art exhibition, they weren't sure if it was fictional,' Fahmi said. 'And I kinda liked that.'

Step Two: Experiment with your newfound weapon

The next time Fahmi was arrested, the story ended differently. Driven by his belief in direct democracy, he had organized Occupy Dataran—a year-long movement intended to gather people at the famous square of Kuala Lumpur and discuss policies. Around 500 university students marched through the historic square of Kuala Lumpur to demand the abolition of higher education loans. By this time, Fahmi already knew his rights.

On 22 April 2012, the eighth day of the camp-in protest, a group of policemen surrounded him when he was sitting around the tent they built. What happened next was all caught on camera. Below is a transcript from the five-minute-and-thirty-five-second recording, with Fahmi giving commentary at present:

> *Police asked everyone to take their belongings and leave. One plain-clothed policeman grabbed Fahmi's arm.*
> **Fahmi Reza:** Why are you holding me, sir?
> **Police:** Can you follow us to the police station?
> **FR:** Why? Why must I follow you to the police station?
> [inaudible passage by the police about the law violation]
> **FR:** Am I under arrest now, sir?

Fahmi commentary: If the police arrest you, you need to ask, 'Am I under arrest?' until you get an answer from them. If they do not answer this, you don't have to follow them to the police station.

> **Police:** Let's discuss it at the police station.
> **FR:** Am I under arrest?

Fahmi commentary: They need to tell me at the point of arrest because the next question is 'On what grounds?' There must be reasonable grounds for arrest. They cannot just catch anyone they want on the street. We have the right to know.

> **Police:** I ask for your cooperation.
> *A few seconds later, two policemen started grabbing both of Fahmi's arms.*
> **FR:** If I am not under arrest, why are you grabbing me like that?

Fahmi commentary: So, at this moment, I knew that this was an unlawful arrest.

> **Police:** Come on, just follow us.
> **FR:** Why are you forcing me?
> *The policemen started grabbing and yanking Fahmi out of his sitting position. The crowd shouted, 'Why are you forcing him?', 'Where is your warrant of arrest?', 'Is he under arrest?'*

FR: If I am not under arrest, why did you grab me like this?
Fahmi was pulled into a van with the number plate WLT 3024.

The police then brought Fahmi to the police station only for him to realize that the plain-clothed personnel were not the police, but the local council, Dewan Bandaraya Kuala Lumpur (DBKL). He kept asking, 'What's the reason for my arrest?' and 'Am I under arrest?' But the police just ignored him and briefly said they didn't know. He sat there for six hours, clueless.

Fahmi commentary: That instance confirmed to me that it was unlawful detention.

Later, when DBKL's witnesses were asked to testify in court, they gave contradictory answers:

DBKL #1: Fahmi was arrested on the offence of obstruction, for putting up camps in public spaces.
DBKL #2: Fahmi was arrested for refusing to follow orders and cooperate.
DBKL #3: I am not sure why Fahmi was arrested. When he was arrested, I was standing far away.
DBKL #4: Fahmi was arrested for pushing the DBKL enforcers, refusing cooperation, and provocation.

What Fahmi did next was characteristic of his growth. He sued the local council, DBKL, and the police for unlawful arrest and unlawful detention.

'You fight them on their grounds. It's like Jujitsu—you use the attack of the opponent, and you redirect it back to them,' said Fahmi.

'The next time you protest, they are put in a dilemma. If they allow it, then you create this culture of criticizing leaders—which the oppressors are not happy about. If they decide to crush it with force, then their [heavy-handed tactics] will be reported to the media and the people will hate them. Either way, you win.

'You should always fight back and shouldn't let them have the final say. Usually, the repression is intended to create a chilling effect—a culture of fear. The message you send [by suing DBKL and the police] is important. It's not about the money. When they kick us to the bottom, we should not stay down—we must rise back up,' Fahmi said.

On the second last day of 2015, the High Court judge ruled that the arrest was indeed unlawful. DBKL and the police were ordered to pay Fahmi compensation and exemplary damages, besides cost, amounting to RM58,000. DBKL tried to appeal the case, but they were denied.

He posted this on his social media after the verdict:

> I am here to announce that I will not take even a single cent from the compensation by the police and DBKL [when it is sent over].
>
> I plan to put the money into a fund to support protest movements and activism focused on fighting against authorities' oppression in Malaysia.
>
> Since the start, this case was never about money. It is to show the importance of speaking up when there is injustice, to fight when there is oppression by the powerful, to be brave in the struggle to protect our freedom and human rights.

Having felt powerless his entire life against injustice, Fahmi finally saw the tangible results of something he had always believed in: Power could and should be in the hands of ordinary Malaysians. Even after being dealt a traumatic incident, Fahmi found enormous strength to keep living and find what is good to keep pushing forward. Like a metal, he was hit, seared, and bent until he finally broke. Instead of wallowing in pain, he built himself back brick-by-brick to a state much better than he ever was before. He became antifragile.

Recalling the 2004 beating incident, I asked Fahmi, 'Do you still view the police beating in 2004 as a negative experience?'

'No, it's very *positive*. Without it, I won't be who I am today,' Fahmi said. 'It sounds strange, but because the incident was so bad the first time, it taught me a lot that I accelerated my growth in activism. Nothing could scare me now.'

Years later, Fahmi Reza would face his toughest challenge yet. He would be faced with the weight of the entire state machinery for mocking the most powerful man in the country. The difference is, this time he was ready.

6

Censorship will never truly work. Don't get me wrong. You can be a dictator and create vague laws and charge artists for work you disagree with, but the outcome will never be as you intended.

That's because of something called the Streisand Effect. The more you try to censor, the more likely it will spread.

Husband and wife Kenneth and Gabrielle Adelman were successful Silicon Valley entrepreneurs who made their money during the dot-com era and retired early. Millions were made after the company founded by Kenneth Adelman, TGV Software, was sold to Cisco Systems and Nokia in the 1990s. For their later life, they have decided to dedicate their lives to environmental causes. Their home at Santa Cruz had the largest residential solar energy system in California and they owned four electric vehicles. Their website, The Adelman Family Homepage, was powered by solar electricity.

In 2002, they realized that the Californian coastline was degrading due to irresponsible and excessive development and pollution.

'There used to be salmon runs on the Pajaro, abundant condors, and pristine beaches anyone could walk on,' Gabrielle Adelman wrote. 'Now we have irrigation ditches, channelized rivers, seawalls, sand starved beaches strewn with garbage and arrogant wealthy homeowners trying to claim that the Pacific coast belongs to them alone.'

So, they decided to do something with a helicopter and a camera. Gabrielle Adelman would steer the Robinson R44 helicopter at around 500 feet. They would remove the port-side rear door, and Kenneth Adelman would use his Nikon camera to take a photo of the Californian coastline. Every three seconds, he would click.

All these photos would be uploaded to a website called 'California Coastline Records Project'. This database, which accumulated

12,000 frames of the Californian coast since 2002, aimed to allow the public to see the 'truth in pictures'—high definition and detailed—so that there was public pressure to save the coastlines from aggressive development. It also acted as a watchdog to see who was destroying it—a copy of a 'before' and 'after' photo would be strong evidence in the court of any environmental wrongdoing.

But one day, legendary artist Barbra Streisand[59] sent the Adelmans cease-and-desist letters because 3 per cent of their entire database had exposed her Malibu home. She sued for $10 million and asked for her home's aerial photo to be taken down. Her attempt at censorship backfired incredibly.

Before Barbra Streisand sued them, the Adelmans' website project wasn't actually popular. Her Malibu home photo, also called 'Image 3850' in the lawsuit,[60] was downloaded a grand total of six times before the suit—two of which were by Barbra's lawyers.

As a result of the lawsuit, the website's visits ballooned to 420,000 per month. As of 2022, the total number of visitors on a Californian coastline website was 10.2 million.

Two years after the failed lawsuit, Techdirt founder Mike Masnick wrote about a similar story. There was a website called Urinal.net that posted photos of urinals around the United States, and Marco Beach Ocean Resort got furious because the website featured its urinal without permission. Mike Masnick wrote:

> How long is it going to take before lawyers realize that the simple act of trying to repress something they don't like online is likely to make it so that something that most people would never, ever see (like a photo of a urinal in some random beach resort) is now seen by many more people? Let's call it the Streisand Effect.

[59] Barbra Streisand is one of the EGOT winners—where she has received the Emmy, Grammy, Oscar, and Tony awards. Only sixteen people in history have accomplished this as of 2022.
[60] Streisand v. Adelman et al., in California Superior Court; Case SC077257

I tell this story because Fahmi Reza was the one who told me about Streisand Effect.

On the last day of January 2016, Fahmi was frustrated with the 'legendary' corruption of the former prime minister Najib Razak in the 1MDB scandal. The 1MDB scandal, a sovereign wealth fund which Najib chairs, was called the 'largest kleptocracy case to date' and 'one of the world's greatest financial scandals'. The scandal involved billions of dollars that ran through the world's financial infrastructure, to which $700 million allegedly went to Najib's bank account.

But what happened after it was found out by international media and authorities was most frustrating to Fahmi. He said:

> After *The Wall Street Journal* exposed the story [in 2015], initially [Najib] kept quiet. He didn't respond, thinking it would just go away. When he couldn't escape any more, he fired the Attorney General who was planning to charge him and hired a new one who miraculously freed him from any wrongdoing. When his deputy constantly raised it in Cabinet meetings, he sacked him. Then he tried to twist it and called it Arab donation.

'The whole 1MDB issue is a farce. We all know it. [Najib] turned the country into a circus—and the biggest clown was he,' Fahmi said. 'The clown face described it perfectly for me.'

To sanitize his image, Najib kept the institutions and the media under his thumb, so that he could continue projecting the image of a clean, moderate, and modern leader. When the 1MDB issue started leaking uncontrollably, he started using repressive laws to silence critics. In the year before Clown Face appeared, the colonial-era relic Sedition Act 1948 was used ninety-one times, which was five times higher than the number of uses in the law's first fifty years of existence, spiralling Malaysia into 'a dark era of repression'. Ninety-one times! That is almost eight times per month. Imagine hearing about arrests twice a week. Wouldn't that make you scared? Only countries like Iran, Uzbekistan, Sudan, and Senegal still retained laws like this.

Triggered by this absurdity, Fahmi Reza drew the Clown Face in fifteen minutes and posted it ten minutes before 2.00 p.m. The police started clamping down on him.

What Fahmi did next was nothing short of extraordinary.

* * *

A mere 166 minutes.

That's how long it took for the police's cyber unit team, Police Cyber Investigation Response Centre (PCIRC), to issue the warning on the Clown Face poster.

It said:

[Fahmi Reza], your account is under PDRM's (police) watch. Use it wisely and in accordance to the law.

'This was an intimidation because they didn't ask me to take down the artwork,' said Fahmi. 'Essentially, they're saying "The Big Brother is watching you."'

The PCIRC's task was not explicitly laid out anywhere. But it spent substantial time cracking down on online content that may violate the law and warning the public on cybercrimes and scams. They would go on Twitter and screenshot a tweet or reply directly to the user with the same 'Use it wisely' warning. Occasionally it would be used as an internal communication tool with the Inspector General of Police. 'Please go after this person,' the Inspector General would say, with a screenshot and the name of the user. 'Got it, boss,' the PCIRC would compliantly reply.

When Fahmi received the warning, he knew that an arrest and a charge might be impending. So, he used the small window of the next few days to practise Jujitsu.

The first Jujitsu was against fear.

Through the PCIRC warning, Fahmi knew that the police were trying to plant fear in him. So, he responded an hour later.

He retweeted the PCIRC's warning with a post that said, 'In a country that uses its laws to protect the corruptor, it's about time we are no longer polite in fighting against corrupt authorities.' In those two days, Fahmi continued to make his defiance clear by defending his right to make satire.

'I wrote a statement to the police to say that I will be more famous if you arrest me. This is reverse psychology on the police to say that "if you decide to arrest and charge me, it will be no good for you. More people will find out about the poster and me, and follow me, and all the political graphics in the past. We will create more rebels if you do this,"' said Fahmi.

In the short space of a few hours, Fahmi's statement had prompted other graphic designers, including the famous political cartoonist Zunar, to create solidarity posters of Fahmi Reza. The hashtag that trailed every poster was #KitaSemuaPenghasut (We are all seditious). If you want to go after this guy, go after us too.

'It's almost a "come and get me" poster, egging the police on,' said Fahmi. They have turned fear around and pointed it back to the authorities.

But there was something else that Fahmi said above: *More people will find out about the poster . . . and all the political graphics in the past.* What does that sound like? The Streisand Effect. That was the second Jujitsu.

Most people didn't know that the Clown Face was an old poster. It was first made and posted in 2014, but it didn't garner much traction. It only had 129 retweets and 37 likes.

'It didn't go anywhere [at that time] because the Sedition Act wasn't a popular issue. It became just another political poster,' Fahmi clarified.

But the PCIRC's warning essentially drew more attention to a poster that would probably have been missed by the public once more. Knowing this and the power of graphics, Fahmi decided to spread it as widely as possible.

He started going around the city to paste the Clown Face on any object he could find. He made high-res versions of Clown Face downloadable in different formats online. He framed this issue as a free speech and censorship issue—then suddenly, the Clown Face was everywhere.

Graphic designers around the country created hundreds of versions of the Clown Face and started sharing it through art groups and the wider public anonymously. There was the happy clown, the sad clown, the inquisitive clown, the creepy clown, the fat clown, the behind-the-cell clown, the Joker clown, the Charlie in the Chocolate Factory clown, the Ronald McDonald clown, the Simpsons clown, the K.I.S.S. clown . . .

At every corner of the city, people started printing their own posters and stickers to be stuck around. A Clown Face even spread as far as Perth, where a Malaysian dissenter stuck one on the Malaysian embassy entrance with a graffiti 'X' sign over it. Many had the Clown Face painted on themselves during Halloween. School students took black and red paint and splattered the Clown Face on their uniforms. The Clown Face design on a pair of Vans shoes garnered the highest votes. T-shirts of the Clown Face were sold in every language with the promotional message as 'The most rebellious T-shirt of the year.'

Then it got worse.

The Deputy Inspector General of Police issued a warning to social media users to stop using the social media platform to insult others, especially country leaders. The earlier passage mentioned the 'individual who defamed the portrait of the country's leader is facing jail and/or fine.' Though without direct reference to the Clown Face, it was evident to Fahmi that it was targeting him and his Clown Face artwork. So, he created a parody poster of it using the Malaysian Communications and Multimedia Commission (MCMC) as its signatory, with a large Clown Face behind the official statement. He was egging on the police and MCMC.

'I designed the warning poster as a piece of political satire and parody to highlight the absurdity behind the warning issued by the government (police) against spreading the clown pictures,' Fahmi said.

This invited a reaction from the MCMC's strategic communication division chief, Sheikh Raffie Abdul Rahman, who said that the parody statement by Fahmi was a false statement. Then he added, even without such a statement by the MCMC, the public should not share edited photos of leaders.

What happened after he said that? The Clown Face spread even further. When you know Streisand Effect so well like Fahmi does, everything that the government attempts to censor runs in your favour. So Fahmi would keep egging the government on.

Whenever the Clown Face died down, Fahmi would prop it back up with a new angle.

He posted his behind-the-scenes drawing and colouring of the Clown Face. Another time, he reassured his supporters that he would continue to fight no matter what happened to him. He used other news reports to maintain his innocence and inject a sense of humour to lighten the mood. On one occasion, he even brought up the 2004 police beating to say, this is why I am not afraid.

The only place that it didn't spread to was the Malaysian mainstream media—there was a blackout. But the online spread was so overwhelming that international press started covering it. BBC went first, then *Bangkok Post*, *The Straits Times*, Mashable, Al Jazeera, and eventually *The Wall Street Journal*. There was no hiding. Fahmi Reza became internationally known as the 'Malaysian Banksy'.

When he was finally arrested and charged in court, Fahmi brought a framed Clown Face artwork with him. He knew the media would take photos of him, so he wanted them to also take a picture of the Clown Face, which would inadvertently create a greater spread.

'Can you not hold it up when we take the photo? This surely can't be published. You know how it's like,' journalists would often say.

But sometimes the media gets careless, and they're not aware of the Streisand Effect the way Fahmi does.

On 6 June 2016, Fahmi was charged under Section 233(1) of the Communications and Multimedia Act 1998 for producing the Clown Face that 'annoy, abuse, threaten, or harass others'. Fahmi Reza would be investigated and charged a few more times under the Act he calls the 'Hurt Feelings Act' (Akta Sakit Hati) because the vagueness and broadness of the Act are often used when the political leaders are hurt by online criticisms or mockery.

Fahmi was liable to one year imprisonment or RM50,000 in fine, or both upon conviction.

The next day, the government's main mouthpiece, *Utusan Malaysia*, published a story on the front page that read 'Graphic designer charged for uploading a false photo of the Prime Minister.' On top of it was a photo of Fahmi Reza standing upright, with his full punk gear of backwards beret, black jacket and jeans, full-frame dark glasses, and a red bandana tied like a scarf around his neck, looking slightly upwards towards the camera without a smile; his right hand held up the brown-framed artwork of the Clown Face. The government's main mouthpiece carried a photo of the Clown Face—it had slipped through the cracks of the impenetrable authoritarian wall; the final piece of the chess has fallen.

The Streisand Effect was complete.[61]

Epilogue

When I met Fahmi Reza in the early part of 2022, his hair had turned grey. The full Fahmi Reza punk gear was gone. He dresses differently nowadays to avoid being recognized. Sometimes, he would tie his wavy hair up in a bun or choose glasses instead of his signature wayfarer sunglasses. We met at a small local café. But it didn't stop the barista from coming over and giving him a salute for his work. He is, unmistakably, a cult icon.

'I'm not above you,' Fahmi would often comment on his fame. 'Don't look up to me. Don't follow me from the back. We go through this struggle together.'

A decade ago, Fahmi mentioned that his role is like Morpheus in *The Matrix*. To him, Neo was the oppressed people, and Agent Smith, the villain, was the government.

Fahmi said: 'Morpheus was the leader just trying to open Neo's eyes to the reality and let Neo decide. I'm not trying to be their [the people's] leader. Just trying to expose the truth. My purpose is to make my role obsolete. If the people are empowered, then they don't need me any more. That's how it should be.'

---

[61] After more than two years since he was first charged, on 11 October 2018, the court freed Fahmi Reza after the prosecution dropped the charges. 'The KL #clowntrial is finally over!' he wrote on social media.

His whole life of activism, including conducting 'Student Power' seminars,[62] producing documentaries, performing political plays in theatres, playing in a band, was driven by the single goal of making people realize the power they have in their hands. Preceding the 2022 general election, he went to public universities to hold democracy classes for university students. He got barred from entering in many of them. But he continued those classes at eateries nearby. Nothing stopped him.

Freedom sounds like the final verse of Fahmi's favourite song, 'Big A, Little A':

> Be exactly who you want to be, do what you want to do
> I am he and she is she but you're the only you
> No one else has got your eyes, can see the things you see
> It's up to you to change your life and my life's up to me

Throughout my interview, I couldn't help but wonder whether the sacrifices that he is making are worth it. Most people in his position would have just quit. How much are you willing to sacrifice for the principles you believe in?

To be Fahmi Reza, he had to sacrifice a life of money. Most of his friends—from school, university, graphic designing groups, activists, and the punk community—have stopped the idealistic, radical decision and pursued more practical choices of working in a company to earn a living.

When Cheng Chean met up with Fahmi a few years ago, he was worried for him. He knew that it wasn't his place to think about Fahmi's material needs, but he told Fahmi that he could recommend a few mid-sized companies that were in need of graphic designers if Fahmi needed help.

'It's okay, Cheng Chean, I'm fine on my own. I'll find a way,' Fahmi replied.

---

[62] Fahmi Reza's 'Student Power' seminar was intended to teach university students the radical history of students organizing, protesting, and participating in politics, which were lost activities after repressive university laws. Fahmi was banned from many universities despite overwhelming support from the students.

And somehow, Fahmi always did.

'I never had a stable income before Patreon,'[63] Fahmi said. 'My lifestyle is minimal. I don't need a lot of money to survive. If I get into trouble, there are many human rights lawyers in Malaysia who are willing to help me for free.'

Until today, Fahmi has never drawn a single poster for commercial use. He turned them down indiscriminately. His art has been, and will always be, only for social good.

He still wears black T-shirts and jeans. Still eats the same food and drinks. Still has the same wavy long hair that doesn't need cutting. Still washes his hair without shampoo. Still cleans his face without skincare.

'The secret to staying young is to not dress like an old man. And don't read online comments,' he said. 'And don't marry.'

To be Fahmi Reza, you also could not marry or have children.

'One reason that I am not married and don't have kids is because that's the choice I made. I would be irresponsible to put them in constant jeopardy of being arrested and going to jail,' Fahmi said. After a pause, he continued: 'The kid might grow up without a father. That would be irresponsible. I don't want to burden anyone when I get caught.'

Anyone who chooses to be with Fahmi must be prepared for a life of constant anxiety. He would tell them to be ready but whenever he is hauled up, it still causes great anguish.

His mother, Muselmah, still worries about him. She attended all the court hearings for the three years the Clown Face was charged in court. Muselmah would call Fahmi whenever she hears about another charge or investigation against him, but she never once criticized what Fahmi did. Live life without regrets—that was her motto. Fahmi would find out that his mother would screen his documentary, *10 Years Before Merdeka* (*10 Tahun Sebelum Merdeka*), a forgotten history of the people's protest against the British's independence proposal accepted by the political elites, to her hundreds of Couchsurfing guests

---

[63] Patreon is a member subscription service that allows the public to pay an artist a monthly sum to support the artist's work. On Fahmi Reza's Patreon, he only allows one membership type, which is $1 (RM4) per month. As of March 2022, he had 722 patrons.

interested to learn about Malaysia.[64] Muselmah would say this is the best introduction to Malaysia, and she might be right.

'That's the life that I choose for myself,' said Fahmi. 'I don't live with any regrets.'

In the recesses of his mind, he would sometimes contemplate the alternate life of being a school teacher. Education remains a tool of empowering Malaysians through their faculties of critical thought. Fahmi had spent a few years in the streets of Chow Kit Road to teach children purposeful use of art to map the best parts of their community that has been stereotyped as a disorderly place with the worst vices. He would do the same for the community in Kota Kinabalu, Sabah. Once in a while, he would also morph into a workshop trainer to teach students and Girls Scouts how to create compelling artwork and how to resist.

If that were the life he had chosen, he would have avoided fines, arrests, and charges. But he wouldn't be able to live with himself. Living an unprincipled and powerless life was more difficult.

'What about the real possibility of going to jail?' I asked.

'The court cases can be quite consuming. I've experienced it before—it's part of my job,' Fahmi said after a long pause. Then he thought about it for a while: 'Nothing will ever prepare you for jail, just like how nothing will ever prepare you to get beaten by the police in a protest.'

His eyes lit up again. 'But sometimes you need the authorities to abuse the law and go after someone like me for the public to realize the existence of dumb laws. So yes, there is a possibility that I might go to jail. But even if I'm jailed, it will still be beneficial to the cause.'

Since the day he found freedom within himself, Fahmi Reza has remained unbothered by what people think of him. 'The Malay community could be quite judgmental against me,' he said. They would call him, more than any other phrase, kurang ajar, a stinging phrase for a community that values honour and avoids shame.

---

[64] *10 Years Before Merdeka* (*10 Tahun Sebelum Merdeka*), created in 2007, won the "Most Outstanding Human Rights Film" award at the Freedom Film Fest in Malaysia.

'My posters are not meant to be *sopan santun* (polite) because I'm playing the rebel.

'A rebel's job is to constantly put pressure on the government, so they pay attention to issues that matter. The rebel is normally extreme in its ways—sometimes breaking the laws, operating outside the system—so the reformists look milder. The reformists are normally the politicians. To create change, the rebels and the reformists need each other. They just have different paths of change. I'm trying to play the role of an effective rebel,' Fahmi explained.

Fahmi referred to his favourite poem, 'Sepatah Kata', created by the National Laureate Usman Awang, which reads:[65]

Sebuah perkataan yang paling ditakuti
Yang tradisional sekali
Untuk bangsa kita yang pemalu.
Sekarang kata ini kuajarkan pada anakku:
Kau harus jadi manusia kurang ajar
Untuk tidak mewarisi malu ayahmu.
Lihat petani-petani yang kurangajar
Memiliki tanah dengan caranya
Sebelumnya mereka tak punya apa
Kerana ajaran malu dari bangsanya.
Suatu bangsa tidak menjadi besar
Tanpa memiliki sifat kurang ajar.

One word most feared,
Most traditional and revered,
For a people who are shy,

Now I teach this word to you my children:
You have to be a kurang ajar human,
To not inherit this shame of your father.

Look at the farmers who are kurang ajar,
Who now own the land with his ways,

---

[65] Antalogi Sajak Teluk Gong (1967), edited by Usman Awang, INSAN.

Before this they didn't have anything,
Because the teaching of shame from his people.

A people will not become great
Without the behaviour of kurang ajar.

Fahmi Reza's kurang ajar posters brought two court cases against him when we spoke in 2022. It was only March. These cases were still 50:50 depending on the judges he gets. Nothing was for certain. A lifelong practitioner of the art of fearlessness, Fahmi still puts out art pieces at a much higher rate after the court cases. For him, sitting quietly in front of the computer, researching issues, and figuring out the right way of conveying a message with sarcasm, humour, and wit was almost meditative.

'Maybe the change that I want will never be seen in my lifetime or the next.[66] But the ethics of activism is that as long as there is still injustice, even on one person, it is still worth fighting for. I don't think I will ever stop. As long as there is still injustice and unfairness, I will be there.'

He still remembers the day in the Pudu Jail cell alone in February 2004. Cold cement touched his body, sending a wave of premonition to his panicked mind. Between the dark and hopeless moments, he heard the protestors' faint chants through the walls demanding his immediate release. *Leave no one behind.*

'Knowing there are people outside gave me a sense of relief that I am not alone. In a way that reduced fear for me. It made me braver . . . knowing that there's always somebody having my back.'

When he walked out of the abandoned Pudu Jail that day, he saw a group of protestors waiting for him. They had moved from the protest ground to the main entrance and chanted unceasingly until they saw him. The sixteen other protestors who were released before him also never left. Fahmi looked at all their faces—strangers whose names he never knew.

He took everything in, clutched his fist tight and raised it to the air.

---

[66] Fahmi Reza's dream is to see a truly people's democracy by having participatory or direct democracy instead of representative democracy.

Key takeaways

- Censorship laws rarely work because of the Streisand Effect: The more you censor, the more people will see.
- Surviving a dangerous situation emboldens you to challenge authority.
- Persevering through fear against an authority's oppression will dissipate the power in the powerful.
- An activist plays the role of the rebel so that the moderates look good.

Chapter 6

Peter Kallang

How an indigenous retiree ushered in one of the largest
environmental victories in the region through the
power of weak ties

*'No one attended the first meeting . . .
not even my family, my flesh and blood.'*

1

Along Sarawak's second-longest river, Baram, was a small village of people who loved folklore.[67] In the morning, men would go into the jungle to grow cash crops, and the women would clean and cook, and weave sun hats for rituals, ceremonies, and daily use.[68] Upon nightfall, the two hundred inhabitants at every longhouse, which was stilted eight metres above ground, would gather on the veranda, listening intently to the stories of older folks. This was their main source of entertainment. There was no internet; mobile lines were poor. Journalists who entered Baram said that there was only one 'telephone booth' located in this village. Three nails were pinned against a wall inside a makeshift plywood shelter, and villagers had to place their mobile phones in a perfect slant for connection; once done, messages would flow in like a water stream.

Surrounded by the rhythms of crickets and cicadas, an elderly man told the story of a place called Batu Gading. It went like this:

> Many years ago, tribespeople, consisting of aristocrats and slaves, lived together in the village of Batu Gading. Whenever an aristocrat died, slaves were forced to offer themselves to be buried with the aristocrat in hopes of being reborn a helper in an aristocratic family. One day, a village headsman of Batu Gading died. An elderly woman knew that her grandson would be offered for sacrifice soon. When she came home and found that her grandson was no longer at home, she cried loudly.
>
> By the time the elderly woman went to the funeral, her grandson was already buried. Angry, she placed a frog inside the tobacco box that was typically passed around in such gatherings. In the middle of the procession, the frog jumped out and the whole crowd started laughing at the frog.

---

[67] The Baram River is 400 kilometres long.
[68] A sun hat is a hat with a fifty-five-centimetre diametre, shaped like an inverted saucer, decorated in bright and diverse colours of wool, beads, strings, velvet, and ink. Only women could weave the sun hats because of a believed spiritual strength.

That night, a huge storm ravaged the village. Many were afraid of what might befall them and started offering animals to the skies. The entire village turned into limestone. Even today, people can still find limestone-shaped cutlery in and around the village. However, the moral of the story was to never belittle animals who live in spirit with humans.

One of the persons in the crowd was a young man named Peter Kallang, who grew up with these folklore. He had heard of the gusty warrior who fired a hole into a giant rock with a blowpipe at the Baram River. The human-turned-crocodile who protected the river from enemies. The assembly of animals, led by the king of the jungle, that protected the sacred mountains against invasions at Batu Kelulong and Batu Uroh. The white beast who turned into a beautiful woman and then sacrificed herself into precious beads.

Born in 1950 to a respectable Kenyah family, Peter was the person you'd turn to at a social function where you knew nobody. He would treat you with warmth and respect, laugh at your jokes, and would not take himself too seriously. If there was a dance party, you could count on Peter to break out a few moves.

After the stories, the village people started singing and dancing to woodwinds and percussions. Plates of leftover grilled wild boar and cucumber were left on the side. Peter didn't know that one day in his adult life, everything that he knew about his village—the land, river, culture, language, dance, and the way of life—would be at risk of disappearing into dust.

2

Peter's father, Kallang Jau, was the only literate person in his community, even though he studied only for a year in school. In photos, his smiling lips and eyes balance out the thick, dark-rimmed glasses and the traditional hairstyle with straight fringes cut a few centimetres above his eyebrows.

Kallang Jau and his elder brother, Gau Jau, an energetic leader who loves to sing and chant in traditional Kenyah, were the Baram community service tag team—Gau Jau as the *Temenggong* (paramount chief) and Kallang Jau as *Penghulu* (number two in the community). Both of them initiated the post–World War II recovery of Baram, fundamentally transforming its economic base.

'They went beyond planting paddy at the fields,' Peter recalled. 'They also introduced cash crops like rubber, coffee, banana, peanuts, sugar cane, durians, and rambutans.'

To the community service tag team, the meaning of service was putting others ahead of themselves. Without trade, Baram villagers would forever be poor. So, Kallang Jau closed his sundry shop, and instead, collected two handfuls of paddy from every house to buy a rice mill. In turn, the rice mill's profits would be used to buy a generator so that every longhouse would have electricity.

Let there be light, Kallang Jau would always say.[69]

The higher rice production allowed them to garner enough profits to buy a ploughing machine in the fields (they became the first Baram longhouse to own one), and then a rubber processing facility, a cattle scheme, and a cooperative that gave them three times the return.

Villagers would describe Kallang Jau as a people's person because he went down to hunt and clean like everyone else. He would pull practical jokes on them that sometimes made them forget that he is the village head.

Kallang Jau was a father to five children. The eldest was Maria Kallang, a smiley and industrious woman whose managerial and people skills (she spoke fluent Hokkien and Mandarin) made the cooperative a hub for commerce in Baram. Peter Kallang was the middle child. In the close-knit family, Peter was most fond of his elder brother, Michael Kallang, who was born six years earlier. Sharp-minded and mild-mannered, Michael Kallang studied difficult subjects like theology and philosophy, preparing himself to be a priest of his community.[70]

'Michael was a very meticulous and organized person,' said Peter. 'The way he dressed, the way he carried himself . . . Even with his

---

[69] At his shop, Kallang managed to push down the bulb price from $3 to $2 so more people could afford it.

[70] The other siblings were Philip Kallang and Irene Kallang.

textbooks, he would still keep them in pristine condition after many years. You flip through the textbook, and it would still smell like it came from the bookshop.'

After Michael Kallang completed his studies, he started working for a well-known British bishop of Miri, who occasionally gave him money that was barely sufficient. Despite persistent hardship, he produced a Kenyah dictionary and hymns and prayers in the same tongue that 'are still used to this day at the Kenyah masses and prayer services'.

'I was not at all like him. I was not the smartest or the best in class. Always average,' Peter recalled.

But you couldn't blame Peter for not doing well in class. Peter had to study at a boarding school in a small town called Marudi, which was a two-hour boat ride from his home village. Like all other boys here, Peter had to learn to be an adult and fend for himself. He only had RM2 per week to buy food, typically purchased on Sundays and Wednesdays. The cheapest ingredients to buy were onions, cooking oil, salt, *ikan bilis*, MSG, and some vegetables they would cook for themselves. Peter would wait for his parents' rice and use it only sparingly. Every Sunday, Peter would cook extra rice to be eaten the next day. Breakfast was leftover cold rice, ikan bilis, and cold water from the river downhill. Lunch was cold rice and vegetables from the day before. When they ran out of vegetables for weekdays, Peter and his fifty-nine other schoolmates would pull out *midin*, a jungle fern curled up like fiddleheads, from the low swampy lands at the forest and eat that for dinner.[71]

The boarding school of Marudi was located at a hilltop, with cool breeze filling the night and dew greeting the morning sun. To get water, the students would have to walk down to the foot of the hill. Peter took a recycled kerosene tin with the top-half cut off and installed makeshift wooden handles to make a pail. Peter and friends would fill their pails with river water, and hold the handle on each side up the hill. 'The basket that has two handles should be carried by two people,' the local proverb goes.

---

[71] Cooked with garlic, shallots, and *belacan* (spicy shrimp paste) over a medium-heat wok, midin is a delicacy in Sarawak today.

But the skinny and clumsy boys would shake and spill the large pails along the way. 'By the time we reached the top, almost half of it was gone!' Peter recalled.

In class, Peter would try to memorize as much English and Latin text as possible. He couldn't study at his dorm room. The early mornings and late evenings were too dark. Lighting a candle was possible, but he still had to squint his eyes through the texts, and this would wear him out fast. There was also another downside to staying up late: Peeing. The toilets were too far from the dorm; the eerie silence convinced the boys that a pee was too dangerous (ghosts). Instead, they would have to sneak out to the grass in front of dorm and pee quietly. During schooling months, the grass outside the dorm turned brown, and only became green again when school holidays came around.

Boarding school was hard on Peter. He could only admire how his brother, Michael Kallang, did it with grace. 'His handwriting was so nice. It didn't take him long to write, but it was so perfect. I don't know how he does it!' said Peter.

When Peter failed his national exams and had to repeat the year at fifteen, Michael wrote long letters to encourage him to carry on.

'. . . Peter don't be disappointed about it, maybe such a situation can successfully serve as an "eye-opener" for you and give you further inspiration and determination to study. The "iron is still hot", so keep on hitting and with further effort you can finally bend it to shape.

Disappointment and loss of hope now, as in any other time, would not do you any good but will only lower your spirit.

The quality of school one attends matters little. What matters most is one's own burning determination to learn. Consider the case of Abraham Lincoln. He did not emerge into fame by having attended an outstanding school nor by the luck of his birth to wealthy parents. Rather, he was born to poor parents in a log cabin, but his will to study and great ambition gave him the key to success. Instead of exercise books he used the blade of a wooden spade and charcoal as chalk. He sat near the fireside at night to have light for studying. In the end he was soaring higher than people of a higher class who had proper school for learning.

So, Pete, please treasure my humble advice. God helps those who help themselves. Please try to let people know that we are not as stupid as they may think.

God Bless,
Michael Balan Kallang'

Years later, the world turned on Peter.

He received a phone call that said something that felt implausible: *Your brother, Michael, has died.* Peter's brother was only thirty years old.

'He died in a road accident when he was riding his motorcycle. Somebody knocked him over,' said Peter, still visibly disturbed by a pain that never eased even after half a century.

Barely half a year later, Peter's oldest sister, Maria Kallang, also succumbed to cancer. Within a year, his uncle, the first Kenyah in the British administration and a part-time entertainer, Gau Jau, also died. All of Peter's closest relatives had died. Suddenly, Peter was alone.

'I remember going to their funerals . . . I saw so many people from the community who came because they admired who [my family members] were. Newspapers even reported about their deaths,' Peter continued. 'I thought to myself, if only I could emulate them—contributing to the community, doing good things—even to a small extent . . . Then maybe I would be a good man.'

3

If you come from a village like Baram, your career choices are limited. Either you stay back and earn a modest living like your parents, or you try to make it big by working offshore for a petroleum company. After the deaths of his family members, Peter was the only breadwinner—he had to pick up a job that was well-paying so the family wouldn't suffer.

'If you worked in the palm oil industry, you might get paid RM3 or RM6 at the highest per day,' Peter said. 'If you worked offshore, you will get big money. The basic salary wasn't that much—around

RM300 to RM400 per month, but the allowances could push it up to RM3,000 per month.'[72]

After four years of technical training in the oil-rich Brunei sultanate, Peter took up an offshore role with an overseas petroleum company. Workers were distributed between onshore (at the office), offshore (at the sea), and off-days (annual leaves). Peter worked two weeks onshore, two weeks offshore, and had one week off.

When they were at sea, they worked on a US$21 million drilling barge called Big John, which has revived Miri's name as a hotspot for new oil well discoveries. Inside Big John was a driller shaped like a Christmas Tree; sets of valves wrapped around it. If gas flew in, a rubber material would inflate and hold the gas down through those valves. A mud-like chemical at the top of the pipe would push the gas downwards to prevent a leak. The reason offshore work was well-compensated was because, aside from being away from family and friends for a long time, the work to maintain and operate a huge drilling barge was high risk and high stress.

Once in January 1971, twenty-one-year-old Peter's offshore work shift was taken by another person named Sebastian Bujang. Peter took off and rested at his home in Long Ekang.

Big John was off the coast of Bintulu, Sarawak, about forty miles from shore. Drilling continued into the night, and they accidentally hit a gas pocket. Back then, safety equipment was not complete; the seismic studies carried out were also crude. They couldn't detect the gas pocket beforehand, let alone prepare for a calamity.

The driller blew up, and as there was welding going around, within seconds, the whole thing burst into a grand explosion.

The entire barge caught fire as the bubbling gas around the vessel ignited at the same time. The derrick collapsed onto the helicopter landing barge; violent flames burned Big John for five long hours.

---

[72] This was in 1970s, which approximately adds up to RM20,000 per month in 2022. This was a lot of money. Once, a housing developer in Miri offered to sell Peter a detached home at RM30,000. Peter said, he didn't want a house, because he had a house in Long Ekang. Today, that house is worth RM3 to RM4 million. 'I was so short-sighted! If only I bought that house, I would be a millionaire now.'

Most of the seventy-seven people on board jumped out, with many badly burnt and helpless.

Peter recalled what happened to Sebastian that day, the man who took over his shift:

> Those days, we weren't required to wear any safety coveralls to work. We could wear anything, so Sebastian was wearing a nylon shirt. When the fire happened, he wasn't actually near the fire. He was outside. But he went in to help put out the fire. As he ran to the fire, the radiation from the burst caused his nylon shirt to stick to his skin. When they took him to the hospital, the doctors and nurses didn't know how to help him. They tried to take off the nylon but they end up peeling him like a banana. His entire skin came off.

The first time Peter heard about it, he thought it must be a joke. How could Big John, the gigantic barge he had worked on just a few days ago, just explode in flames? The blast killed six of his friends. After that day, Peter sent in his resignation letter; he even paid off the notice period with his salary so he could leave immediately.

'God spared me that day,' Peter reflected. 'For a purpose, I think.'

* * *

To know how 'mind-bogglingly diverse' Borneo was, consider this fact: Borneo's biodiversity concentration of 700 species for every fifteen hectares of land is equivalent to the whole of North America. Borneo's 15,000-plant status ranked it the highest in the world for plant diversity, and it was only one of two places left where the orangutan (the smartest ape) still survives. The island received visitors from around the world, including famous naturalist Charles Darwin, who called Borneo a 'luxuriant hothouse made by nature for herself'. Rich forests like those in Borneo are an unending secret, revealing unknown species in a mysterious shroud.

Corruption and deforestation, however, have torn Peter's home state, Sarawak, to shreds. Since 1973, 86 per cent of lowland forests have been logged or cleared, leaving only a quarter of the forest intact.

The aggressive and blinding pace of destruction compelled the former British prime minister Gordon Brown to call it 'probably the biggest environmental crime of our time'.

Lukas Strauman, author of *Money Logging: On the Trail of the Asian Timber Mafia*, described how it started and its long-term impact to common Malaysians, in an interview with *National Geographic*:

> Initially, logging companies come in for so-called selective logging, taking the oldest and most valuable trees out.[73] A couple of years later they come back and get the rest of the bigger trees. Often, they return for a third time, after which nothing much is left to be harvested.
>
> If indigenous communities living in the rainforest want to build a school for the children, they can't find the timber to construct it. They frequently don't have access to clean drinking water because all the rivers have been polluted. And while the timber barons have become billionaires, the communities have remained very poor. Maybe there is a road. But do these people have a car to drive on the road? Most of them don't.

The brown water in the Baram River is evidence that the villagers, too, were not spared. Soil from logging and palm oil plantations leaked into the river, killing fishes and contaminating drinking water. The government's rampant development reached its crescendo when the government announced the RM420 billion (target) Sarawak Corridor of Renewable Energy (SCORE) to make Malaysia a developed country. One of the main thrusts of the plan was to transform the rainforest state of Sarawak into an industrial powerhouse—by using seven mega dams, among others.

The first mega dam was the Bakun Dam, the second tallest concrete-filled rockfill dam in the world. Despite multiple stages of

---

[73] A February 2022 edition of *Nature Plants* found that rare, old, and ancient trees (often ten to twenty times older than the individual tree in the forest) are vital to the forest's long-term survival. These were the 'lottery winners' that have genetic resilience that span centuries and would help in the forest's 'long-term adaptive capacity, substantially broadening the temporal span of the population's overall genetic diversity'.

resistance, the dam was built. Nearly 10,000 Sarawak natives lost their homes, lands, and livelihoods. When Bakun Dam was operational in 2011, it had a capacity of 2,400 megawatts, making it Asia's largest hydroelectric dam outside of China. But the resettlement turned out to be a disaster with settlers 'given substandard houses and infertile farmland', famished and diseased, forcing some to return to Bakun to live on 'floating houses'.

Peter saw, with his own eyes, the difficulty of resisting a giant government oppressor that had the power of corporations with deep pockets. During a protest against another mega dam, Murum Dam, the police shot a few bullets in the air as a sign of intimidation. Finally, they bulldozed their way in, like many other mega dams and rural developments in the past.

According to SCORE, Murum Dam will be followed by Baram Dam, a 150-metre land above sea level, that would guarantee to flood vast land areas and displace the entire community. For Baram, 412 square kilometres of rainforest (half the size of Singapore) and 20,000 indigenous people's homes from twenty-five villages would submerge under water.

A year after Murum Dam's construction, Peter attended a meeting organized by NGOs to rally against the Baram Dam. At that time, Peter had chosen early retirement and was working as a casual consultant.

The representatives from eight NGOs decided to form a coalition called SAVE Rivers Network, with a singular mission of stopping the Baram Dam. They learned that compromise with the government, like in Bakun and Murum Dam, only ended in a disaster for local communities. For the thirty indigenous communities, once they lose their land, they would also lose their language, culture, and way of life— the things that contributed to the beauty of the world. Never again.

At the end of the meeting, they looked at Peter and asked, 'You're not working, right? Why don't you become the chairman?'

Peter thought about what happened to past environmental and indigenous rights activists around the world. Murders, mysterious disappearances, constant harassments. He thought about the Swiss activist, Bruno Manser, who fought for indigenous Penan rights in Baram, and how he was regarded a persona non-grata by the government, targeted for bounty, and eventually disappeared against his will. Global Witness found that more than 700 environmentalists were murdered since 2001, many of whom were defending Brazil's Amazon. Columbia, Mexico, Honduras, and the wider Latin America are some of the deadliest places for activists who defend our planet. A few of them Peter knew personally.

But Peter also remembered a quote by the late Dr Martin Luther King Jr, which he had since made into his email byline: Our lives begin to end the day we become silent about things that matter.

That night after the meeting, Peter took a boat to cross the once-clear, now-yellowish Baram River that has served as his life source since he was young and entered the world of activism as the face of resistance to one of the biggest environmental fights in the region.[74]

4

'Activism' is a dirty word in Sarawak. In Baram, the people call the authorities *perintah*, which means 'order' or 'instruction' in Malay. Villagers held on to the adage 'Jangan lawan perintah' (Do not fight against the order) like an edict.

They were not wrong to place their full trust in authorities. Past community leaders like Peter's father, uncle, and brother had served Baram all their lives. The villagers could see that the schemes and initiatives introduced pulled Baram out of a subsistence economy to a more hopeful future. Trusting the government had served them well, and the obedience benefited Peter's family.

Why would they defy?

Baram villagers had no reasons to doubt the benefits of the proposed Baram Dam. The deputy minister of international trade and industry Datuk Jacob Dungau Sagan, who was also the parliamentarian of Baram, said, 'life would be much better [with the dam] than it is now . . .

---

[74] Baram Dam was a project with a RM4 billion development cost.

[it will] eradicate poverty, have better facilities, new towns flourishing, new schools being built, water and electricity supplies, clinics . . .'

The Sarawak government and the appointed consultants were ready to exploit the 'Jangan lawan perintah' mindset to the fullest. Instead of obtaining free, prior, and informed consent, as is required for high-stakes projects under the UN Declaration on the Rights of Indigenous People (UNDRIP), consent was forced or coerced. By the time the government went to ask the people, most of the early work like drawings, planning, and earthworks had already started.

Here was what Peter saw at the beginning of that so-called consultation process in May 2015:

> There was a townhall meeting. They held a large event with slaughtering pigs and celebration of around 1,000 people. Once, they even had a townhall where 90 per cent of the attendees were not from Baram. They just took indigenous people from other places like Limbang and Lawas, some of them were even government officers, teachers, and students. They started collecting signatures and took pictures with the chief minister and government officials. And they treated that as consent.

In the months before, government-appointed consultants told villagers that if they did not comply with the requests to fill up the survey for the social and environmental impact assessment, they would not receive their compensation and might regret their actions later. They also asked the villagers to fill the form with pencils (erasable) and sign them with ink (unerasable), raising questions of potential manipulation.[75]

Peter was rushing against time. As the new chairman, he needed to coalesce villagers' resistance against the dam before the government bulldozes the project without full consent. But he was struggling to even explain what a dam was: A 100-metre-tall concrete barrier that stopped water flow from a reservoir to generate electricity through

---

[75] Some villagers refused to give their identification information and only wrote 'I don't want the Baram Dam!' at the top of each page of the survey form.

a powerhouse; most Baram villagers had not even been exposed to common infrastructure like highways or bridges.

He talked to neighbouring friends and families, but they were unconvinced. When he called for a meeting to explain the Baram Dam, no one attended. More people started turning their backs against Peter, even people closest to him.

'Some were good friends and close relatives, they tried to distance themselves from me,' Peter recalled with a bitterness he still could not numb. 'They labelled me as a public enemy and they called me an opposition in politics, which was a damning remark because of the "Jangan lawan perintah" mentality.'

They told Peter they were no longer comfortable being seen with him. They did not want to be seen going against the government; they were afraid of being arrested.

The saddest day of Peter's life came when his close relative, the late Paul Kallang, who was also a Penghulu, lodged a police report against him and made a press statement with other high-ranking government officials, accusing Peter of spreading lies about the Baram Dam.

'We, the leaders of the Orang Ulu people in Baram, have never appointed Peter Kallang and his friends to speak for us,' Paul Kallang said. 'We have worked so hard to promote the benefits of Baram [D] am project to the local community . . . [Peter's actions have] caused mental anguish among us.'

Peter tried to laugh off the simmering despair: 'It hurt me, it affected my relationships, they were my flesh and blood.'

The only people left were the loose connections among the activist circle—the people he met at the first SAVE Rivers Network meeting. He barely knew them; merely acquaintances brought on a common mission. It would turn out that this was the most important connection he would ever make.

* * *

No matter how many times Peter warned about Baram being totally destroyed underwater, or showed numbers and evidence of how bad Baram Dam would be, he knew that the villagers didn't buy any of it. It wasn't enough for the villagers to know about the impending devastation, they needed to *feel* how bad it could be.

'If it's just me talking, they won't believe how bad it will be,' said Peter. 'They need to see it with their own eyes and listen to the people who were affected by the dam.'

Through SAVE Rivers, Peter went to Bakun Dam and invited two resettlers, Miku Loyang and Ngo Jok, to Baram in March 2014 for two weeks to explain in vivid details what Bakun Dam had done to their lives.

Miku Loyang was a fit, bespectacled man with thinning white hair parted to the right of his head. The lines on his forehead and neck showed his years, his dark and coarse hands showed a lifetime of manual labour under the hot sun. He was a crowd favourite, often telling jokes to the longhouse villagers who would sit on the veranda's long bench or lean against the wall. Ngo Jok, on the other hand, was quieter and more serious-looking; his indigenous tattoos were still visible on his scaley arms. Though small in size, Ngo Jok's voice would reach the ends of the longhouse, and everyone would stop and listen. No amplifiers or microphones needed.

Miku and Ngo went to as many longhouses as they could in the fourteen days, giving speeches without rest, rising before the sun, setting after the moon.

'We have been victimized by the Bakun Dam! They're all fake promises!' exclaimed Miku. 'The house given to us [for resettlement] was different from what was promised and worse than what we had at Bakun. In Bakun, our house was wide, beautiful, and comfortable. Over at Sungai Asap [the resettled area] the wood is low-quality and the workmanship is horrible. When it rains, our entire house would be flooded. The toilet is small and stuck. It makes the whole place smell like pee and faeces.

'The government even said the Sungai Asap house was free. That the electricity and water would be free. But after we moved here, nothing was free. They even asked us to pay RM52,000 for the house. The compensation given was only 30 per cent of what was promised. We didn't move out of Bakun on our own—we were asked to leave!'

Other resettlers like Bengo Telang, a middle-aged man always wearing faded clothes and a bucket hat, and Intan Kutok, a youthful mother of nine, shared similar sentiments. The agricultural lots given were narrow and infertile. They would get fifty or hundred cocoa fruits per tree at Bakun, but in Sungai Asap, they would only get five. Their children stopped going to school because of unaffordable fees; most of the time, they starved at home.

Every night, the resettlers of Sungai Asap cried themselves to sleep. There was regret, sadness, anger, and frustration. A few were desperate to turn back the clock, so they spent hours walking back to Bakun, only to see their village drowned underwater, without the slightest chance of revival.

The story of Bakun Dam was disturbingly similar to Murum Dam that was built a few years after. Infertile and small lands, low-quality homes, and the spectre of a future worse than before.

Perhaps nothing was more damning than what Miku and Ngo told the Baram villagers next. In the still and chilly night, young and old from the longhouse at the Long San village sat closely in a circle. On a long bench at the back sat the old matriarch of the house, Janda Balo. She only had a few teeth left, her face with deep lines from the centre, and earlobes stretched long to her neck as a sign of power and cultural pride.

After watching a documentary of Bakun and Murum, and making a few self-deprecating jokes about their helpless condition, Miku lowered his voice and said: *Our ancestors' graveyards would be submerged underwater too.* In Kayan culture, when an ancestor is buried after death, the families are not allowed to visit the grave. When the dam is built, their graveyards would surely be flooded. To villagers, this meant that their relatives and foreparents would suffer a second death.

Miku reminded them of the high stakes of the Baram village as the last protector of the indigenous tribes:

There are only two places in Malaysia that have native Kenyah and Kayan people. Bakun had flooded the land of Balui and the native village there is gone forever. Baram is the last native place.

If the Baram Dam is built, our native land will be gone . . . it would
demolish our entire land, property, territory, birthplace, ancestors . . .
Why do the Kenyah and Kayan have to suffer this destiny?

For the indigenous people, their land is the single most important
asset. If you have land, you live. If you don't have land, you die. Forced
displacement resulting from dam constructions disproportionately
affects indigenous people, and it is indeed what Peter Kallang said, 'a
cultural genocide'.

Janda Balo stared blankly at Miku and Ngo; her mind wandered in
disbelief. Like many Bakun resettlers, Janda Balo could not sleep that
night. She woke up early and sat alone in the wee hours of the morning.
Light rain began to wash off the morning dew. She thought about her
children and grandchildren's future, and her late husband's grave.

'People in the longhouse don't want this dam!' she shouted in
her native Kayan tongue. 'I like it here. If I want to eat ferns, I eat
ferns. If I want to eat fish, I go to the river and fish. If this place is
flooded, there will be no more plants, ferns, fish . . . nothing to eat.
Nothing will be left for my grandchildren. I want to die here—this is
my native land!'

Her family consoled her, and for the first time, started asking what
they could do to stop the decimation of their village. Peter started seeing
signs of change among his neighbours, who were often treated like
animals in the jungle without rights. They started collecting signatures,
holding seminars and workshops, and protesting in front of the village
heads' homes. The village heads were shocked to see such defiance
among usually compliant and submissive villagers. No longer just a
safe deposit for elections that could be bought with simple promissory
goodies, Baram finally took charge of their destiny.

With Janda Balo and other family heads joining the fight, the
protest evolved into a spirited struggle, with more starting to say: I'd
rather die than to see the dam built on my native land.

'The chief minister should just come here and bomb us [if he
wants to build the dam],' an old villager, Balan Sigau, said. 'Let me die
drowning. I will not move!'

5

Suppose you have just graduated with a marketing degree, and you are now looking for a job. Which way do you think gives you the highest chance of securing a job? Choose one of the following:

1. Applying through a vacancy advertised online
2. Asking your close friends whether they know of an available job
3. Ask for your family's help in finding you a job
4. Messaging an acquaintance asking if a job is available
5. Writing to the company asking for a job

If you had chosen any answer other than '4', you would have gotten it wrong. In his 1974 classic book, *Getting a Job*, the well-known American sociologist Mark Granovetter made a groundbreaking finding that people were three times more likely to get better jobs faster when they tapped into their personal contacts. It is who you know, not what you know that counts—this much was obvious.

But then it got even more interesting. From the personal contacts that successfully helped find a job, he found that a whopping 80 per cent of them were people the job-seekers only met 'occasionally' or 'rarely'—mere acquaintances.[76] This was the case for white-collar and blue-collar workers alike.

Isn't this strange? Why would people we barely know benefit us the most in times of need?

Turns out, it all came down to the *flow of new information*. You, the fresh marketing graduate, could only apply for something you've heard of. It didn't matter if you were the most qualified or fitted for the role. If the vacancy information does not flow to you, you will not get the job.

To Mark Granovetter, a close friend might be predisposed to helping you look for a job, but he/she would likely fail because he/

---

[76] 'Occasionally' (55.6 per cent) here meant more than once a year but less than twice a week, and 'rarely' (27.8 per cent) meant once a year or less.

she will not know much beyond what you already do. In other words, there is simply too much overlap in contact and information you and your close friends and families possess that they will prove less useful. An acquaintance with whom you are weakly tied, on the other hand, is more 'prone to move in different circles than one's self.' The structure of your network, said Mark Granovetter, matters more than your motivation to apply for a job.

Your job hunt process would actually look like this:

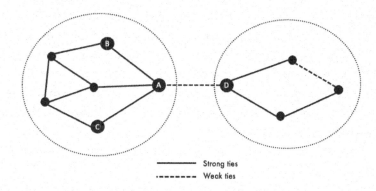

-------- Strong ties
- - - - - - - - Weak ties

For this purpose, you are 'A' in this diagram, and all connections on the left side of the diagram are strong ties—people with whom you are close. This includes 'B', who could be your father, and 'C', who could be your close friend. You'd notice that even though there are more connections on the left side—six people and eight chains of connection—they are all still part of the same social circle. This means that the information passed between A and B is similar to information passed between A and C. To learn about new information, A needs to tap into D's circle. Even though D has far fewer connections than A, the information passed to A is far more valuable because they are *new*. And when new information is known, a job opportunity arises. That's how you get a job.

But if D is merely your acquaintance, wouldn't they be less open to help? Mark Granovetter found that there are a few reasons why acquaintances have an incentive to lend a hand. First, it's part of the interpersonal transaction of being nice to someone and doing them a favour. It makes the helper feel good. Second, if D succeeds in recruiting someone competent, D's reputation in the company would be enhanced—he would be known as the guy who 'knows how to get things done'. Third, a general sense of self-efficacy would also arise as D would be known as the 'kind of guy who likes to put people to places'.

Mark Granovetter's 'weak ties' concept applies similarly to activism. In another 1973 paper called 'The Strength of Weak Ties', he studied a working-class Italian neighbourhood in Boston during the 1960s when they were opposing an 'urban renewal' project. Even though the sentiment against the project was overwhelmingly negative, they still failed to mobilize a resistance action. Why? Because the Italians were *too* close-knit. Your friend's friends are your friends too. At every social gathering, you meet the same people. You didn't have new information to mobilize a group. Compare this to Charlestown, a working-class community that was far less close-knit than the Italians in Boston. Even though their sentiment was more mixed, they succeeded in resisting the urban renewal project because of a richer, more diverse organizational life.

When ties are strong, organizational strength is weak. You need weak ties to create strong organizations.

Shunned by family and close friends who deemed him a public enemy, Peter Kallang found himself in a network of mere acquaintances—weak ties which turned to be his biggest strength.

* * *

SAVE Rivers Network was a coalition of weak ties. It consisted of eight separate NGOs that have worked on different environmental and indigenous projects. Among others, they consisted of—

HARRISON NGAU
Award-winning environmentalist who started the Sarawak branch of Sahabat Alam Malaysia, a Malaysian environmental NGO established since 1977

TONG JALONG
President of Jaringan Orang Asal Semalaysia, an NGO fighting for indigenous rights

MAK BUJANG
Geologist and activist against the land-grabbing in Borneo

But there was one weak tie that proved particularly useful for an international pressure campaign: Bruno Manser Fund, an NGO named after a tireless environmentalist who disappeared in the Borneo jungles.[77]

'In the second half of 2012, Bruno Manser Fund connected me to a group in Australia who were against the logging in the state of Tasmania,' said Peter. 'There was a Sarawak logging company in Tasmania called Ta Ann Holdings and its chairman was Hamed Sepawi. Hamed also happened to be the chairman of Sarawak Energy Berhad (SEB) (the contractor for Baram Dam) and also the cousin of the former Sarawak chief minister Taib Mahmud.

'SEB at that time appointed Hydro Tasmania, a state-owned company, as a consultant for the Baram Dam. So that connection was made. We went there to mount an international pressure for Hydro Tasmania to get out of Sarawak.'

Through that multi-layered network of weak ties, Peter and a village headman, James Nyurang, launched a twelve-day campaign in Australia (Melbourne, Canberra, Hobart) in December 2012 to urge Hydro Tasmania to pull out of Sarawak.

Peter sought help from Australia's Greens' leader Christine Milne and MP Bob Brown to highlight Hydro Tasmania's involvement in a dam that had a massive environmental and human rights impact.

In Hydro Tasmania's annual report, it highlighted what an engineer who worked on Murum and Baram Dams said about his work in Australia:

> Safety and environmental compliance are not given as much importance here (Sarawak). But before we become too judgmental, we need to think back to how Australia did these things a few decades ago and that is the state of practices in Malaysia today.

---

[77] Bruno Manser Fund was set up by the late Bruno Manser, a Swiss environmentalist who spent six years living with the Penan tribe, where he adopted their way of life by dressing in a loincloth, hunting with blowguns and eating primates; he helped organize efforts against timber companies and shed light on the Penan's plight. He was last seen carrying a thirty-kilogram backpack up a hill and never since.

Australia has stopped building hydropower dams in its country because of its devastating damage. 'If they stopped building dams in Australia a long time ago, why do they continue building dams in Sarawak now?' Peter said.

'One of Hydro Tasmania's downstream subsidiaries, Entura, proclaimed that their energy business was the greenest in Australia,' Peter continued. 'I went to the Australian press and told them, "But they are not too green in Sarawak!"'

When Peter met the CEO of Hydro Tasmania, he didn't mince his words. He asked them to leave Sarawak immediately. By the end of the Australian tour, the CEO of Hydro Tasmania, Roy Adair, released a press statement announcing that they would be leaving Sarawak and will not return. Soon, another Australian company, Snowy Mountain, was appointed as a replacement, but they, too, pulled out because of pressure.

In this successful case, Peter's weak ties diagram looked like this,

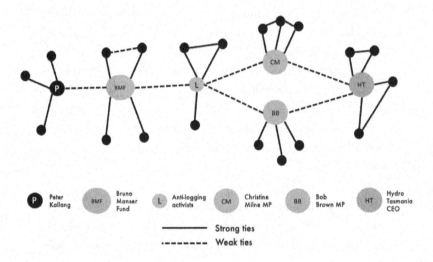

To compel the Australian companies to pull out from Sarawak, Peter used the multi-layered weak ties network to get to the most important people. To succeed in activism, Peter did not seek help from his close-knit family like the Italians in Boston—he acted like the working-class men in Charlestown.

Around the same time, Peter met another weak tie by the name of Cynthia Ong. She was the short-haired, pronunciation-perfect, no-nonsense founder of Land Empowerment Animals People (LEAP) in Sabah. She told Peter the success story of resisting a 300-megawatt coal-fired plant in Sabah, preserving the ecological 'Eden' that still housed the endangered Sumatran Rhino. She also told Peter how academic support was pivotal in persuading authorities to change their minds—to win the battle, you must first win the argument. That was where Cynthia Ong referred Peter to the academics from the University of California, Berkeley, one of the top fifteen universities in the world.

Peter made an inquiry into the university's Renewable and Appropriate Energy Laboratory (RAEL).

'We engaged a professor called Daniel Kammen (who worked with Cynthia in Sabah) and his PhD student, Rebekah Shirley, where they spent two years on the ground at Baram, talking to villagers and travelled to Borneo and West Malaysia to speak to people from SEB and other developers,' said Peter.

The research paper found that the electricity that will be produced right up to Bakun Dam had already far exceeded the energy needs of the people of Sarawak for decades ahead. There was no need for the Baram or Murum Dam.

The energy demand growth projected by SCORE, in percentage terms, was outrageously high at 16 per cent. No country has ever needed that much energy. Not even China during the peak of its industrialization. Turns out, the additional electricity was meant to cater to dirty industries like oil refinery, aluminium and steel manufacturing, livestock, and coal—to transform Sarawak from a biodiversity sanctuary to an industrial complex.[78]

Generally, most large dams do not make financial sense. Seventy-five per cent of dams suffered from cost overruns, typically double their initial estimates.[79]

---

[78] Even then, poor governance and disputes on finances resulted in Rio Tinto mining group scrapping their $2 billion aluminium smelter project in Sarawak.

[79] In an Oxford study by Dr Atif Ansar et al. where they analysed 245 large dams between 1934 and 2007, they found that the cost of most large dams overweighed their benefits.

Alternatives were better. Rebekah Shirley suggested that 'micro-hydro and solar, and even small-scale biomass could supply energy in these communities more efficiently and at a lower cost.' We could avoid large power grids, which are costly and environmentally damaging; instead use minor island grid, where we tie smaller solar and mini-hydro networks, without bringing the grid to the interior. The future of energy sources, Rebekah said, is small, localized, diversified. No longer mega dams.

'With the academic studies, I could show the government and the public how ridiculous the Baram Dam proposal was,' said Peter. 'I could also show what we ought to do instead to generate electricity. It made a constructive contribution—I'm not just a troublemaker.'

Peter grew close to the Berkeley academics. He still wears a blue T-shirt with 'BERKELEY' printed across.

You could already guess how Peter's weak ties diagram looked like for this:

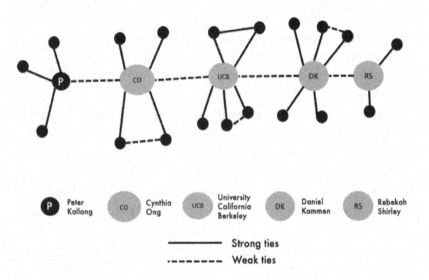

In his innumerable other resistance actions, Peter followed the method of weak ties. Take a look below:

No.	Things Peter Did Using Weak Ties
1.	Protest in front of the International Hydropower Conference
2.	Protest against the Norwegian company, NorPower, in Norway as part of his European tour[80] [81]
3.	Multi-coalition police report against SEB
4.	Fundraising for blockade villagers (blockaders)
5.	Lawsuits against the state government, chief minister, and the forestry department
6.	Malaysian Anti-Corruption Commission report against the SEB's CEO
7.	Press release with the dam victims
8.	Stopping the Asian Development Bank loan to SEB
9.	Official complaints letter to the state government
10.	Coverage on the *National Geographic* website
11.	At least sixty police reports to different authorities

What was initially seen as a weakness turned out to be the greatest advantage in building an effective network against a giant opponent.

---

[80] SEB appointed NorPower, the subsidiary of Norconsult, as the engineering and design consultant. With a full Kenyah regalia, Peter and two activists protested in the headquarters of Norconsult in Oslo, Norway, where he was featured on Norwegian TV. He did the same in Sweden and Switzerland, which prompted the involved companies to review their projects in Sarawak.

[81] Peter was referred by Jonas Ådnøy Holmqvist, Director of The Association for International Water Studies (Fivas), who referred him to the building of the Norconsult CEO, the Norwegian media so that the TV would broadcast his sentiments, and the Norwegian natives against the Alta Dam in Norway. (The Alta Dam was substantially reduced in size and no villages were flooded due to the protests by native Norwegians. It was considered a 'turning point' for Norway's treatment of its natives.)

But it wasn't enough. Everything that Peter did so far only delayed the Baram Dam construction, it didn't stop it.

In 2012, tens of excavators, bulldozers, trucks, and chainsaws moved into Baram. The main developer, SEB, started constructing access roads into the intended dam site. The earth-shaking crawler excavator vibrated the soil, rock, and clay, and the smell of premixes gave the clear air a striking pungent smell. Chainsaws were heard cutting trees in an activity ironically called 'salvage logging', where the workers would cut everything in sight on the premise of supposedly reducing methane from organic material once the dam was built.

On April 2012, the SEB organized a ritual ceremony called Mayau Dalleh to kickstart Phase Two of the project—perform geological studies on the site before moving to construction.[82] Out of the forty-three community leaders invited, only ten turned up. Protestors gathered around the site with protest banners and signs asking for the dam to be stopped.

But they were ignored. The CEO of SEB said that moving the villager's lands and graveyards were very painful, but he would spend time educating the villagers about the project's benefits. Local assemblyman, Dennis Ngau, was more forthright in reminding the Baram villagers to not adopt a narrow mindset, echoing the tone-deaf spirit of replicating the Bakun 'success story'. They gathered in front of the banner for photos and hit a gong that was tied to a tree branch.

Baram villagers felt helpless, disappointed, but mostly, angry. Would more seminars, protests, petitions, signature-collections help at all?

During the SEB geologists' site examination,[83] Baram protestors stopped them in their tracks. They asked the SEB workers to leave that instant as they had no right to encroach on their native customary land. The SEB workers refused and said that they had the legal right to do

---

[82] Locals complained that the ceremony was premised on a butchered understanding of the traditions and culture of Orang Ulu. The Mayau Dalleh ceremony was traditionally used to cleanse the land after a disaster that struck the community. 'What was the disaster here?' asked Philip Jau, one of the local organizers.

[83] SEB geologists were checking the topography, soil conditions, vegetation, and structures of the site.

geological works. Back and forth they went about asserting their rights, until a Baram villager suggested a tiebreaker.

'If you claim that this is your land, prove it!' said one Baram villager. 'I dare you to grab some soil on this land and eat it. The soil here protects its true owner. Whoever dies first from eating the soil is not the true owner!'

They both grabbed a handful of soil in their hands, but no one dared to put it into their mouths. The Baram villager kept taunting the SEB workers and, in the end, the workers decided to leave the site.

After the workers left, a few young and energetic group of Baram villagers took the sampled rocks and smashed them into pieces. They then threw everything into the river. Months of geological work and thousands of ringgits spent evaporated within seconds.[84]

But the villagers knew that fighting this way wasn't sustainable. They needed something more concrete, something that would physically disable the SEB workers from entering their land: A blockade.

* * *

During his trip in Bakun in 2012, Peter Kallang saw something he could never forget. In a large palm oil estate was a red-bricked house erected at the entrance to prevent any vehicles from entering. Decades passed, and still no one dared to bulldoze their way through the house.

The blockade was against the plantation project of one of the most powerful timber tycoons in Malaysia, the mysterious, hunchbacked Chinaman, Ting Pek Khiing.[85] Locals who passed by would stop their

---

[84] Peter Kallang and twenty-two others were later sued for RM3.5 million for destroying the rocks for geological studies.

[85] Ting made a name for himself as the sixth-largest private concession holding group in Sarawak, with license to 310,000 hectares of timber land in Sarawak. In the construction industry, he was known as a prefab wizard who could build at lightning speed. Once, the prime minister Mahathir needed to build a five-star Sheraton Hotel at Langkawi Island for an aerospace exhibition, and Ting used only 100 days to complete the project. His reputation earned him the right to work on the cursed Bakun Dam; its cofferdam (a temporary wall to keep water away from built site) collapsed twenty times. During his lifetime, he faced two bankruptcy claims which he called a 'small matter'.

footsteps and admire the simple, yet impossible resistance: No one trespassed this land, not even Ting Pek Khiing's men.

'See! This blockade is what we should do in Baram,' Peter told his Baram villagers on their visit to Bakun. 'Even Ting Pek Khiing doesn't dare to harvest plantations here!'

The Baram villagers were not convinced. One of them said, 'I think the Baram people wouldn't dare to do something like this . . . Baram people are too mild.'

Anger, however, changes even the mildest people.

'On 23 October 2013, we started the blockades in two main sections,' said Peter. 'One was at Long Lama, to prevent the works department from building roads into the site. The second was at Long Kesseh to stop SEB from conducting their geological research.'

At the earliest stage, a blockade was simply a wooden log lying on the road to prevent vehicles from going through. But with large-enough excavators, the SEB workers could remove even large logs of wood without much resistance. A successful blockade, like the one in Bakun's palm oil estate, required tough people to monitor the site. When they sensed the person entering the site was from SEB or the state government, they would have to be bold enough to ask them to leave the land, with sufficient legal knowledge to back their arguments. In other words, the blockade needed people who were tough (unafraid of authorities), knowledgeable (able to cite legal rights in the face of competing claims or lies), and patient (day and night, for months and years).

'I started raising funds to keep the blockade alive. We use the funds to make up for loss of income of subsistence farmers who spend time at the blockade. We need to build a settlement there,' said Peter.

On the first night, Peter and the villagers built a small settlement with a plastic canvas as a roof and bushes that they cut as cover. They lit up a few candles and burnt a kerosene lamp for light. Raindrops fell repeatedly on their makeshift shed; winds blew against their faces. The canvas started shaking and it finally fell on them. Everyone was drenched from head to toe, struggling to put back a collapsed tent.

As the night went on, Peter and the men took turns for quick shuteyes. They could not all sleep at once—no one should leave the blockade unwatched. Around 4.00 a.m., Peter suddenly shouted loudly. He awoke from a nightmare, with his heart racing and breath rapidly shortening.

'I dreamt that people were coming to attack us, and they were going to kill us!' recalled Peter.

Everyone around him was jolted awake. 'What happened?' they asked.

'Nothing, nothing.' said Peter. 'Don't worry—you know what, better don't sleep lah . . . It's dangerous after all.'

They made some coffee and sang to some indigenous tunes that kept them company until the morning light.

6

In October 2015, the Baram blockade entered its twelfth month. Still no dam in Baram; the village was safe for now. Baram villagers planned a celebration of the blockade's one-year anniversary. They wanted to invite people who helped them on this journey: Their Bakun and Murum friends, SAVE Rivers' committees, lawyers, activists, and other NGOs. For them, this felt like something they'd succeeded together.

Baram villagers knew that one year hadn't gone by peaceably. They had to fight for it. Different authorities had tried to dismantle the blockade. They had brought heavy machinery and armed personnel to do so. But every time they did this, the defiant villagers had put back a new one. Sometimes, they'd done this in front of the authorities.

'They removed it, we put back in. They removed it, we put back in,' said Peter. 'We did this for at least twelve times. The authorities were so frustrated that they installed a police station to monitor us. Once they even tried to remove our blockade and put up their own. But our men removed their blockade and installed ours again. Imagine that—twelve times!'

The blockade now looked more like a settlement. No more amateurish plastic tents and bushes to tie things together. Instead, it was a military-style barrack for blockaders to rest and sleep. In the barrack were a toilet and a table tennis table. Outside, there was a clothesline to hang their coloured clothes, mostly printed with protest slogans; behind, there were chickens and plants, with garden tools lying on the side. In front of the blockade was a slogan written on a brown jute sack that read,

OUR FOREFATHERS FOUGHT AND DIED FOR THIS LAND.
STOP THE BLOODY DAM! BARAM IS OURS FOREVER!

'We even had a "telephone booth", a self-identified perfect location for the mobile phone reception,' Peter chuckled. 'The line actually belonged to the logging company nearby. They didn't even know we were using their lines while protesting them!'

Three days before the first-year anniversary of the blockade, 21 October 2015, Peter received a phone call while on a protest trip in Kuala Lumpur. It was one of the Baram villagers.

'The police are here, and they're asking us to follow them to a police station in Miri,' the villager told Peter, with a shaking and mumbling voice.

'Do not follow them! It's a trick!' Peter reminded them. By then, Peter knew that this was a way of luring the villagers away from the site so that the authorities could remove their blockade once and for all. By putting the blockaders in a town that was at least five hours away from the blockade site, the authorities would have ample time to enter and start construction.

'If they want to arrest us, they do it at the site. And they have to tell us what we are arrested for!' said Peter to the villagers on the phone.

Peter knew that he could not make it back in time. A flight from KL to Miri takes two hours and twenty minutes. A four-wheel drive from Miri to Baram takes another five hours. A lot can happen in that period. He knew he had to count on the villagers to resist on their own.

The authorities came in droves. Fifty police personnel from the General Operation Force (GOF), ten Forestry Department officers, and 'a handful' of loggers from the logging company MM Golden Sdn Bhd dismantled the blockade at Long Kesseh.

The villagers remembered those loggers who were allegedly spotted felling and transporting one of the tallest tropical trees, the Tapang

'Ironwood' trees, illegally.[86] The use of threats and intimidations, even supplanting brawny bullies, was something the villagers had seen before.

The ten Baram blockaders quickly informed the rest of the villagers to gather in a show of strength.

'When we first started, the villagers were not that brave. But when they started to defy authorities more and more, with know-how and experience, they started to become fearless,' said Peter.[87]

When authorities allegedly tried to bribe the locals with RM3,000, the Baram villagers didn't take a single cent. Instead, they lodged a police report against the briber. When the logging company tried to persuade the locals of the benefits of Baram Dam, the villagers could already see through the deceit.[88]

One of the blockaders was a man named Johannes Luhat. He confronted the authorities and asked, 'Who authorized you to dismantle the blockade? This area is still under dispute, and there is no court order to lift the blockade.'

They were breaking the law, said a Kenyah-speaking Forestry Department officer named Asan Udau. By putting up the blockade, the company could no longer enter the site to extract timber but they had a permit to do so.

Johannes replied that the land the company was logging on was native customary land belonging to the villages of Na'ah and Long Kesseh. In fact, logging here was illegal as they hadn't conducted an environmental impact assessment (EIA) study.

---

[86] Used as a valuable nesting ground for honeybees, the Ironwood is protected under the Second Schedule of the Sarawak Wildlife Protection Ordinance 1988.

[87] Being mild-mannered and unconfrontational, Baram villagers knew that they had to compensate with their knowledge. Villagers who manned the blockade learned about basic knowledge of human rights, including the UNDRIP (international consent requirement), as well as the rights of native customary land and how to prove it. They also underwent paralegal training so that they would be able to fight with authorities on facts. Baram blockaders also established an efficient alert system so that hundreds of villagers would storm the site in case of an emergency. They also learned to record audio or video of any instances of confrontation as a sign of proof.

[88] In the Orang Ulu tradition, if you take someone's money, you have to return a favour. The villagers were afraid that taking the money would mean that they agreed to the Baram Dam being built. They made it clear that they didn't.

Then he showed the rest of the villagers behind him. None of us here agree to the logging on our lands, he said.

'We've already lodged a police report with the police and the Malaysian Anti-Corruption Commission (MACC) against the illegal logging by the company,' the natives said.

Both parties wouldn't budge. Then the natives sought a compromise.

Give us a three-day grace period, the villagers offered. This was the same strategy they used in July that year when the villagers asked for a fourteen-day grace period. It helped ease the tension and ensured the authorities leave. Instead of relenting in the next three days, the villagers began to 'dig in' and 'fortify' their positions, making their blockade more elaborate and entrenched to the ground. It made every dismantling attempt harder than the last.

True enough, when the authorities came back three days later, on the 365th day of the blockade, the blockade was still intact. This time, there were already at least 120 villagers at each blockade, and the settlements around the area showed that the villagers were not moving an inch. *The chief minister should just come here and bomb us. Let me die drowning. I'm not moving!*

The blockade leader rose from his seat, kept his cool, and spoke to the Forestry Department officers in a nice way—typical of a mild-mannered Orang Ulu. He told the authorities that they were not willing to move. Instead, they asked the officers to relay the discussions to their boss. Sensing too strong a resistance, the authorities didn't attempt to dismantle the blockade this time.

Before the authorities turned away and left, the protestors even requested for them to take away the contractor's bulldozer. 'We don't need that here.' At 1.00 p.m. that afternoon, the bulldozer was removed and never seen again.

7

On the day the late Adenan Satem was appointed the fifth chief minister of Sarawak, he knew he was living on borrowed time. Barely a year before, he was lying in a hospital in Singapore with tubes running through his weakening heart. 'I called all my relatives, my children, my grandchildren . . . I was ready to go,' Adenan recalled of a time in 2013.

'[B]ut then God is great. I recovered, I was back to normal.' God gave him a new 'lease of life', to do what needs to be done for the disenfranchised state of Sarawak.[89] He was willing to make bold decisions, oftentimes in opposition to the federal powers (called for more oil royalty, defended non-Muslims' rights to use Arabic term for God in Islam, and the recognized Chinese schools' United Education Certificate), and sometimes in direct contradiction to his predecessor, Taib Mahmud, who was also his former law classmate and brother-in-law. Long plagued by massive corruption in timber, the imposing figure of Adenan Satem told a roomful of timber tycoons that he would 'put fear of God into the people who are dishonest'. Those who pretend they don't know are either 'stupid, cowards, or corrupt'.

While Taib was extravagant and embroiled in massive corruption scandals, Adenan was unglamorous and down-to-earth. While Taib was cold and mysterious, Adenan was warm and grandfatherly, often seen in the wet market doing groceries with his wife. While Taib was small, Adenan was big. In Sarawak, a chief minister's role was seen as comparable to a prime minister, an office all Sarawakians deemed most prestigious. Adenan fitted in every way.

In June 2015, Adenan Satem wrote back to Peter Kallang. He was the first government official to respond to mountainous meeting requests by Peter Kallang and SAVE Rivers. The chief minister asked to see Peter as soon as possible.

'See me next Monday,' said Adenan Satem.

Peter didn't know what to expect. This was his best, and perhaps only, shot to persuade the government to abandon the Baram Dam once and for all. He needed to condense three years' worth of work into

---

[89] The Malaysia Agreement 1963 was the cornerstone document that laid down the rights and autonomy of the Sabah and Sarawak, as part of the condition during the formation of Malaysia. This, however, had been deemed repeatedly violated. Among others, oil royalties to Sarawak had been a contentious issue. The federal government only gives 5 per cent to the Borneo state although it produces around 26 per cent of the country's oil.

a one-hour meeting and put the best case forward. He brought three weak-ties acquaintances, with specific purposes:

1. Daniel Kammen from University of California, Berkeley: To bring in expert opinion on the massive oversupply of electricity by the proposed Baram Dam based on a two-year academic study on the ground.
2. Gabriel Wynn from the Green Empowerment: To provide opinions on feasibility and cost in implementing alternative sources of electricity.
3. See Chee How, Batu Lintang assemblyman: For political persuasion and networking.

At the back of his mind, Peter was worried about facing the person he had publicly denounced. He had sued the government multiple times, besides releasing countless press statements criticizing the project and lodging police and corruption reports. The blockade itself was an aggressive physical protest. Would the chief minister take any of this kindly?

On Friday, 26 July 2015, Peter received a call from Adenan Satem's private secretary. 'Could you come over tomorrow instead? Chief minister has to fly to Kuala Lumpur on Monday. He can't see you then,' he said.

The next day, Peter, Daniel, Gabriel, and See drove to the residence of the chief minister of Sarawak. The clock had not turned ten, the morning was already warm.

'We knew that there would be many protocols, so we dressed our best, complete with suit and ties,' Peter recalled.

When they came out of their vehicle, the private secretary rushed to greet them. 'Take off your jacket and ties, please. Hurry!' he said.

The private secretary brought them into the house and when he opened the door of the sitting room, there he was—the chief minister of Sarawak. Adenan Satem was dressed in a simple white round-collared T-shirt, sitting on a sofa waiting for them to arrive. No drinks or food around him—it was the fasting month of Ramadan.

'Please take a seat,' he said. After introductions and pleasantries, he said, 'Talk to me.'

In the next hour, Peter told Adenan Satem of the Baram villagers' concerns that the chief minister hadn't heard before. At the elite level, the 'people's voices' were typically only the pro-government community leaders' voices. Sometimes, the community leaders were not even from Baram to represent the villagers' plight properly. There was a strong tendency of establishment bias, especially in a feudalistic country like Malaysia.

'The newspapers misquoted me [at the gathering in Miri],' Adenan assured. 'I didn't give my go-ahead to the Baram Dam construction. I will listen to you like how I listen to the proponents of the dam.'

Danial Kammen distributed physical copies of his presentation slides to explain the severe oversupply of energy, even on the worst projection of Sarawak's energy demands. Sarawak simply didn't need that much energy. The controversial Bakun Dam was only half-used now—Baram Dam and many other megadams would face the same outcome of severe under-usage. Then, he showed his recommendations for cleaner, cheaper energy: Biomass, solar, micro-hydro, wind.

The chief minister seemed intrigued. He started asking about the opportunities, benefits, and costs of clean energy. Gabriel then talked about his experience in building alternative energy supplies in Malaysia, Southeast Asia, and Africa. He talked about the feasibility of building an island system that integrated different alternative energy sources into a centralized channel to be used by all. The idea was to pilot in some villages and scale them later once they were proven to work.

'I don't care what [method is used] but let there be light,' Adenan Satem said, referring to the rural areas he cared about deeply. Adenan requested Daniel and Gabriel to show him a proposal that he could then distribute to dam proponents for a balanced view.

Before the end of the meeting, Peter handed a petition that contained the 10,000 signatures of the Baram villagers who were opposed to the dam. This represented half of Baram's population.

'Chief minister, please also visit Baram if you can. Don't just listen to the community leaders. They're not representing all, they are only representing themselves,' said Peter.

The chief minister understood what Peter meant. 'After Hari Raya Aidilfitri.' Adenan Satem gave them his word.

'I will listen to you. But please don't be so rough on me,' he pleaded, referring to the court cases and police reports launched by SAVE Rivers against the state government. The room burst into laughter.

Peter smiled, and they left his residence, promising a proposal as a follow-up.

A week later, Adenan Satem arrived on a helicopter at the small village of Long Lama in Baram, the same place Peter attended his boarding school. He was well-received by the cheering crowd and they became even more excited when Adenan Satem said he was willing to put the dam construction on hold while he listened to views from both sides. But then he asked the Baram supporters, specifically calling out its leader, Peter Kallang, for a favour: Remove the blockade as a sign of good faith.

The crowd's mood changed. Claps stopped, replaced by boos. Sitting among the crowd, Peter didn't say a word—he only smiled.

Four months after Peter's visit to Adenan's residence, the state government officially announced that the Baram Dam will be stopped indefinitely.[90] The blockade remained unmoved for another two years.

Epilogue

Documentarian Leerang Bato was interviewing Bakun Dam resettlers when he stumbled upon four drawings by a child. They were drawn with colour pencils with basic shapes, each drawn two years apart. We see the stories of Bakun before and after the Bakun Dam (built in 2011) through the eyes of an innocent child.

---

[90] The gazette that earmarked the customary land for Baram Dam was officially revoked on 18 February 2016.

2009: A half-dressed man with a red feather on his hat was rowing his boat on the blue river with gentle waves. Behind him was his abode—a wooden longhouse, surrounded by leafy trees and mighty mountains. The sea reflected the colour of the sky, the cloud was pillowy white above his head.

2011: The water waves turned rogue, blue had given way to purple, navy, and black, reflecting its inner monstrosity. Trees were uprooted, the mountains were barely visible; the shocked rowing villager suddenly had tears falling from his eyes.

2013: The water level had risen to cover the entire village. All the tree leaves were gone, leaving only torn branches scattered on the ground. The blue water was mixed over with brown dirt. Two fishes swam around the broken pieces of a longhouse that once belonged to the rowing man.

2015: Two fishes were now tilted upside down at the surface of the river; dead. The remaining trees and longhouse had disappeared entirely, turning into dirt and dust. Nothing was left in the drawing, except shades of brown and black, speaking of the eternal, irreversible tragedy of a ruthless Bakun Dam.

The Bakun children who were born in the 2000s were the unluckiest. They lived to see their childhood village, a place of happy memories and a communal livelihood, washed away by the waves in a matter of years. Would they grow up with a generational trauma that they would pass on to their children, or would they develop a vengeful sense of resentment for the government that did this to them?

The exact same thing could have happened to the children of Baram if Baram Dam had been built. But it didn't. Baram children's homes were safe because a seventy-year-year-old indigenous Kenyah retiree named Peter Kallang decided to keep trying even without money, influence, and the support of his family.

When you meet Peter Kallang in person, it is hard to imagine the risks and burdens on his shoulders. At the Seacology Prize ceremony at Berkeley, California, a prestigious award that recognizes outstanding efforts of preserving the island environments and culture, the audience would only remember seeing Peter Kallang dancing on stage in exuberance receiving his prize, before bringing laughter and warmth in his speech.

But this was the same man who paid a personal price. In a land where going against the word of government is treated as a sin, championing environmental causes was dangerous business.

'I'm scared. Because I know the government doesn't like people who go against them. I know people like Bruno Manser who fought against logging disappeared in the jungle. I've seen what they have done to people in the past. Like my friend [People's Justice Party's political secretary] Bill Kayong, who was shot on his way to work [because of resisting unjust causes],' said Peter.

As bitter as it is, you know this is a man who could not be stopped. He loved Baram and the environment too much to weigh its cost and benefit before acting. Today, Peter still takes five-hour four-wheel car drives from Miri (where he stays) to Ulu Baram for urgent meetings or actions. Baram had tasted a small victory with the government moratorium on Baram Dam, but to Peter, that was hardly the final line.

He continues to work on micro-hydro projects to electrify the community and make them believe that their lives are not worse off without the Baram Dam. He also puts in time and effort in launching the coveted Baram Peace Park.

The 2,835 square kilometres peace park is the last forest that has been relatively untouched since ancient times. To ensure its success, Peter had to continue campaigning against logging in Baram, that was threatening the core area of a relatively undisturbed forest. 'We need them to "stop the chop!"' he would say.

The water in Baram is slowly turning blue.

'It's everyone's job to imagine the world we want to live in,' Peter said. 'When we started the fight against Baram Dam, everyone said we would lose, but we did not give up. Hope, imagination, and determination can change the world.'

Interviewing Peter Kallang for this book has given me first-hand insight to how he works. Often, when I sent him a question over WhatsApp, he would reply with long messages, photos, and multiple links as though he had the sources at the back of his hands. If he wanted to show me a particular passage in an article, he would copy the online article on a separate Word document, highlight the relevant passages, convert it to a PDF copy and send me the PDF alongside the original article.

Working with Peter was easy. He was extremely meticulous—like his late brother, Michael.

I asked him about the friends and family who walked away from him when he started SAVE Rivers. He told me that they have since come back to him after the Baram Dam was stopped. But there were some things that will never be the same again.

Then I asked, 'If your brother, uncle, and father was still around today, and they saw what you've done with the Baram Dam, what do you think they would feel?'[91]

He paused. His eyes wandered across the ceiling.

'I think if they understood what I was trying to do—to serve the people in the community they worked hard for—maybe they would appreciate. My method may not be something they approve. But the end result—I hope they would be happy,' he said, with a twinkle in his eye.

Key takeaways

- The most useful networks are the informal, weak ties—the acquaintances, the people you barely know.
- Resistance can be at once firm and gentle.
- We might not need as much power as we think we need.

---

[91] Peter's uncle, Gau Jau, was also remembered fondly as a hero in the Japanese resistance movement during World War II.

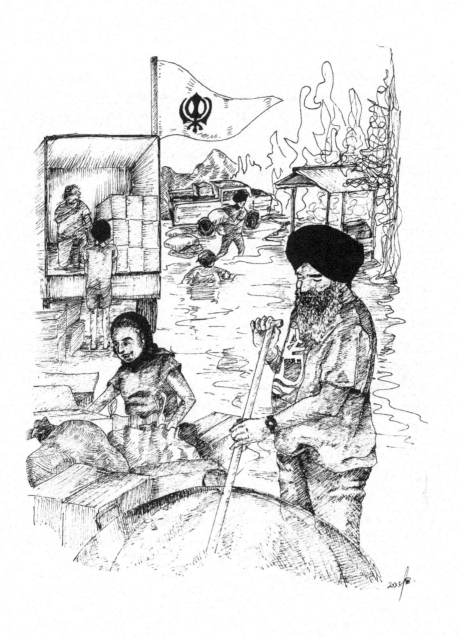

Chapter 7

Gurdwara Sahib Petaling Jaya

How a group of gurdwara-going Sikhs saved thousands
of lives in the largest flood in modern Malaysian history
through an organization without leaders and hierarchy

'If you drown or go missing, we cannot come to save you.'

1

Jagdave Singh still refuses to tell anyone what he saw on the night of 18 December 2021. It had been raining for two continuous days. What initially looked like the usual end-of-year monsoon started to feel strange.

Strong winds rattled neighbourhood windows, jolting up sleeping children. Sporadic cloudbursts formed amidst hail and thunder in an ominous background, before flushing urban cities with heavy waterfalls.

In the morning, the Malaysia Meteorological Department (MetMalaysia) issued a yellow caution of poor weather. By night, the colour had changed to orange, and then red. Water seeped in from the door gaps of low-rise houses, into the kitchen and bedroom. The residents of Taman Sri Muda, a diverse working-class neighbourhood in the populous Selangor state, were not too bothered by the water that rose from their shins to knees.

On paper, the area, with low topography near the long Klang River, was meant to be a water catchment area to prevent water overflows. Development projects in Taman Sri Muda and its vicinity of Kota Kemuning, however, were aggressive from the 2000s. Not only was more water flowing from residents, industries, and commercial units in Taman Sri Muda to its drains and canals, but other developments around were also piggybacking Taman Sri Muda's irrigation systems. Residents estimated that Taman Sri Muda's irrigation systems were taking in water volumes three times the load it was initially designed. Since 2019, residents of Taman Sri Muda already had a premonition as knee-level floods were increasingly common. When the rain started to pour fiercely and unrelentingly in December 2021, it prepared for the perfect condition for a massive flood.

Typhoon Depression 29W that had an intensity resembling a mild typhoon filled up the drains and breached the riverbanks and suddenly the water was at chest level for many residents. Families rushed to put their electronic appliances to higher ground. Eventually they had to pull each other up to the roof as the entire living area would be submerged under water. A few people posted photos of muddy waters flooding their houses; debris and waste floated on the surface, families stood on stools and chairs staring out the windows.

Jagdave, a forty-something events manager, got a call from Pavandeep Singh, a committee member of Gurdwara Sahib Petaling Jaya (GSPJ).

'I heard the flood is bad in Taman Sri Muda. Do you mind going there to check and see what is going on?' Pavandeep asked.

Jagdave took his motorcycle and rode to Taman Sri Muda. On the way there, he tried calling the firefighters and police for help, but no one picked up. As he was calling others for help, he feared the worst. Victims would be starving without food, cut off from telephone lines, shivering under the rainy night. He must save them if he could.

The only problem was he wasn't sure if he could go in and come out alive.

'We needed to find a boat. Any kind—a kayak, an inflatable rubber dinghy of some kind,' he said. For the next two hours, he called friends and boat sellers around the state. Eventually, he found one.

He rushed to the flood scene alone, slightly before midnight. He circled the area a few times to find a higher ground as an entryway to the residents' houses. Eventually, he found a petrol station on a highway that had a lower flood level that would come to serve as his temporary base. When he was sure of the coordinates, Jagdave called two other gurdwara friends to come along with their truck of dried goods supplies.

Taman Sri Muda was without a sound. The entire neighbourhood was pitch dark. Some of the houses were emptied. The murky water that reached their chests was still.

'Everything was destroyed,' Jagdave said. 'It was the first time in my life that I'd seen something this horrible.'

Before going in, he took off his slippers to avoid dragging. A barefooted Jagdave tied his arms with two other friends' and walked in unison, pushing an engineless boat, one small step at a time. They were swerved around by the fierce water, failing to walk straight.

'We took an hour to walk a short 100 metres—we couldn't walk at a normal pace,' he said. 'The water is so dirty you cannot see anything.

We don't know where the holes are, or where the drain is. At times we would accidentally step on a nail or a car. We really prayed not to walk into a deep drainage—because if you fall, you don't know where that would lead you.'

At a distance, echoes of shouting and crying reverberated and faded in a flickering wail in that eerie night.

'In those few hours, you could really see things you didn't want to see.'

2

Along the busy road of Jalan Utara in the satellite city of Petaling Jaya is a narrow alleyway most drivers would miss. The narrow road is covered with overgrown trees and fallen leaves. A small entrance between two painted concrete walls is a modest Sikh temple, called Gurdwara Sahib Petaling Jaya (GSPJ). It sits on half an acre of land, with five blocks of three-storey buildings in gradients of beige and yellow. Every building is accessible through four doors on every side: Peace, Livelihood, Learning, Grace.

More than a place of worship, it is a place for food. Half of the floor at the annex is taken up by a community kitchen called Langar, which serves vegetarian food to thousands on a daily basis. Everyone is welcomed to sit at one of the long stainless-steel tables and help themselves with hot food, traditional sweets (*adhirasam*), savoury *poori*, and the classic Punjabi *cha* that patrons drink like water.[92]

Men wearing different-coloured cotton turbans wrapped around a hair bun would greet you as they pass. Women dressed in salwar kameez with their heads covered with dupatta would smile at you as though you are kin.

In the darkest nights, the small domes at the edge of the buildings would give out a flavescent glimmer. Soft light shines on a triangular, orange flag called Nishan Sahib, a sacred flag remembering the

---

[92] These are the ingredients to make a good cup of Punjabi cha: 1 tsp fennel seeds, 4 cardamom pods, 1¼ cups of water, 1 tbsp loose leaf black tea, 1 tbsp jaggery, ½ cup of homogenized milk.

sacrifices of Sikh warriors in the name of human rights. The flag is kept pristine, only ever washed with water and milk. Every Vaisakhi, it must be changed anew. A pilgrim, outcast, or passer-by who felt shunned, rejected, or shamed must look at the flag and know that 'no matter where you come from and who you are, you are always welcomed here at the gurdwara'.

This was the core lesson in GSPJ's annual youth camp, called Gurmat Parchar Sammelan, which was attended by Sikhs from around the world.[93] Being small in numbers,[94] every Sikh person had to be involved with organizing at a young age. Children and teenagers were involved with packing, carrying, counting, cleaning, arranging, and the adults were involved in logistics, distribution, cooking, and management. Naturally, this pulled a small community close together. Every Sikh knows of another because they would have met them in the past.

In that four-day Sammelan, Sikh boys and girls would be involved in the entire preparation process for the spiritual team-building, gurmat training, and knowledge development programs.

But the Sammelan in 2021 was cut short. At the end of the third day, one of the youth leaders, Jagmeet Singh, a twenty-nine-year-old banker, received a phone call from a Sikh friend of another temple.

'He told me that, "Something is really, really bad."'

The Gurdwara Sahib Petaling Tin was in trouble. Continuous rainfall had flooded the temple. Besides the facilities being submerged under water, there was also something important at risk: The holy scripture, Guru Granth Sahib. In a gurdwara, there is no statue, idols, or religious paintings. There is only a holy scripture placed on a throne, which is placed under a canopy, and covered in an expensive sacred cloth. This single object is more valuable than everything combined at the gurdwara. They knew that the holy scripture must be saved.

---

[93] Gurmat Parchar Sammelan is one of the largest and longest-running annual Sikh youth camp outside of Punjab. Held first in 1963 by the organization Sikh Naujawan Sabha Malaysia (SNSM), it attracted 1,000 participants and 200 stay-in volunteers, and a huge number of visitors.

[94] There are approximately 80,000 Sikhs in a population of 32 million.

When the GSPJ team went to the gurdwara to save the holy scripture, they saw that the flood was worse than what they heard. The predicted continuous rainfall would mean that more people may be stranded. GSPJ started receiving more calls.

'We started asking what we could do to alleviate the troubles of flood victims,' Jagmeet recalled. 'So we thought, "Food!" Let's give out food. GSPJ already had a langar kitchen ready for mass cooking. I asked Pavandeep (a charismatic forty-something with a greying beard) how much we could prepare. He told me, "However much you want, we can cook." So, I took it as a challenge. The only thing left to do was to bring in the demand.'

* * *

Flood relief is fundamentally about economics. Even if you are ready to help, you will not succeed if you do not know where and what to help. Ideally, you help the neediest first with an order of assistance of rescue, food, and ration. To do that, Jagmeet figured that they needed a helpline for victims to self-locate. Based on the collected information, GSPJ would decide what needs to be done first.

'We were enthusiastic about helping,' Jagmeet said. 'The only problem was we were inexperienced. We never ran a helpline before. But we knew enough that this was a fundamental feature in a relief effort, and that it was a difficult operation.'

Jagmeet and his team couldn't do it themselves, but they knew someone who could. They knew three women, led by Ajib Kaur, who had been part of the Global Sikh's Aceh tsunami relief efforts in 2014. It was the largest relief effort by any Sikh organization, and the three women ran the helpline. Within half an hour, GSPJ approved the suggestion, and they were ready to go.

The three women agreed to form a secretariat at an office using their telephones. Within two hours of putting up the posters and online messages, calls started coming in.

'This was how it worked: We would get a call for 250 packs of food, and then we would check with the ground team to cook. Then volunteers would send the food with their trucks to the location, and the site person (usually a local) would coordinate the distribution from there. We always make sure we work with the local coordinator because they are more familiar with the ground—and of course, we made sure there was enough food.'

Numbers shot up at a blinding pace. Before the afternoon, the secretariat was receiving continuous calls, at a rate of one call per second. Calls became increasingly desperate. Days without food, a fainted grandmother, a lost family, drowned animals, lost cars, appliances, documents, house . . . all gone.

* * *

The worst part about being stranded in the flood is you that have to go through the dreadful five hours from 12.00 a.m. to 5.00 a.m. The only safe place is at the top of the roof. Rescue boats dwindle during these hours; around you there is neither light nor sound. Hours of starvation leave you too weak to continue shouting for help. You stare at the rising water level in your soaked clothes. Then the night breeze blows at you and gives you an intense shiver.

'It was a harrowing time . . . All I could think of was death,' said one victim.

Megala Murthi, a thirty-something resident of Taman Sri Muda, knew that she and her husband needed to escape from their house when the water rose to their chests. When they walked out of their house, they saw an immobile grandmother and two old ladies who could not run out as they could. So, they swam to bring the elderly folks to a nearby shop lot's first floor with twenty-five others. It was relatively safe, like an island amidst a deadly sea, but they were stranded without food and drinks.

For the next three days, Megala Murthi would shout out 'Help' and 'Food' until her voice cracked. A police boat would come, and she would yell for them to evacuate the victims, but they only took police officers out of the site. She would yell again and again in the direction of the police and beg someone to help.

'Nobody came. In the end, we were rescued by private boats and civilian volunteers, and a few NGOs,' Megala Murthi said. 'No government authorities came to help at all. The army only came after everything was over.'

Another resident, Thinesh, faced a similar ordeal. He swam out of the flood area after two continuous days without food and drink, only to find authorities standing without boats or transport to help other victims, including his seventy-eight-year-old grandmother left stranded at his flooded house.

Victims who swam up ran to the nearby mini-markets like 7-Eleven, KK Mart, and Mydin and looted these shops for food. Having lost everything to the flood, the victims took what they could to reduce their losses, even though the efforts were futile in the big picture.

Throughout the most critical first three days of the flood, victims admonished the then government's slow response. When the MetMalaysia's warning indicator turned red, some ministers were either giving stump speeches about power in their party's general assembly[95] or were still on a year-end vacation abroad.

The government's response was described as a 'disaster of epic proportions'. They were either severely delayed or ruefully inadequate. The former youth and sports minister Faizal Azumu, and the former women, family, and children minister Rina Harun held separate volunteer 'launch' ceremonies to commemorate government assistance even though that caused delays in a crisis where time was of the essence.

Ministers who arrived at the scene were booed and berated by locals for coming when the water had subsided, and they were criticized for showboating. Rina Harun wore high heels to the flood scene, and was seen using a water jet to spray off a clean floor for photo ops.[96] The then finance minister was seen waving from a truck and boat with an entourage of photographers. The former prime minister had a team edit a video with sombre background music of him visiting a flood-stricken area, holding biscuit containers, nodding his head, strolling gently in

---

[95] The general assembly of the former prime minister's party, Bersatu, ended with grand fireworks.
[96] 'Washing imaginary mud on the floors?' a Twitter user asked.

the water, and giving a Korean heart-shaped sign to the victims at a building. At the time of writing, the video on Twitter received only 176 retweets (typically a sign of support) compared to 2,693 quote-retweets (mostly in criticism of his obvious showboating).

The December 2021 flood was the worst tropical cyclone–related disaster in Malaysia since 1996. Around 136,030 people were affected, fifty-five died, and two were missing. The estimated loss was around RM20 billion (5.9 per cent of GDP), excluding the historic, cultural, and sentimental value of items lost, as well as water-borne diseases and long-term mental health effects.

GSPJ had to stand in for a government that wasn't there.

3

How do you do a job the government could not do well? Flood relief efforts may sound simple in theory, but, in reality, they are logistical and operational nightmares. Told to me by five GSPJ members, this was how they looked at the problem, shown in Figure 1—the Flood Relief Triple Threat.

The efforts were divided into three parts: Input, Operations, and Output. For the first, the focus was on getting the right flood information via the helpline, and sufficient human-power via a volunteer network. For the second, it came down to how fast food and ration were organized and pushed to the vehicles for transportation. But GSPJ told me that it was important, as a matter of principle, to ensure that the food and ration were also high-quality and not just the bare minimum.[97] Additional quality inspection was conducted. Lastly, Output refers to the on-site work that was handled by the lionhearts. Volunteers must travel to the flood scene where no authorities had, figure out the terrain, and then risk their lives to save others.

---

[97] Amarraj Singh, a GSPJ volunteer, told me that a few flood victims told him that they preferred GSPJ's rations because they were 'barang premium' (premium goods), which refers to items above the bare minimum. It is also a GSPJ policy to exchange items upon the flood victims requests.

INPUT	OPERATIONS	OUTPUT
Helpline • Channel to gather information • Filter accurate and genuine information • Capacity to handle high volume of information continuously without loss of insight	**Food** • Capacity and expertise for mass cooking • Standardised process for ingredients preparation and packing and organizing of food packets • Quality control for food	**Rescue** • Capacity (equipment and manpower) and expertise of rescue • Quality of rescue operations (time taken, people saved, area covered)
Volunteer • Recruitment and training of volunteers • Distribution of volunteer	**Ration** • Call and collection of ration by order of most-needed • Organisation, loading and offloading of ration	**Distribution of food and ration** • Identification and recce of site • Large-scale convoy coordination to affected areas • Distribution and stock-check

Figure 1: Flood Relief Triple Threat

At this point, flood relief efforts looked slightly more complicated than theory. But simply laying out the three areas involved was merely the first step. To capture reality in its full complexity, we need to consider a crucial element in disaster-related operations: Risks.

The risks for the December 2021 flood looked something like Figure 2: Flood Relief Risk Matrix.

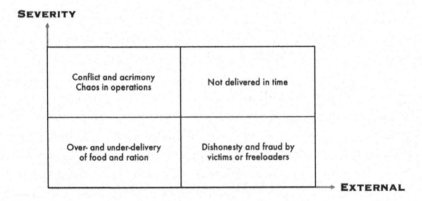

Figure 2: Flood Relief Risk Matrix

The most severe external risk in a flood-relief effort is when the food, ration, and rescue are not delivered in time to save victims from their plight. Most things must move fast—time is of the essence. That puts another severe internal risk to play: Conflict and acrimony among GSPJ members and volunteers, as well as an utter chaos in operations. For instance, there may be disagreements on what needs to go where first, and differences in opinions on what is most important may drive a wedge among unpaid helpers. If you only have fifty bags of rice, do you send it to a large village of eighty families or a small village with only thirty families? To send to the large village of eighty, do you wait for another thirty bags of rice to arrive tomorrow before giving all eighty bags out or do you send out the fifty bags to the large village first?

Most of the time, there is no clear answer. It depends on whose opinion you follow. Sending fifty bags (thirty short) to a village of eighty families will give the receivers some certainty that they wouldn't need to starve in the coming days, but it also risks creating communal tension from frustration and jealousy.[98] Victims' frustrations would spill over to the volunteers and without proper management, this sentiment could drive out Good Samaritans which would, in turn, make recruitment harder in a vicious cycle.

To mitigate these risks in the largest private flood relief effort, GSPJ's plan was to implement a management strategy that has become too familiar to them: A leaderless management style.

Although Pavandeep Singh and Kuldip Singh were de facto co-leaders of the flood relief effort, there was no hierarchy with position-based authority flowing from top to bottom. While Pavandeep was president to Sikh Naujawan Sabha Malaysia (SNSM), where he served for twenty-five years, he was just an ordinary committee member at

---

[98] This was precisely what happened in one of Amarraj Singh's expedition to Bukit Serok, Rompin. The village was divided by a highway into Hulu (upstream) and Hilir (downstream). The flood struck Hilir first, and because of lower ground, it was totally submerged under water. Hilir villagers ran across the highway and Hulu villagers, who had shin-level flood, offered Hilir villagers shelter. When Amarraj brought bags of rice to Hilir villagers, the Hulu villagers were frustrated. They said, we helped the Hilir villagers, and now only they get help, and we don't? 'Coming from GSPJ we needed to be fair,' said Amarraj. 'We brought extra vehicles the next day, thirteen vehicles with a one-tonne lorry carrying rice, family packs, utilities, medicine, milk powder, and so on. We helped both Hilir and Hulu. We didn't want to create a situation where if a flood happens again and Hilir needs help, Hulu villagers refuse to help because of this. We didn't want to make their relationship worse—we needed to leave things better than they were before.'

GSPJ, and on the first few days of the flood relief work, he was busy mixing curry in the kitchen.

Pavandeep told me that the leaderless management style relies on three fundamental strategies: Extreme delegation, autonomy, and a volunteer-first approach.

'All the members and volunteers needed to do was to update me about the general need so that I could push things forward,' said Pavandeep. 'Most of the time, they solve the problems on their own.'

This is how this strategy is implemented throughout the three areas of Input, Operations, and Output.

1. Input: Volunteer-first

'From the very beginning, we knew that we couldn't do it on our own,' said Pavandeep. Although the weak ties in the Sikh community became a useful launching pad to kickstart relief efforts, they were too small in numbers to cater to the demands of the relief work. Pavandeep and GSPJ knew that if they were to make this work, they would have to count on a huge number of volunteers.

'We needed to make volunteers feel welcome as many do not know what to do. It's their first time at a gurdwara, and their first time volunteering for a disaster like the flood,' said Pavandeep. 'So, we made it a point to take care of our volunteers first. If we take good care of them, we could scale up our flood relief efforts.'

All volunteers who walked into the gurdwara would be greeted warmly like an old friend. Those who do not have a headscarf would be given one, and they would be brought to the airy kitchen before anywhere else.

'The first thing we told them was to have their food first. We had a dedicated corner in the kitchen that was just to cook for volunteers who came through. It's part of our gurus' teaching—to make sure everyone who comes through is fed well.'

Then, volunteers would be guided to one of the several departments, either ingredients preparation, cooking, packing, arranging, lifting, driving, or collecting . . . In all, the GSPJ members made sure the volunteers felt comfortable while volunteering. For Muslim volunteers, GSPJ even opened up one room on the first floor for *solat* prayers.

As a measure of accountability and engagement, GSPJ posted constant updates about the floods and relief efforts so that volunteers feel the actual impact of their help and attract further volunteers.

'Very soon, we became the main hub for volunteers in the December 2021 flood. Thousands and thousands of volunteers walked in during those few days, to the point that there was no walking space in the gurdwara any more,' recalled Pavandeep.

What was even more encouraging was that the hours spent by volunteers and the number of repeat volunteers increased rapidly. Most volunteers stayed longer than they initially planned, with many who stayed from early morning till midnight to help as much as possible.

'There were a few drivers who had taken at least thirty round trips throughout the flood relief week. They used their own cars, and by travelling to flood zones, they damaged their cars, but they still did it because they really wanted to help,' one GSPJ member told me. 'We were so comfortable with each other by the end of it, we became friends. We were just happy that we were helping others next to each other.'

2. Operations: Rapid promotions

When I arrived at GSPJ on a Sunday evening, I saw a group of volunteers lifting boxes of supplies into a giant truck. Amidst the men passing goods in a straight line was a small twenty-something woman with a loud voice. Jagmeet told me her name was Dilpreet Kaur.

'Hey, buddy, a few more boxes in,' 'Can you do it? Do you need help, buddy?' 'Family packs, women's packs, children's packs, fifteen, ten, ten.'

She was pacing back and forth between writing on the whiteboard and taking stock in her rubber slippers, occasionally bantering with the volunteers whom she treated like family.

The way she spoke was like how she worked: A bullet train that couldn't be stopped.

'I'm all about execution. If I see something needs to be done, I go in and do it—pah, pah, pah,' she said.

'You see the trucks and cars coming in? They'll all be put under the orange or blue listing. Orange listings are those who we knew were coming. Before the truck comes in, we look at the number plate, we already know what we will put in. The boxes are ready. Once the engine stops, we form a line. First person starts count, last person keeps count. We try to load a four-wheel drive in a few minutes, so they could move along fast. The blue one is for self-pickup. We direct these cars to form a circle around the Astaka field next door, and we load them the same way. After some time, if I need to pack for 100 families, I already know how many trucks I would need. For every volunteer car coming in we have a quick registration process to keep track. The whole point is to make sure there are no empty trucks going out.'

Behind her were eight tents with different item categories. Every item donated to GSPJ's flood relief centre was segregated into one of the eight tents, before individualizing every item to be fitted into packs. She then listed down what they put into the packs: Biscuits, salt, sugar, cooking oil, baked beans, three-in-one coffee powder, instant noodles, mosquito coils, candles, matchsticks, Panadol, charcoal pills, plaster, face masks, toothbrush. Pah, pah, pah—fifteen. Dilpreet manages all of them.

Her meteoric rise as the primary manager of the relief effort was symbolic of the leaderless belief that GSPJ held: Quick promotions upon performance.

Dilpreet started as an ordinary volunteer who was working in the backgrounds when the flood relief work started. Then she started to coordinate the packing of one division. Her obsession with coordination meant that she was able to streamline and scale her work by loading and offloading tons of items in a short time.

'Don't underestimate her small size, she is the fastest around,' one GSPJ volunteer told me.

Then she took charge of the unnamed middle coordination section, where she was inside three-tonne trucks shouting for all the items to go in. Then she handled the stations, and finally all the tents, including registration, organization, and distribution—from start to finish. At the point of interviewing, she was agonizing over the finer details of how to best handle electrical appliances and monetary donations. Both were more tedious than usual because both are highly valuable and required the highest level of accountability. She set up physical protections for the appliances and a more rigorous process for distributing public money.

'GSPJ gave me authority because they knew I was familiar with my work,' said Dilpreet. 'The thing about how it works here is that Pavandeep never really interferes with what I do. He entrusts me to keep him updated on the big picture and run the team. I do the same with my volunteers—I realize that giving them acknowledgement will motivate them to take it further. If I noticed that they could handle it, they would be the coordinator almost immediately.'

The method worked so well that Dilpreet started to inject recycling into the relief work—a rare consideration in urgent disaster efforts. She knew that they couldn't use paper bags for family packs because they would break easily. So, she tried to offset the waste by reusing plastics, recycling waste, and repacking better.

Dilpreet's rise in the ration department was also seen in the food department. Initially, volunteers in charge of cooking were Sikhs from other gurdwaras. Past camps had created weak ties that GSPJ could call up and build a sizeable foundation to start. But this rapidly changed by the third day, when the non-Sikhs coordinators who had been consistent were promoted to lead other volunteers. At its peak, 60–70 per cent of the lead coordinators were non-Sikhs. Malay aunties would be teaching newer volunteers how to cut onions, the Chinese uncles would lead the packing, Indians would be stirring the curry in the big metal cauldron . . .

'The kitchen was non-stop morning to night—breakfast, lunch, dinner,' Pavandeep told me. 'We needed to cook something that was fast, filling, and easy-to-eat. So, we decided to make

Nasi Lemak (rice and onion sambal) and potato curry. We needed
to continuously boil potatoes to make the masala and gravy—the
thickness is important so that the gravy doesn't spill over when the
victims eat. In the end, we must have used at least eighty to hundred
bags of onions and fifty bags of potatoes every day. And these are
the really big bags.'

The food that left the kitchen was an unbelievable amount.
They delivered 18,000 packs in the first day, 7.2 times higher than
the maximum estimate of Jagmeet, the GSPJ youth leader, a day
before. On the second day, 22,500 packs went out, and then a day
later, close to 25,000. In the end, a total of 107,000 food packs left
GSPJ to help the flood victims in December 2021.

Jagmeet told me, 'In a place where there was no obvious leader,
we saw natural leaders who moved seamlessly to carry out tasks
bigger than they initially imagined. I saw people of all races coming
together, drinking cha, feeling comfortable in a sacred place we've
built for all.'

'Since young, we've been told that the gurdwara models on
the Golden Temple in India where there are four doors in every
direction—to show that it's open for everyone. This was the first
time I saw that my gurdwara became that ideal. Politicians can
divide us and tell us we are different, but I realize, in the end, we are
all the same. And there's something so beautiful about that.'

3. Output: Maximum autonomy

Flood relief work would have been easier if the flood victims were
concentrated in only one place. But they weren't. Flood ravaged
small towns and villages all across the country, and some of the
worst-hit areas were trapped deep inside unfamiliar terrain. For
GSPJ, it was also essential to ensure goods delivered reach the hands
of those most in need rather than being stuck in the process due to
bureaucracy, delays, or corruption.

Thus, GSPJ decided to work directly with locals with maximum
autonomy given to those involved. Rather than going back and
forth from GSPJ to the site, Pavandeep decided that it was best to

set up smaller bases near the worst-hit areas, like Bentong, Shah Alam, Mentakab, Kuala Krau, and Kuala Lipis. Being masters of weak ties, GSPJ was able to reach out to Sikhs in those bases to find other locals to 'take us and go'.

'They will recce the site and collect a list of names and households who needs help, together with what they need and how much. Then they will roll out in droves to deliver those goods, before doing a final round of check to make sure everyone got what they need,' Pavandeep said.

In all of this, Pavandeep was invisible in the process, except for some high-level coordination. 'They were on the ground, not me. Why would I presume to know better?' he said. 'Any major decisions on the ground, the team makes them on their own and decides among themselves.'

Before long, the locals who were trustworthy and familiar with their village were entrusted with more coordinating work of surrounding areas. They provided GSPJ with further information about other areas not reported by the media who were also in dire need of help.

'We need to trust people. If we control everything from the base in GSPJ, nothing will move. We can't afford that kind of delay,' said Pavandeep.

4

Inside the bestselling author Jim Collins's Colorado office, the strangest thing you will find is not the extra-large Curious George chimpanzee stuffed toy sitting on a leather chair. Instead, it is the stopwatch Jim Collins holds in his palms that has three different timers. Born in 1958, Jim Collins is known for living his life in a hyper-methodical manner. Every time he starts and finishes a task, he will click on the stopwatch and record how much time he had spent on them. His goal, he said, was to reach 1,000 creative hours a year. 'Teaching at Stanford University' and 'Others' would thus have to compete for his time.

To reach that target, he has made several dramatic changes in his life. He keeps a 'sleep log' that is calculated on a rolling average, visiting a sleep lab to learn how to optimize a good seventy-hour sleep every ten days. He has also developed a habit of saying 'no' to consulting and speaking invitations. It didn't matter if they were offering $65,000 per talk or a million per engagement. To him, his creative hours spent answering big questions about management were most important.

That was the same approach he took in producing the book, *Good to Great*, which has sold four million copies worldwide and has become one of the most widely read business books in the past two decades. In a six-month financial analysis 'death march', he created a highly rigorous process to search for twenty-one student researchers (primarily from Stanford and Colorado, with a penchant for perfectionism and irreverence), studied all 1,435 companies on the Fortune 500 list, and spent $500,000 and five years to answer one of the most difficult questions: What differentiates a great company from a good one?

What Jim Collins found was so surprising that no one could stop him from telling the world—not even for $100 million. Let's try something. Look at the list below and give yourself a point every time you recognize the name of a company. This is a low recognition game—you don't need to know the company fully, just having heard of its name is considered valid.

1. 3M
2. Boeing
3. Coca-Cola
4. GE
5. Hewlett-Packard
6. Intel
7. Johnson & Johnson
8. Merck
9. Motorola
10. Pepsi
11. Procter & Gamble

Then, go through another list using the same scoring method. A point for each name that you recognize.

1. George Cain
2. Alan Wurtzel
3. David Maxwell
4. Colman Mockler
5. Darwin Smith
6. Jim Herring
7. Lyle Everingham
8. Joe Cullman
9. Fred Allen
10. Cork Walgreen
11. Carl Reichardt

For the scores of the company name on the first list, convert the total score into negative, and keep the scores on the executive names positive. You will only pass the test if you have a positive score. Most people, as expected, did not get a positive score.

Here comes the most surprising part: The eleven executives on the second list had led companies that beat the 'marquis set' companies in the first list by a few times. The takeaway is this: Truly great companies were not the popular ones; instead, they were led by people who most people have never heard of.

We are so used to seeing larger-than-life, Trumpist chief executives as the reasons for great business successes. But Jim Collins found the opposite was true. Celebrity leaders were *negatively correlated* with companies that turned good to great. Based on his research, leaders who used the word 'I' significantly more than 'we'—indicating an enlarged ego—were less likely to create a world-class company that sustains through time.

He called it 'Level Five Leaders', with the formula of,

$$\text{Humility} + \text{Will} = \text{Level Five Leaders}$$

Level Five Leaders are like Darwin Smith from the old-paper company, Kimberly-Clark, who always shies away from the limelight and credits his success to others. With no airs of self-importance, he found companions among plumbers and electricians, and he never cultivated a hero or cult-like status for himself. When asked about his success, he always mentioned his colleagues and successors, or if he couldn't, he would attribute it to luck.

The graph that showed the stock price of Kimberly-Clark before and after Darwin Smith's tenure was illuminating. The twenty years before Darwin Smith took over, the share price of the company never breached above $10. In the next twenty years after Darwin Smith stepped in, Kimberly-Clark jolted to more than four times that amount.[99]

Compare him to Al Dunlap, CEO of Scott Paper, who thumped his chest during his $165,000-a-day tenure and called the Scott story 'historic' as one of the 'most successful, quickest turnarounds ever' in his first nineteen months, gave many newspaper interviews, and wrote a book about himself by drawing comparisons to Rambo—the one who 'gets rid of bad guys'. Safe to say, his company didn't make it to the *Good to Great* hall of fame.

Level Five Leaders seemed to come from Mars. When asked about their success, they would often say things like,

'I hope I'm not sounding like a big shot.'
'If the board hadn't picked such great successors, you probably wouldn't be talking with me today.'
'Did I have a lot to do with it? Oh, that sounds so self-serving. I don't think I can take much credit. We were blessed with marvellous people.'
'There are plenty of people in this company who could do my job better than I do.'

[99] Out of 1,435 companies, only eleven made the cut as a *Good to Great* company. It's shocking how similar the chief executives were in the eleven companies. Another example was Gillette's publicity-shy Colman Mockler, who upon receiving a copy of himself portrayed as Conan the Triumphant, crumpled to the floor and had a massive heart attack.

If we extend the word-list game at the beginning, a Level Five Leader would have descriptions like,

1. Quiet
2. Humble
3. Modest
4. Reserved
5. Shy
6. Gracious
7. Mild-mannered
8. Self-effacing
9. Understated

If the first and second word lists were the general stock market price worth one dollar for each word recognized, the final list here is worth 471 times more. That was the difference in a Level Five Leader.

* * *

Interviewing GSPJ for this chapter was hard. Instead of interviewing one person deeply for hours—like I did for the other chapters—I had to talk to five GSPJ members, each averaging forty-five minutes. I first reached out to the youth leader, Jagmeet Singh, for an interview, and his first reaction was, 'Are you sure you want to talk to me or someone from GSPJ?'

When I arrived at the gurdwara, Jagmeet introduced me to others who were involved and, as became typical, downplayed his role significantly. He would find others who were willing to speak to me and asked me to interview them instead. It became evident that no one was willing to take credit for the flood relief success. When I told them that they would be quoted in a book, they shied away even more.

Another volunteer at GSPJ told me that they have stayed away from most media coverage unless it directly helped put the word out for more volunteers. Otherwise, they were not interested in getting themselves known. The interview with Pavandeep Singh, the co-lead coordinator, was his first ever, even though he was the main person running the entire operations.

'I don't like talking to the media, having the spotlight on me,' said Pavandeep. 'I'm just a normal volunteer here.'

Just a normal volunteer here?

That can't be true, can it? He was the President of SNSM, one of the largest Sikh organizations responsible for a few of the world's largest Sikh events and a key contributor to the tsunami relief efforts in Aceh. With Kuldip Singh, Pavandeep was also in charge of making sure everything in the flood relief of December 2021 ran smoothly. He was also the main person running the kitchen that delivered 107,000 packs of food. He was comfortable sharing power and leading a team that does not listen to just one powerful man.

In fact, that was how all five interviewees introduced themselves: I'm just a normal volunteer here.

You could tell whether a leader was at Level Five in times of success and failure. Do they look out the window to credit or blame others, or do they look into the mirror to credit or blame themselves? When the flood relief was successful, GSPJ's volunteers chose to look out the window to credit others, like the thousands of volunteers who came through to lend a hand. In my forty-page-long interview transcript, you couldn't find a single part where they thought they directly caused its success. Instead, they lamented that they hadn't done enough.

Does that sound familiar to you? GSPJ is like Darwin Smith from the old-paper company, Kimberly-Clark, above.

But it wasn't enough to just be humble. Jim Collins also mentioned that every successful Level Five Leader had an enormous, insatiable will to succeed for the organization. The only difference, compared to a larger-than-life leader, was that their drive is not directed at themselves but at the organization.

I interviewed GSPJ members in January 2022, six weeks after the flood happened. Although most of the volunteers were no longer active, the GSPJ members still went there from morning till night, seven days a week. One member, Dilpreet Kaur, had even stayed at the gurdwara for most nights since the relief started.

'I live so far, like forty-five minutes away,' said Dilpreet. 'So, I brought my clothes over and just slept here . . . it's easier, so I don't have to go back-and-forth since I'm coming here every day anyway.'

At that point, they were the only organization left helping the remaining flood victims. The central principle they held on to was that no one should be left behind. Even when the cameras and social media attention were no longer there, it didn't stop them from lifting boxes up the truck and driving out to the victims' places.

'Our first Sikh prophet, Guru Nanak Dev Ji, talked about the three pillars of Sikhism. *Naam Japo* (meditation on God), *Vand Chhako* (sharing money, possession with others), and *Kirat Karo* (working hard and earning an honest living). This flood relief is the second pillar in full, of sharing your means. Whether you are flooded or not, we are helping whoever is in need—regardless of who they are, and where they come from,' Amarraj Singh, a volunteer told me.

Once, Amarraj Singh was at a toll station, a pitstop before going into the deep ends of a village. Suddenly a mother and son pair walked to him and gave him money.

'I asked them, "Do you know me?"' Amarraj recalled. 'They said, "No, but we know about you people—you help," and pointed at my turban. Both of them took out as much as they could from their pockets and just gave it to me. The turban is a sign of help. And if you ask a Sikh to help you, they will rarely say no. In the end, the mother and son gave a total of RM137.50.'

After the toll stop, he continued to lead thirteen others in his convoy. He was driving a four-wheel drive at 100 km/hour when a Range Rover started accelerating to catch up with them.

'We made way for him because he was driving much faster than us. But when we were driving in parallel, he rolled down his window and passed me an envelope before speeding off again,' Amarraj continued. 'Inside the envelope was RM500 for the flood relief. We only had a small, laminated sign at the back of our car windows that read, 'GSPJ'.

They were rushing to help us as much as they can—we became a sign of help.'

Humility + Will = Level Five Leaders

Humble non-leaders turned out to be the best leaders of all.

5

'To be honest with you, I couldn't swim much,' Amarraj Singh told me. 'When I reached the indigenous village in Pahang, it was raining heavily close to midnight. We have made our way to the deep ends of the village in a forest because nobody wanted to. The roads were totally submerged—water was at least ten-feet high. It was pitch dark inside—nothing but the few of us. No light. No telephone coverage or data. Nobody would hear you even if you shouted. Our cars floated like boats.

'Those people at the entrance told us that, "It's better for you to not go in. If you drown, go missing, or if there's an accident, we cannot come to save you. It's just too dangerous."'

But Amarraj knew that no one had given help to the indigenous people because the village was hard to reach and, frankly, people had forgotten about them. A few days before, a Twitter user in one of the flood-stricken areas tweeted in all caps:

PLEASE DON'T JUST FOCUS [ON] SELANGOR OR SHAH ALAM (Urban), WE HERE IN BENTONG, PAHANG ALSO HAD TERRIBLE FLOODING AND ARE IN NEED OF HELP IN FOOD AND CLOTHES. PLEASE HELP US.

One of the reasons relief efforts were concentrated in urban areas, Amarraj said, was simply because it was easier to help brick-walled houses compared to wooden houses. The payoff was also lower in the rural areas because, like Amarraj, you would have to travel from 7.00 a.m. to 2.00 a.m. to get help to a handful of villages.

'As I was driving the truck in, I was not sure where we were going. There was no Waze to help you . . . Even we were worried whether we could come out alive,' Amarraj recalled. 'But the cry for help was so much greater than the risk we would take. So, we went in with brave hearts, taking one step at a time.'

At a distance, Amarraj saw an indigenous man squatting on a piece of metal rod, and he stopped to ask him to bring the GSPJ team to his house. The man was walking with only one leg, and he could only see with one eye.

'He asked us to stop after a few hundred metres in, and he pointed to the right and went down the truck,' Amarraj said. 'That's my house, he said. But there was nothing there—it was just an empty land. That's when we realized that his wooden house was beside the river, and the water was so strong it washed off his house entirely. This guy lost his entire house! And that was where he will sleep for that night.

'Then I asked him where the light was. He only showed us a Bunsen burner that would go off in a few hours. This was terribly heartbreaking for me. Because I was standing there, having everything, and he was there, beside me, having nothing at all.

'We gave him everything we had on the truck and came back the next day with electrical appliances and Gensets to help him for a few days. We helped him to build a plywood home . . . Despite everything, he was still in high spirits (Sikhs call it *Charhdi Kala*) and smiling. But deep down, we knew that was not enough. This was the Hidden Malaysia.'

Amarraj and his team committed to a principle: Never leave anyone unhappy. If it meant they had to go deeper into the jungle, they would do it. Before leaving every site, they would ask the locals who else they knew in the village who hasn't received help. 'I ask them, be honest with me. If it meant we had to go back and come again the next day we would do that,' Amarraj said.

He paused for a few seconds and continued, 'Maybe that's why what initially was a 2,500-hot-meal assistance turned out to be a full-scale relief centre with warehouse of every item. Maybe that's why what was initially a one-day relief event turned out to be a continuous one. I thought it was going to be a one-day thing, but two months later, look—I'm still here.'

* * *

On the same day as my interview, there was a wedding at GSPJ between a couple who were volunteers at the flood relief. Volunteers from every walk of life became friends and started holding events at the gurdwara because they felt connected to the place where they shared a higher purpose.

'As human beings, we must have a purpose,' said Dilpreet. 'This whole flood relief thing screwed up my sleep cycle, and I haven't been home for weeks. But you know, to be able to give more than we receive, that gives me so much joy.'

When I asked her about what she thought of the success, she grew uncomfortable.

'What success? Yes, it's rewarding to see that victims appreciate what you give . . . But it's also heartbreaking because we know after this—what? How are they going to rebuild their house? How to rebuild their life from scratch? How do they be mentally resilient in all these challenges?

'People keep telling me, Dilpreet, you've done a lot, but I honestly don't think so. I keep thinking that we're not doing enough, because how much help is truly enough for people who have lost everything?'

'When will you stop helping?' I asked.

'Until the day I close my eyes.'

Epilogue

Every December, the volunteers at GSPJ would look out the window. If it rained too heavily—they were ready to go out to the waters again.

Key takeaways

- The most successful leaders are the Level Five leaders who are quiet, humble, and shy.
- Ordinary people could organize and replace a mighty government machinery if they are motivated by common kindness.

Chapter 8

Marcus Yam

How a photographer went from being expelled from school to winning the Pulitzer Prize and what it shows about the value of going where nobody goes

'Another Taliban came back with cold water and
Monster energy drinks [and another asked for a selfie] . . .
I'm thinking to myself, "This is surreal."'

(This chapter may contain disturbing photos. Viewers' discretion advised.)

1

Three Months Before the Fall

For a long time, Afghanistan was considered the worst place in the world to be born. Out of 1,000 live births, 257 ended up dying, and 70 per cent of the population does not have access to clean water.

The country was especially bad for girls. Schools were regular sites of attack by terrorists; girls prohibited from education. In public, women were watched for what they wore, where they went, and even what cell phones they used.

In a secluded building surrounded by tall ancestral trees in Kabul, the capital city of Afghanistan, there was a quiet symphony of defiance. Thirty-five young girls between ages thirteen and twenty, covered in hijabs, shuffled in and out of a small room with closed windows. Twice a week, a soothing mix of Beethoven's Ninth Symphony and classical Afghan folk songs emanated from aged instruments, Western and traditional Afghan, from the Zohra Orchestra.

It came from the Afghanistan National Institute of Music, that was founded in 2010 by Dr Ahmad Sarmast, the son of a well-known conductor who triumphed during the country's golden age of music in the 1960s and 1970s. He wanted to continue his father's aspirations of enriching Afghan life with the music, but he knew that they lived in vastly different times.

During the thirty-year Taliban rule between 1978 to 2001, the golden age was reversed dramatically. Music was deemed to have a 'corrupting influence' on the populous, such that musicians were tortured, imprisoned, and some brutally murdered. Even after the Taliban was ousted in 2001, freedom existed only in small pockets.

Dr Ahmad Sarmast knows the Taliban's oppression personally. In 2014, he was nearly killed in a suicide bomb at the French Cultural Center. His students from the music school were performing in a concert to an audience of 500. A suicide bomber infiltrated the concert and sat at the front row before blowing himself up. Among the dozens injured was Dr Ahmad Sarmast. He was rendered unconscious, and almost lost his most prized asset as a musician—his hearing.

The Taliban, who claimed responsibility for the bombing, stated that the concert was 'against Islamic values' and specifically mentioned Dr Ahmad Sarmast, accusing him of corrupting the youth.

'[W]e realized the Taliban knew about us,' said one of the Institute's earliest faculty. 'That was the first time we realized we could lose our lives.'

Dr Ahmad Sarmast's response to the incident was characteristically defiant. Instead of backing down, he made another bolder ambition: To start an all-female ensemble. Education and music were already dangerous ingredients that brought about the Taliban's admonition. Adding 'female' to the mix was something no one even dared to dream of.

'The initial idea was to form a pop group of four to five girls,' said Dr Ahmad Sarmast. 'We can't build a democratic society in Afghanistan if we will be neglecting half of the population of the nation.'

'[The Talibans] can send bombers. We respond back to the beauty of music,' he said.

Interests grew rapidly and the small ensemble grew into a a strong, all-female, thirty-five-member orchestra—the first in Afghanistan history.

Inside the small room at the Afghanistan National Institute of Music, smiles, jokes, and laughter filled the air. The girls knew how lucky they were to be drowned in the pure joy of music. Playing music in the building was a contrast to their lives outside—dusty, noisy, isolating, with people policing their every move, and fearing that they could die in a bomb blast.

'When I play music [here], it makes me feel safe,' said an orchestra member.

Through pockets of goodwill and luck, Zohra Orchestra managed to perform at some of the most prestigious stages in the world.[100] They performed at Davos for the World Economic Forum, the Sydney

---

[100] Others were not so lucky. A male friend of one of the orchestra girls were seen holding a guitar in public. To make sure he didn't play music again, the Talibans cut the boy fingers' off.

Opera House, British Museum, and the University of Oxford. A few girls even played for the Carnegie Hall and the Kennedy Center in the United States. Wearing the red, green, and black of the Afghan flag, they showed the world a picture of courage and resilience in the face of oppression. But the prospect of a Taliban return hung over their heads.

Since being removed from power, the Talibans picked themselves up through the decades and have built up substantial strength in the rural communities. Unlike the first regime, Taliban 2.0 is not only more tech-savvy but also more strategic in their pursuit for power. They used Twitter, through their spokesperson Zabihullah Mujahid, to publicize their attacks in real-time, with posting frequency and followers significantly higher than the Afghan Defence Ministry. Encrypted platforms like WhatsApp and Telegram also became information battlegrounds for the Talibans to spread their propaganda at scale and speed.

Internationally, the Talibans were conscious of their extremist image and sought to portray a misleadingly moderate one. They wrote op-eds and gave interviews to The *New York Times*, cooperated with the international community in calling for investigations in the Christchurch terrorist attack, brokered ceasefire with the Afghan government, and arrived at a peace settlement with the United States. The renewed international standing was meant to distract and make people forget about their inglorious past, remembered for flogging, amputations, mass executions, strict restriction on women's rights, and destruction of cultural and religious sites.

From a ragtag guerrilla insurgency, the Talibans grew to a size of 100,000 in 2010, and proceeded to take over rural areas, mostly without much resistance. Streets after streets, provinces after provinces started to fall.

'We don't know whether the Taliban are coming or not,' said the Zohra Orchestra girls. '[Our] future is totally in the air.'

Even without complete power, Taliban-minded conservatives were already launching attacks on schools. On 21 May 2021, a car bomb followed by two explosive devices blasted targeted schoolgirls at Sayed al-Shuhada, leaving 90 dead and 240 injured.

'It's a crime against humanity,' said Dr Ahmad Sarmast. 'It's a war crime, a genocide. Girls deprived of their education rights. People slashed publicly for no reason. For listening to music or watching movie or caught with a mobile phone.'

No one expected the speed of the Taliban's progress. They expected the Afghan military forces to fight back all they could—they could not, and would not, imagine a Taliban return.

'If there is no music, then no one can survive,' another orchestra member said. 'Music is the soul of human. It can make you happy. It can [also] show the pain of your country to another.'

I hope they don't take my instruments away from me, one of them said.

2

Two Days Before the Fall

In the scorching heat of August 2021—it was thirty degree Celsius—in Beirut, the electricity at Marcus Yam's apartment went off. No air-conditioning, no fan in the humid weather. Marcus laid on the marble floor to cool down, scrolling through the laptop for the latest news.

Marcus, born on 27 April 1984, is a staff photographer and foreign correspondent for the *Los Angeles Times*. He grew up in the suburbs of Kuala Lumpur with three other siblings and was raised by a father who specialized in sewerage engineering ('My dad would often tell us, "Shit pays for everything here"') and a mother who worked in real estate. Over the years, Marcus had been internationally recognized for his heart-wrenching photos of war that are at once tragic and hauntingly beautiful. He has won the Robert F Kennedy Human Rights Journalism Award for the violent fights at the Gaza Strip, an Emmy Award for News and Documentary, and was twice part of the Pulitzer–prize winning team that covered the terrorist attack at San Bernardino and the deadly Oso Landslide.

On his profile page at the *Los Angeles Times*, Marcus is described as a 'roving' foreign correspondent, because he is always travelling and on the run—a man without a home base. In August 2021, Marcus and his colleague, Nabih Bulos, were dispatched to the capital city of Lebanon to cover the first anniversary of the Beirut ammonium nitrate explosion—one of the 'most powerful accidental artificial non-nuclear explosions in history', that even physically shook neighbouring countries of Turkey, Syria, Palestine, Jordan, and Israel.[101]

'I'm having this very bad feeling that Afghanistan is going to fall in a few days,' said Marcus to a shirtless Nabih Bulos, who was lighting up a cigarette. 'I don't know what it is, but something's telling me that the Taliban is almost there.'

Marcus's suspicion was not without basis. For the past few weeks, large swathes of Afghan territories had fallen to Taliban at lightning pace. Residents in Kabul assured themselves that while the Taliban was strong in rural areas, they would not get into provincial capitals. That was until the province of Zaranj fell in almost the same fashion as the rural areas—without resistance. More and more Afghans were internally displaced from the new Taliban territory, fleeing to the capital of Kabul, where they lived in makeshift tents made of fabric and tree branches.

Nabih Bulos dismissed him and said they should only go to Afghanistan in September 2021, as originally planned. The United States had announced that they would be withdrawing their troops on 11 September 2021, to coincide with the twentieth anniversary of 9/11. At that time, most analysts also surmised that it might take a few months before the Taliban could defeat the Afghan forces that were trained and funded by the Americans, if they succeed at all.

'It's not going to be in September, I'm telling you,' said Marcus. 'It's much sooner than that. We have to leave now!'

Marcus called for an emergency meeting with his editors and the team of the *Los Angeles Times* that afternoon.

'I wasn't expecting the Taliban to win that quickly and easily, but things are going at a faster pace than anyone imagined,' said Marcus in the call. 'I'm pitching to be there on the day of the last stand. If the Afghan forces decide to circle the capital city of Kabul and set up a defence perimeter against Taliban, I am going to be there from the start to the very end, side by side with them to fight off the Taliban.'

After hours of arguing, the editors finally agreed.

---

[101] 'I mean, the question is why did the cargo of 2,750 tonne of ammonium nitrate sit in one place without any proper safety measures?' said Marcus. 'It's absurd.'

His colleague, Nabih Bulos, did not follow him because he still hadn't applied for a visa, unlike Marcus who had applied a year before. 'I still don't think you should fly out so soon,' insisted Nabih Bulos. That meant that this would be the first time Marcus would be travelling to a war-torn country alone.

This was characteristic of Marcus Yam, who never took 'no' for an answer. He would find ways around the 'no' to get his way and prove the naysayers wrong.

The meeting was over at 6.40 p.m., leaving Marcus with less than two hours to reach the airport gate before the last flight out. He stuffed everything he needed into his bag in twenty minutes and called a taxi. Because of the fuel crisis in Beirut, many taxi drivers did not work that day. It took him forty-five minutes to get into one, and when he arrived at the airport, there were only five minutes left before boarding. He made it.

The only way to reach Afghanistan from Beirut was via a connecting flight from Dubai. At the Dubai airport, he was assigned to wait at Terminal 2—a contrast to the other terminals as Terminal 2 flies to the most 'unsavoury places'—for almost eight hours.

'It was the most uncomfortable terminal. No amenities, no charge points,' said Marcus. 'No one brings a suitcase at these terminals; instead, they have boxes wrapped in plastics. Everyone stayed awake throughout their wait, not sleeping while clutching their bags tightly, so that no one stole their belongings. There was very little to do other than pray.'

The airport gates opened, and the word 'Boarding' flashed on the screen.

'Good morning! Going for a vacation?' said the air stewardess, cheekily.

'Yes, going for a honeymoon,' replied Marcus. 'You wanna come?'

Marcus was among the handful of people who boarded the commercial flight into Kabul, Afghanistan. In that quiet flight, he thought about his past and the stubbornness in never taking 'no' for an answer.

When Marcus was in school, the feisty and shy late bloomer found nothing more interesting than playing the online games of Counter Strike and StarCraft.

'I was at the cusp of figuring out a career in e-sports. I really thought that I could just drop out and play,' said Marcus.

Out of 300 school days, Marcus skipped 200 of them to play online games. To limit his gaming, Marcus's engineer father bought an intercom system with all the phone wires connected. Anybody who used the phone or internet would trigger an alert in the parents' room. It would say where the usage was coming from and the length of usage—'like a Big Brother watching you,' said Marcus. That meant Marcus could no longer play in the middle of the night any more, like he always had.

But that didn't stop him.

'I went to the hardware store with the little money I had and bought a 200-metre telephone wire,' recalled Marcus. 'When my dad wasn't around, I went to the intercom box and figured out which plug would bypass the system. I replaced the plug with mine and connected the wire to my room. I made a couple of tries to make sure that the internet worked for me—and more important, to make sure my dad's intercom system wasn't picking up on the signals.

'So, when I knew that it was going to work, I made it my modus operandi every night. An hour after my parents went to bed, I would sneak downstairs, plug in my wire, pull it to my room, and start my proper gaming, which would continue into the morning. My dad normally wakes up at 6.00 a.m., so if I start at 1.00 a.m., I get a solid five hours of game time,' said Marcus. 'Before anyone wakes up, I would roll the wire and sneak it into my drawer. I learned early on that you want to roll it in a certain way to prevent entanglement.'

One morning, Marcus's father woke up an hour earlier than expected to get water from the kitchen. He accidentally tripped over the 200-metre wire that passed through the living room, stairs, hallway, and the room.

'My father was so pissed. I haven't seen him so angry before,' said Marcus. 'Safe to say I could no longer play video games at home in the middle of the night.'

Throughout school, Marcus failed more subjects than he passed. But he continued his gaming ways despite being kicked out of his school, admonished by his teachers, and chased by his mother with a metal hanger.[102]

Marcus's mother was so frustrated that one day she burst through Marcus's room with a huge pail of water and poured it on Marcus's computer.

'I had to let go of the computer—the whole thing went up in smoke!' recalled Marcus. 'My mom didn't say a single word. She just walked out, and we didn't talk for a very long time. If there was a list of Malaysia's most rotten children, I would be at the top of the list.'

Oddly enough, the most effective way of keeping Marcus from online games was to send him to this giant library at a suburb of Selangor called Shah Alam, which was a half-hour drive from Marcus's home. Every Saturday, Marcus's mother would go on to pursue any one of her obsessions—crystals, baking cheesecakes, marathons—and drop Marcus to the replacement babysitter, the Shah Alam Library. Her mother would give him RM20 for lunch and off they went their separate ways.

'Most of the time I would just be walking aimlessly at the library to kill time,' said Marcus. 'I slowly gravitated towards the science section. I don't know why that became my fascination. I started drawing and copying stuff from the books, like military equipment, airplanes, rockets, and satellites.

'My favourite was the Jane's series that served as an encyclopaedia for all war equipment. I learned about the Humvee and how it worked, as well as how to throw a grenade. By the time I was twelve, I already had notebooks filled with drawings and schematics of military vehicles and equipment.'

More than two decades later, the knowledge gathered in a small library in a sleepy town of Shah Alam would prove useful in one of the most historic war events of the twenty-first century.

---

[102] 'Normally my mechanism was to jump over and hide behind furniture,' said Marcus. 'I would tell people I must be the first one to invent parkour as a child just to survive unscathed.'

'It's strange to see weapons in the war field now and tell yourself, "Oh, I read this as a child." No knowledge is wasted—it is all just a matter of time.'

The commercial flight to Kabul, Afghanistan, landed safely. Marcus had been here a few times before, the most recent of which was three months ago, where he interviewed the women of Afghanistan including the Zohra Orchestra girls, among others.

Anxiety, fear, and desperation defined that day. Marcus left his belongings at a guesthouse and went to Hasa-e-Awal, a park at Kabul that turned into temporary safehouse for internally displaced Afghans who fled the Taliban. The Taliban fighters were inching closer to the capital itself by the day. The latest count of displaced Afghans reached 250,000.

'Men and women tugged at my shirt, grabbed my arm, held my hands,' said Marcus. 'They wanted somebody to help them.'

A house cleaner, who was displaced from her province by the Taliban, told Marcus how her heart was beating fast at the thought of Taliban taking over the country. They had already fled their abode without looking back, and they were prepared to flee again if the Taliban came after them. But they did not know where to go.

'As night fell . . . scared voices whispered over sleeping children.'

The next day, Kabul fell.

Marcus Yam 1

3

The Fall

'Afghanistan is dead. I am dead,' a trader told Marcus Yam.

As the Afghan President Ashraf Ghani fled the country, it was over for Afghanistan before it began. Afghan residents expected the government and the military forces to put up a fight against the Taliban, but it became clear that they gave up as soon as the Taliban encircled the capital. Soldiers took off their uniforms and sought refuge. Marcus remembered that the defeat was so swift, like 'a film [that] was suddenly fast-forwarded'.

Traffic was congested, with honks and shouts heard from every direction. People were rushing to any ATM that worked, shops were closed down, finger-pointing and fist fighting broke out. Images of women in mascara were taken down from beauty salons.

'"Chaos" was an understatement,' said Marcus.

Marcus took a taxi and planned his emergency exit route in case he needed to rush out. He booked up a few flights for different hours of the day in case flights were cancelled. Another plan was for him to exit via Pakistan. Another was to use his Malaysian passport to be smuggled into Iran from the west of Afghanistan. None were ideal.

He started receiving messages and phone calls from other Western reporters. The Taliban's rapid takeover was beyond anyone's wildest imaginations. Nobody knew how dangerous the country would be for the next few days.

Marcus's long-time friend, Fatima Fauzi, a *New York Times* reporter, called him.

'Marcus, I want you to leave right now,' she said. 'All of us are leaving. *New York Times, Wall Street Journal, Washington Post*—we are all leaving, and you should too.'

Thousands had swarmed the Kabul International Airport in the hopes that they could board a flight to leave. Gunshots fired randomly and incessantly in the background. Smoke grenades blurred off the scenes. People climbed on top of one another to get on a plane. Many who did not get on ran alongside taxiing flights. A few hung on to the wings of aircrafts only to fall after take-off. Desperate to find a way out no matter what, where, and how.

But Marcus insisted on staying.

Fatima Fauzi started to cry and begged for him to leave.

'If that's what you're going to do—good luck, then, Marcus,' said Fatima Fauzi. 'I'll see you on the other side.'

'I'll see you, Fatima,' said Marcus.

Marcus called his editors at the *Los Angeles Times* and had the same disagreement. Everyone in Los Angeles said that it was imperative that Marcus left Afghanistan given the unexpected escalation, and especially when every other international media were evacuating. 'Can you please get out of there?' they said.

Once again, Marcus said no.

Marcus's long-time mentor and *Los Angeles Times* director of photography, Calvin Hom, suggested in the call that he talk to Marcus one-on-one after the team meeting.

'Man to man, what do you want to do?' asked Calvin privately.

'I want to stay,' said Marcus.

'This is not something you *have* to do. This is not a company directive at all. You don't have to stay if you don't want to,' said Calvin.

'I want to stay. I've come this far, I'm not going to turn away now—it's cowardice,' said Marcus. 'This is what the American government is doing—withdrawing. If we do that then we are no different. I am one person. I can take care of myself easily. I can hide anywhere if I have to.'

Marcus also gave Calvin Hom the three exit plans that he had devised earlier in the standstill traffic of Kabul.

'This is a historic moment,' said Marcus. 'We are the last Western publication to stay behind. It is our duty and responsibility to document history. We need to stay and commit to this coverage and do whatever it takes. I won't turn around.'

'Okay, then. If that's what you want, then I will back you up,' said Calvin Hom. The trust that Marcus and his mentor had was years in the making, as Marcus had proven time and again the lionheart he was.

Calvin Hom told the other management team about Marcus's final decision and asked for everyone's support in the company.[103]

In the next few hours, Marcus Yam and the *Los Angeles Times* decided on a mission statement that would come to define how the world understood the Afghanistan fall. They were not going to follow the Taliban around as they establish their dominance over governing institutions. No, they were not going to see the fall through the lens of the victor.

'We have to keep in mind that this is not just a country falling apart. It is a whole generation who grew up in post-Taliban world of 2001 and don't know of the harsh and repressive reality their parents spoke about,' said Marcus. 'Now they are at the brink of losing everything they know about their country and themselves.

'Our mission statement was to cover this conflict from the eyes of ordinary Afghans. Not the victors—but the losers who were at risk of losing everything they knew.'

4

Day Two of the Fall

The Taliban now enjoyed a firm grip on Kabul. Taliban flags in black and white were erected and waved across the city. Fighters held Kalashnikov rifles close to their chests, guarding every street. A few held grenades between their fingers, others with machine guns aimed at any passer-by. The unrelenting heat continued to burn the city.

Marcus Yam found a new driver, Zabi, a calm, centred, tall man with sunken but kind eyes. 'I want to go to the airport,' said Marcus. 'I want to know what's going on. I'm a photographer with the *Los Angeles Times*.'

---

[103] Reflecting on that moment, Calvin recalled that it was 'perhaps the hardest and most stressful time [as] a director of photography.'

'There's a fight there?' said Zabi nonchalantly. 'Let's drive up there then.'

Unlike other taxi drivers, this was not the first invasion Zabi had seen. He was a driver during the 2001 US invasion, also helping the media to get stories. He had an amazing ability to remain stoic in the face of chaos.

When the taxi reached the entrance of the airport, Zabi told Marcus, 'I can't go in any further. I need to look after my car. You go in, do your work. I will wait here.' He then proceeded to light up a cigarette as Marcus exited the vehicle.

Marcus saw thousands of Afghans waiting outside the blast walls and barbed wires of the airport, looking for a slither of chance to leave the country. They had bloodshot eyes, having traversed sewer-filled streets, carrying their only belongings, and waving their documents in the air. Bearded Taliban fighters, dressed in traditional suit and baggy trousers, with odd pairings of gold watches and high-top sneakers, stopped desperate Afghans from entering the airport. This was the Taliban's first test of crowd control.

Every now and then, the Taliban fighters shot to the sky as warning. They would also beat back the crowd with 'sticks, rubber hoses, knotted ropes, and rifle butts'.

Marcus found a few kids to get a sense of their story. Suddenly, a sharp sound zipped through their ears. It went on in rapid succession for a few times. Then it came closer. Before long, they realized the Taliban fighters were firing at the crowd.

The kids asked Marcus to go behind a tree, so that at least there was a cover.

'The machine guns started to rattle off, longer than usual,' recalled Marcus. 'Then, I heard a loud scream.'

When he turned around, he saw a woman lay bloodied on the street, losing consciousness. People from the crowed dragged the woman and her child to the side of the road for safety. Marcus ran across the three-lane road to see what was going on. A mob started to surround them.

This is what happened in the next five minutes:

An elderly man in a bloodstained sports jacket carried a limp child whose eyes had rolled back. Another child shrieked. People sobbed. Men loaded the wounded mother and the children into a yellow Toyota Corolla taxi that sped away.

'Those shortest five minutes will stay with me forever,' said Marcus, in reflection. 'It happened right in front of me. And I thought, this horror is truly unlike any other.'

Marcus didn't file the photos immediately, breaking his regular routine. Instead, in the late afternoon of the same day, he went to the first press conference of the Taliban where the shadowy spokesman, Zabihullah Mujahid, finally revealed his face. Other freelance journalists were there too.

'Where did you go today?' asked a journalist.

'To the airport,' replied Marcus.

'What? Why? With whom?' the journalist asked in disbelief.

'Alone.'

'What? Are you crazy?'

That night, Marcus went back to his guesthouse and opened his laptop to review the stories. 'I just sat there and kept looking at the picture of the bloodied child at the airport.'

The bloodied child was unconscious in the arms of a faceless man whose back faced the camera. His black blazer and light-brown trousers were splattered with scarlet blood. Another boy came to look at the child, worried, and another adult gestured for help. In the background, cars were stuck in traffic, with a man seemingly yelling in pain. At the foreground was a boy who was defeated by the inexplicable violence he'd seen, relenting to a country that has far too many times descended into chaos and terror. Blood everywhere.

'Do I hit "send?"' Marcus remembered asking himself. At that point, everyone was still unsure whether the Taliban would act differently compared to their first regime rule. In the Taliban press conference earlier that day, its spokesperson Zabihullah Mujahid was intent on persuading the world that the Taliban now was different—no longer harsh nor violent as it was in the past.

The man who used to issue 'bloodthirsty statements' made several assurances in a calm and measured language: Independent journalism, prevent base of terrorism, amnesty for enemies, rights for women and minorities.

'This photo [of the bloodied woman and child laying unconscious] will make the Taliban look so bad. Nobody went to the airport, so nobody knew how bad things had escalated with the Taliban's crowd control measures,' said Marcus. 'But people deserve to know the truth.'

He thought about the personal consequences that may come with posting the photo. Would this anger the Taliban? How would the international community respond? What will they do to Marcus Yam?

His eyes never left the photo on the screen. He finally hit 'send'.

Immediately his editors called him. 'What the hell just happened?' they asked, worried.

That night, Marcus showed the world the truth—the shadows of the Taliban that never left.

Marcus Yam 2

5

Day Five of the Fall

'Once again, I would like to assure the media, we are committed to media within our cultural frameworks. Private media can continue to be free and independent, they can continue their activities . . .'

—Zabihullah Mujahid,
spokesperson for the Taliban on its
first press conference in Kabul, 17 August 2021

On the anniversary of Afghanistan's Independence Day, 30 August, 200 Afghan men rode on motorcycles and bicycles to the street to protest against the Taliban. They draped the Afghanistan flag over their body, in defiance against the Taliban flag, and chanted 'God bless Afghanistan!' The Taliban wanted the people to raise its new Taliban flag and start calling the country the 'Islamic Emirate of Afghanistan' instead of its old name, 'Islamic Republic of Afghanistan'.

The protestors met with the Taliban guards. They shouted at each other, and a physical scuffle quickly broke out. Marcus Yam, who just came out of a nearby mosque for interviews, saw the fight and ran towards it to find out what was going on.

'I moved out of the direct line of where the rifles were pointing, and started snapping,' recalled Marcus.

The Taliban got mad at the crowd and started beating and pointed their guns at them. A big, burly Taliban fighter pulled Marcus's camera strap and sucker-punched him, yelling in Dari, the local language.

'He asked me to stop taking pictures and delete the ones I took,' said Marcus.

When Marcus refused, the big man hit Marcus in the head five times in a row. A gunshot fired and temporarily distracted the big man. Marcus used this to escape but before Marcus could run, the big man grabbed and swatted him with a huge knock—Marcus's glasses flew off his face.

The big man's face turned redder and continued to yell at Marcus while clutching on to his rifle.

Marcus's thoughts were in a swirl. His head throbbing in disorientation. He raised his hand and pleaded, 'Please do not hurt us. We're journalists, we're foreigners, we're media. We're allowed to work.

'I'm from the *Los Angeles Times*.'

As if awakened from a slumber, one of the Taliban fighters rushed over and asked for the beating to stop. He knew English. He asked how Marcus was feeling and if he needed to go to a safer location. With a few men, the English-speaking Taliban fighter carried Marcus to the shade.

'Another Taliban [Hamid Nazri] came back with cold water and Monster energy drinks,' recalled Marcus. 'And I'm thinking to myself, this is surreal.' The Taliban even asked for a selfie, which Marcus, still in haze, had to oblige.[104]

Perhaps the Taliban was conscious of Marcus's status as a high-profile international journalist and that hurting him would damage the Taliban's reputation in the eyes of the international community. It would have shown that they were not more moderate as they claimed.

On Marcus's way out, the Taliban fighters continued to apologize, and said that they would not have treated Marcus so poorly had they not mistaken him for a local because of the traditional dress Marcus wore.

Though Marcus was relieved—having recovered his glasses—he knew that the Taliban fighters were only half-joking. Certain privileges were given to him only because he was a foreign journalist.[105]

Local journalists, on the other hand, were not nearly as lucky.

A few days later, the Taliban proved that the notion of free press was nothing but a façade. *Etilaatroz* reporters Nemat Naqdi and Taqi Daryabi, both in their twenties, were grabbed and dragged by the Taliban for photographing the women's protest in September 2021.

---

[104] Marcus did not smile for the camera.

[105] In a Zoom call with the newsroom that same night, Marcus told the team about what happened in the most nonchalant way: 'Oh yeah, and I got beat up by the Taliban.'

Both of them, like Marcus, pleaded that they were journalists, but the Taliban did not care in this case. They beat and ridiculed the reporters as though they were prepared to kill them.

The Etilaatroz reporters were beaten so badly they could not even walk after the Taliban released them. Long, deep wounds run through their backs like a map. The lines on their flesh were raw—burning upon the slightest touch.

'The Taliban haven't changed a bit. Journalism doesn't mean anything to them,' said Taqi Daryabi. Violence, censorship, and intimidation remain hallmarks of their regime. Unlike Marcus, Nemat Naqdi did not get his glasses back.

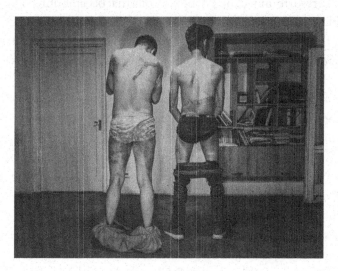

Marcus Yam 3

6

Day Sixteen of the Fall

Before August 2021 closed, Marcus Yam heard news that a family of ten had died in an explosion at a working-class neighbourhood of Khwaja Burgha, three kilometres west of the Kabul airport. Forty-year-old Zamairi Ahmadi, an aid worker, reached home in his Toyota Corolla, waiting to see the rest of his family, including a twenty-five-year-old relative who was about to get married, and five kids below five years of age, including the youngest Sumaya, who was only two years old. They had applied to be evacuated and were waiting for the final step—a phone call to set them free. Zamairi Ahmadi loaded several containers of water in the car boot.

A loud bang hit the neighbourhood, shaking houses. A propane tank exploded at once, igniting a fireball that incinerated Zamairi Ahmadi's car, part of his house, and took all ten family members' lives. The plasters on walls fell off and spread on the ground, blood splashed on nearby building—dark red that faded into brown.

Marcus was the first few journalists who arrived at the scene. Neighbours surrounded the Toyota Corolla that became unrecognizable. It was blackened and reduced to mere metals and plastics, with scraps of human flesh. A sombre mood took over any remaining hopeful spirit.

Marcus climbed to the roof of the house for a better view of the wreckage.

'At this point, nobody was sure what happened,' said Marcus. 'Neighbours could only describe what they heard. Everyone seemed to have a different version of the story.'

Something convinced him that it was not a typical explosion. The shockwave pattern and the large bowl-shaped cavity from the impact looked very unusual.

'Do you have a shovel?' he asked one of the neighbours.

He started to dig into the soil on the ground, and about a foot in, his shovel his something hard.

'It was orange and it had serial numbers on them,' said Marcus. 'Nothing in nature is curved like that. It is definitely not part of a car. Nothing would be buried underground like that.'

The confluence of Marcus's past interests began to converge. His reading of Jane's military encyclopaedia at the Shah Alam Library when he was young gave him a hint that a Hellfire missile could only be launched from either an Apache long bow helicopter or a predator drone. Since there was no long bow helicopter in Afghanistan, that was only one possibility.

He took a photo and showed his friend, who was a military weapon geek like him, and asked him to verify.

'Jackpot!' said Marcus. 'No other country in the world has a Hellfire missile except for the US. It's confirmed. It's a pneumatic accumulator—in other words, a drone.'

The *Los Angeles Times* became the first to push out the drone story. It was followed by other newsrooms subsequently confirming the validity of the drone strike.

The US forces meant for the drone to target an imminent threat by ISIS-K, which killed more than 180 people at the airport a few days ago. The Ahmadi family insisted that there was no way their family could be linked to the terrorist group; if anything, they were potential enemies of ISIS-K. One of the victims, Ahmad Naser, was even a translator with the US forces.

In a later statement, the defence secretary Lloyd Austin later confirmed that there were no connections between Mr [Zamairi] Ahmadi and ISIS-K, and that they were not an 'imminent threat' as claimed.

'We apologize, and we will endeavour to learn from this horrible mistake,' said the Defence Secretary. Such civilian casualties angered Afghans and partially contributed to the Taliban's popularity over the years, a regional newspaper claimed.

Marcus met Zamairi Ahmadi's brother, Emal Ahmadi, and his relatives at the house that day.

'He was my brother!' said Emal Ahmadi, helplessly, pointing to his brother's portrait. The windows in the house had shattered into sharp pieces, cracked lines and darkened explosion marks filled the walls. 'America is doing a bad action. Next time you don't try to kill a civilian.'

Emal Ahmadi then sat in his brother's room and cried alone, looking through the broken windows that the drone struck. The home was filled with items of people who no longer lived. Marcus grabbed Emal Ahmadi's hand and said, 'I'm sorry.'

A funeral was held a few hours later.

Ten caskets were carried by Emal Ahmadi's family, neighbours, and good Samaritans—seven of the caskets small. The caskets were laid flat in the pattern of a Japanese fan. More than 200 men attended the procession.

'I crawled and made myself small to be part of the crowd. One of the brothers looked at me and nodded [as consent to take photos],' said Marcus. 'That was when I knew I was allowed to be there, to mourn with them at a time like this.'

'They stood in rows, faced Kabul's airport and folded their arms to pray,' Marcus remembered. 'I've never attended a funeral with ten dead family members all at once.'

He knelt in front of the coffin, opposite to the praying men, and wanted to capture a shot like a classical Renaissance painting to remember the moment of quiet dignity.

In that moment, a US jetfighter F/A-18 Hornet flew lower than usual and made a loud, thundering roar that disrupted the procession. Amidst the wailing and crying, everybody looked up at once in utter disbelief.

'Why would you do this?' reflected Marcus. 'I don't know what happened. The pilot must've stepped on his afterburners to make that roar. What a desecration of a solemn and private moment.'

'It struck me that this was a sad ending to a chapter in Afghanistan. For twenty years, the US invasion brought about many misgivings. And on its way out, it inadvertently killed more civilians. As they were leaving, they were making the same mistakes again.

'A tragic coda to an end of the war.'

Marcus Yam 4

7

Day Forty-Nine of the Fall

On 3 October 2021, Marcus Yam went to the airport for a flight bound for Doha, Qatar, leaving Afghanistan for the first time as a Taliban country. He had stayed longer than initially planned. He had not had a proper night's sleep since he had first come, running from one assignment to the next. As he boarded the flight, Marcus ruminated about the people he'd met. Unlike Marcus who lived in a comfortable Los Angeles home, the Afghans did not have the choice to leave.

'How well Afghanistan does will come down to how they treat their women,' said Marcus. 'I've met so many female activists who just couldn't get out to the airports safely to board out. One woman told me that she's become very, very suicidal, and I don't know what to do when people tell me that. I'm just a journalist.'

He thought about the seventy-three-year-old women's rights activist, Mahbouba Seraj, who still intended to spend the rest of her life fighting for a space for women in business, education, medicine, media, and government. The twenty-seven-year-old Lida's continued ambition to be a policewoman, despite her burnt face from roadside bombs. The thirty-two-year-old university dean of social science, Tabesh Noor, who was bound for promotion before the Taliban came looking for her. 'I was crying every day, every day,' she told Marcus. They typically had to shop at different markets, walk different routes, or change their looks to avoid people recognizing them. Life as a woman in Afghanistan remained tough.

All-enveloping garments sales, like burqa, went up multiple folds after the Taliban took control. No more Ministry of Women's Affairs; all-men cabinet line-up, half of them under US or United Nations sanctions. The ultraconservative brand of Islam was back. At the time of writing, the Taliban continued to break their promise on women's rights as they banned university education for women. Teenage girls were still not allowed to attend secondary school. Women banned from seeing male doctors. Most sectors were closed for females to work.

Once again, proving the point that the Taliban's hard-line approach was an eventuality—only a matter of time.

Music was one of the first things the Taliban came to control. At the National Institute of Music, which once housed the Zohra Orchestra, a picture of Jalaluddin Haqqani, founder of the Haqqani Network (with ties to Taliban and al-Qaeda), now hangs at the metal front gate. Dr Ahmad Sarmast, the leader of Zohra Orchestra, showed the *Los Angeles Times* pictures of disfigured piano and a smashed guitar. 'Music is not in our religion,' said a Taliban commander. The Taliban have ransacked wedding halls and declared musical instruments 'haram'.

The Zohra Orchestra girls' escape was not smooth sailing. Dr Ahmad Sarmast had to reach out to international parties for help, to create a pathway for safe exit. When Dr Ahmad Sarmast thinks about the final batch of orchestra girls who boarded the commercial flight out, it still gives him goosebumps.

Although the girls were safe, many of their family members were left behind. They became the most stressed teenagers in their schools, always worrying about their family's safety and future. The Zohra Orchestra girls would send e-books to their sisters and female friends to learn. But they had to hide their books and convene in secrecy, studying in the quiet, whispering the words they were trying to learn.

Many of them still carried hopes for their country. No matter what they became—doctors, teachers, or musicians—they all hoped to contribute to their country one day; to build the best schools and give the best education.

'Wherever we are, we will be Zohra, and we will again stand as one community,' said one of the girls. They still cling on to the hope of uniting Zohra one day, however faint that hope flickers.

In the words of Dr Ahmad Sarmast, they will always try to 'defeat the beast with the beauty of music.'

Marcus Yam still remembers his first time meeting the internationally renowned Zohra Orchestra girls.

After the interviews, he asked if he could take a portrait of each of them. He was conscious of the danger his photographs would bring. Outside the four walls of the rehearsal room, the girls could not be seen with their instruments. They lived a double life in Afghanistan. No one was allowed to know them as musicians—even though that was how they saw themselves.

'How would you like to be photographed?' asked Marcus Yam.

'With our instruments,' they said.

In separate monochromatic portraits, Marcus Yam captured them at their best. Many smiled widely, others slightly, a few with their eyes—all with their instruments held closely in their arms.

Marcus Yam 5

8

How did Marcus Yam go from a failing student kicked out of his school in a suburb in Kuala Lumpur to one of the most established, Pulitzer-winning war photographers in the world?[106]

Marcus Yam is the classic underdog. He grew up in a satellite town in the developing country of Malaysia. He failed more subjects than

---

[106] 'I'd never imagine myself doing what you do in a million years,' I said to him in an interview. 'Me neither,' Marcus replied. 'If you told this boy from the suburbs of Kuala Lumpur that one day he would be living a life where he goes from country to country, keeping stash of things in lockers and storage, and running into danger, that boy would think, "No way, I don't want to join the army."'

he passed in school, skipped 200 out of 300 days of classes, and got kicked out of a school for playing truant. In university he did not take a single course in photography; instead, he took aerospace engineering. He didn't pick up a camera until he was nineteen. He didn't start war photography until 2017. He was a late bloomer to the craft that made his name—he was an underdog.

Perhaps the answer could be found in the most popular sporting game in the world: The Olympics.

In 2016, political scientist Danyel Reiche published a book called the *Success and Failure of Countries at the Olympics* to answer the question of why some countries succeeded at the Olympics and others did not.

Other researchers had tried their hand at this question, but their answers were unsatisfactory. The most common explanation was population. The more people you have, the more likely you are to win a medal at the Olympics. That is a tempting explanation because China and the US always topped Olympic medal charts. But Danyel Reiche argued that it was incomplete. How do you explain India's meagre ten gold-medal performance despite having the second-largest population in the world, and being on track to becoming the most populous? Cuba, on the other hand, with only 0.8 per cent of India's population had eight times more gold medals than India.

Another explanation was money: The higher the GDP per capita of the country, the more likely it was to win the Olympics. Once again, this was unsatisfactory, Danyel Reiche argued. 'Saudi Arabia's per capita GDP is seven times higher than Kenya's per capita GDP, but Kenya has won more than seventeen times more medals than Saudi Arabia,' he wrote. Similar line of arguments could be said for the Olympics success of East Germany, Hungary, Cuba, Bulgaria, Jamaica, and Ethiopia.

The key reason, Danyel Reiche argued, was finding a niche. This meant specializing in an area you are naturally endowed and/or going where nobody has gone.

Choosing to play where you are naturally good at was crucial for smaller countries. Where do you think Kenya and Ethiopia's medals come from? You guessed it: Running. The top ten medal-winning countries had 42–100 per cent of their medals come from only three sports.

Additionally, choosing to play in an uncrowded field where no one has gone was also important. When the International Olympics Committee introduced women's archery as a category, South Korea doubled down its investments into the area. Until today, their 'reign' in this sport is undeniable, winning all but one of the gold medals ever awarded. They did the same for short-track speed skating at the Winter Olympics, dominating the charts as an undisputed leader.

If Danyel Reiche's theory was illustrated as a Venn diagram, it would look like Diagram 1.

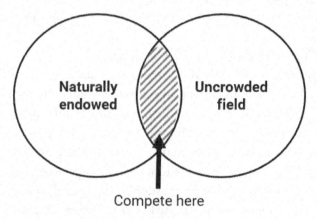

Diagram 1: Underdog Venn diagram of success

You don't necessarily need both to secure an Olympics medal, but playing at the intersection is where it could give you the maximum advantage.

1. Naturally Endowed: Testing until Something Sticks

If you asked Marcus Yam what got him started in photography he would inevitably say, 'Laziness'. Nineteen-year-old Marcus Yam needed to take English credits at the largest public university in New York, the University of Buffalo, because he was an international student.

'I argued with the university advisors and said, "No, you don't understand. I grew up speaking English. Our TV is English. I don't need to take English as a language any more,"' recalled Marcus. But he was unsuccessful in persuading the university to give him an exception.

A mopey Marcus Yam walked down the crowded Student Union one day and was given a flyer of the student newspaper, *The Spectrum*, recruiting students.

He asked them, 'What kind of credits do you give? Do you cover for English classes?'[107]

'Yes, we do!' said the newspaper recruiter.

'Great, what options do you have?'

'You can either work in design, reporting, or you can take pictures.'

'I'll go with the easiest: Photography.'

His encounter with the camera was not a eureka moment. When he started taking photos for the student newspaper, he wasn't particularly interested in the technical intricacies as well. He barely edited his photos beyond the basic editing software from the CD that came with the camera. Nor did he even contemplate photography as a viable career to replace aerospace engineering.

But that is precisely how 'passion' is discovered, argued famous professor and author Angela Duckworth. 'Before hard work comes play,' she wrote. To discover what you really love is based on your best guess at that time. Not only must you goof around—or in Marcus's case, go with the 'lazy' or 'easiest' choice—but you ought to be exposed to things to trigger and retrigger your interest. Passion means 'a little bit of discovery, followed by a lot of development, and then a lifetime of deepening.'

Photography at university allowed Marcus Yam to tap into his storytelling side that he was naturally endowed.

'I was a natural busybody. Working for the newspaper gave me a license to go to the most interesting places. I would drive up to

---

[107] The university newspapers could not pay a salary in return for a job, so they paid in class credits instead.

farms and make my long way up these long driveways and just say, "Hey, how's it going? Can I take some pictures?"'

Since he became a photographer for the university newspaper, Marcus walked around the university campus with a camera around his neck. Even though he didn't like basketball, he stayed until each match was over and hung out with the players and learned about their stories. Unlike most photographers who attended a match or concert for the first five minutes to take the most performative shots, he stayed for the stories—anything interesting that was worth a shot.

Eventually, he made enough friends to get invited to exclusive underground events at hidden warehouses, which got him access to rarer events and even more interesting friends.

'Photography was fun not because of the settings and equipment—it was fun because it allowed me to find all these interesting stories. To do that I had to figure out how things work and how people are,' said Marcus, with a smile.

His drive to chase the right stories caught the attention of a *Buffalo News* design director, John Davis, who persuaded him to take up a paid internship with them and introduced him to photography as a career.[108] That allowed him to hunt stories to its fullest, including staying up late every night to find a serial arsonist with firefighters and the police. His ability to burrow into a story earned him important gigs with the top publications of the world like *The New York Times*, *Seattle Times*, and most recently, *Los Angeles Times*. Shooting wildfires, deadly landslides, protests, and terrorist attacks.

At their best, Marcus Yam's photos tell stories of intimacy amidst conflict and struggle.

'I grew up with little intimacy from my family. Maybe my work is an intersection with my professional and personal curiosity. I naturally chase for moments of intimacy because I'm curious to know how it feels.'

---

[108] *Buffalo News* is the only newspaper fully owned by Berkshire Hathaway, whose owner is one of the richest men in the world, Warren Buffett.

'And when I get to capture those moments, I get to feel like I'm alive. It helps me become more understanding to people around me, more forgiving.'

Over time it became undisputable that telling these stories through photography was something Marcus was naturally endowed to do.

2. Uncrowded Field: Go Where Nobody Goes (Even into Conflict)

Marcus Yam only started war photography in 2017. The Battle of Mosul in Iraq was the single largest battle of that decade. The Islamic State of Iraq and the Levant (ISIS) control of Iraq's second largest city had resulted in public beheadings, imprisonment of men without beards and women without burqas, and the persecution of minorities. More than a million people had since fled the city, resulting in a large-scale humanitarian crisis. The Iraqi government and its allies' effort to retake Mosul was bound to be a tough, but necessary, thing to do.

When Marcus Yam heard about the war, he volunteered to cover it.

'I was doing work like the wildfires and landslides that were high stress and chaotic,' said Marcus. 'I wanted to see what else I could do. Like any job in an industry, you kind of want to try everything first and see what works and what doesn't work for you.'

But the managing director at the *Los Angeles Times* thought he wasn't ready. This was a full-blown war, requiring intense hostile environment training and deep military knowledge. Plus, at that time, very few photographers covered war because of the risks involved.

Great photographers who went to war were not afraid to admit how difficult the experiences were to their physical and mental health. Even though they did good and important work, the risks always outweighed the rewards. The war photography scene shrunk even more after the death of great photographers like Tim Hetherington and Chris Hondros, who died while covering the war in Libya of 2011. Photographers started to reassess their goals, and diverted to doing safer work like political photography (e.g. covering the White House and Presidents), breaking news photography (e.g. mass shootings, natural disasters), and celebrity portraits.[109]

But as was common in his career, Marcus ran into danger. When every international journalist and photographer left Afghanistan at the fall of Kabul, his choice to remain made all the difference.

Around this time, one of Marcus's long-time mentors, Calvin Hom, the executive director of photography with thirty years of experience at the *Los Angeles Times*, told him something that proved prophetic.

'Everybody in the photography business is trying to do multimedia—audio and video—juggling between multiple things to give their employers or clients value for their money,' Calvin Hom told Marcus. The shift towards wedding photography, budget packages of photos and videos, happened in many parts of the world as photography became more accessible.

'That is going to erode their photography skillset because everyone is trying to do too much and lose focus,' Calvin Hom continued. He predicted that fewer people of Marcus's generation were going to reach the pantheon of great photographers. So, he advised Marcus to drop video and audio, and focus on still photography.

What that meant was that the field of pure photography became uncrowded, allowing people who focused solely on it, like Marcus Yam, to gain a competitive advantage over others.

But success in war photography came at an incredible price for Marcus Yam. Like battlefield combatants, he suffers from post-traumatic stress disorder that requires him to recuperate for months after every assignment. Going to war, after all, 'goes against every instinct we have.'

He ran into conflict when most were running away. His most recent coverage of the Ukraine War exposed him to the most carnage he'd

---

[109] Marcus Yam also covered a few celebrity portraits in his career, like Natalie Portman, Rami Malek, and Benedict Cumberbatch.

seen in his life. The deaths of fellow journalists, Fox News cameraman Pierre Zakrzewski and crew Oleksandra Kuvshynova, and documentary filmmaker Brent Renau, were reminders of the occupational hazards of his career.

The senselessness of wars did not escape him. In these war-torn countries, people took up arms for the silliest reasons. 'Violence is easy, and life is cheap,' as Marcus put it.

'How do you console a grieving mother who has just lost her child from a mistaken drone attack? What do you say to her?' said Marcus. 'Honestly, I would rather run into bullets than to talk to some of them. It's the most difficult part of my job and the most painful.'

What he holds on to is the other side of conflict—the best side of humanity.

'I saw men who put their lives on the line to defend their countrymen. Soldiers on their knees, willing to fight on the spot with the enemy combatant, just to make sure the innocent civilians are safe,' he said.

In 2022, Marcus was announced the winner of one of journalism's highest honour, the Pulitzer Prize for the 'raw and urgent images of the US departure from Afghanistan that captured the human costs of the historic change in the country.' For his work, Pulitzer described Marcus as having a 'warrior's courage and a poet's heart'. The highlighted pictures included:

> A young boy's face, crumpled in anguish as a bloodied child is carried to safety; Taliban gunmen, bowing in prayer over their shoes and assault rifles; a family, praying for loved ones killed in an errant US drone strike, as another American aircraft flies overhead; and two local journalists, stripped to their underwear to reveal the scarlet wounds of a savage beating.

The moment Marcus got the news of his Pulitzer Prize, he broke into tears, recounting the road he had travelled.

'My gosh, a Pulitzer Prize. I am still in shock. But I am grateful,' he wrote on social media.

'The bravery and courage really belongs to the everyday Afghans who pay the highest price. [W]e have the privilege of leaving but they do not. They have to remain to face the unknown. This is for them.'

Epilogue

Seven other extraordinary things that Marcus Yam had captured through the years:

1. Sorrow and Defiance

Marcus Yam stayed in Taliban Afghanistan longer than planned in 2021. He interviewed women who did not make it to the flight out. This was a photo of a former police officer injured while on duty—two-thirds of her body still had scars from the burn. Marcus Yam could not take a photo that revealed who she was and how she looked. She was still on the run. She'd changed phones and her numbers, burned all her documents and uniform. The biggest challenge for Marcus was to bring these women to life but not reveal their identity. For this, she stood behind a dream-like curtain as though she was ruminating the day of being a police officer again.

Marcus Yam 6

2. Afghan Soldier Looking Out the Window

Marcus Yam was boarding the UH-60 Black Hawk (Marcus called it the 'Ferrari of helicopters') on a resupply mission to Shah Wali Kot district, north of Kandahar, Afghanistan. At this point, the Taliban had taken key territories. The Afghan soldiers were trying to drop soldiers and food to their men in the area now surrounded by Taliban.

The soldier photographed here was about to be dropped off at the outpost.

'It was a look that maybe this was a war they could not win,' said Marcus. 'And maybe he could not make it.'

This photo made the front page of the newspaper. A few months later, Marcus was informed that the soldier did not make it home.

Marcus Yam 7

3. Death from Above

At Al Jadida, Marcus Yam found that civilians died unnecessarily from a US airstrike. ISIS fighters stood at the rooftop as a bait for the allied troops to attack them. But ISIS also hid many civilians in the same building.

'How could you order an airstrike when you hadn't confirmed that there were absolutely no civilians in the building?' said Marcus.

He had followed a few children who brought him around. Then the children disappeared, and a few men suddenly urged him to follow them. Sensing something untoward, Marcus ran back to where he came from. He was just a few blocks away from enemy frontline—he could have been kidnapped.

Marcus Yam 8

4. Iraqi Bomb Defuser, Wissam Daoud

Marcus Yam met Wissam Daoud, a twenty-five-year-old bomb defuser, who followed his father's footsteps of taking a high-risk job that paid $1,000 a month. Wissam Daoud operated at the frontlines—even to the forbidden zones. His job was to defuse the enemy's bombs or turn them against the enemy. Two hundred of his friends had died in the war. Without wearing protective gears, Wissam Daoud brought Marcus into warehouses to defuse bombs.

'The innocent-looking rooms are the deadliest,' said Wissam Daoud. 'Boom!'

Marcus Yam 9

5. California Burning

Marcus Yam has covered almost every major wildfire in California, including the largest one, Thomas Fire. He waited longer than he should have at the top of the hill, and he had to drive through a wall of flame, searing his skin. Another time, a victim named Darl Synder wrote Marcus a note that read:

'Dear Marcus Yam,

I stood a few feet from you when you took this picture of my home. I thought to myself, another vulture sensationalizing on people's misery. After seeing this photograph and looking at your portfolio, I was wrong. You portray human emotion without all the makeup and glamour. You have my respect. My home withstood the test that night, and Old Glory still waves. Today, I replaced that tattered flag with a new and shiny one. I would like you to take care of that old flag for me.

Sincerely,
Darl Snyder.'

Marcus Yam 10

6. Great March of Return

The confrontation between Palestinians and Israelis was the deadliest since the war in 2014. Sixty Palestinians died and 2,700 more were injured.

Marcus Yam 11

7. Oso Landslide

A 'traumatic' disaster that killed forty-three people, the Oso Landslide was memorable to Marcus Yam. 'Within sixty seconds, the neighbourhood vanished, consumed by the thunderous wall of earth . . . Some homes exploded. Others were ripped from their foundations only to be swallowed in a sea of churning mud,' he wrote.

Marcus ran where everyone was leaving. The editors called and urged him to get out. 'Are you crazy? It's still sliding!' They finally found a helicopter to take Marcus out of the scene.

Marcus Yam 12

Key takeaways

- Go where nobody goes. That's how some small countries win Olympic gold medals.
- There is beauty on the other side of conflict. Run into conflict.
- Sample enough by trying different things to find what you're naturally endowed with. Then burrow all the way.

Chapter 9

What We Can Do

Universal Lessons to Make the Country Better

'It used to be thought that the events that changed the world were things like big bombs, maniac politicians, huge earthquakes, or vast population movements, but it has now been realized that this is a very old-fashioned view held by people totally out of touch with modern thought. The things that change the world, according to Chaos theory, are the tiny things. A butterfly flaps its wings in the Amazonian jungle, and subsequently a storm ravages half of Europe.'
— from *Good Omens* by Terry Pratchett and Neil Gaiman

Throughout my year of writing this book, the hardest question to answer was not 'What is this book about?' After multiple refinements, I could answer that question with something to the effect of 'It's about underdogs in Malaysia who applied unconventional tactics to overcome a giant.' The characters in this book were outstanding. Just by describing who they are and what they have done, I would succeed in capturing a moment's attention of a potential reader.

The hardest question, instead, was 'What is the purpose of this book?' It is perhaps insufficient for a person to pick up this book, read the stories, and just feel good about the country, and by extension, humanity. The seven characters did things that were worth learning, but inspiration without action will not make the world better.

The theories found in every chapter explain *why* they succeeded in what they did. But there were also broad themes of action that were universal across all chapters, which may be worthwhile to consider. I have found seven of these universal themes of action, and they were highly persuasive to me to do things bigger than myself.

If you are, like me, eager to see how we could make the world better, you may find these seven themes helpful:

1. Believe in Something and Get Involved

Before the country knew her as 'Aunty Bersih', Anne Ooi was already well known in her community. It was hard not to know who she was, because she was always around her community doing something: Pulling out weeds by the roadside, talking to hawker stall owners about politics, cleaning the common staircase, planting flowers in the balcony, joking with children who were playing football, having tea with the homeless . . . Anne Ooi believed that the world should be left better than how we found it. She also felt strongly for hygiene—she wanted everything clean. Anne Ooi would often take things into her own hands. She did not wait for the local council to cut the grass or pick up the rubbish. She did it herself. The experience of doing community work exposed her to people from different walks of life and gave her a sense of purpose.

When the Bersih rally came about, she had no fear. She already knew her community, her people, and her country. Bersih's message of cleaning up the country of corruption and abuse of power became just another belief she held dearly. Community work and protesting are driven by a common set of beliefs; only the methods were different.

Having a strong belief and acting on it was a common theme for all seven characters of this book. Marcus Yam believed strongly that the world deserved to see the raw images of humanity's worst moments. Nor Salwani Muhammad believed that government audit should be honest and transparent. GSPJ believed that you should help a person in need regardless of race and religion. Peter Kallang believed that his community and its culture ought to be preserved and protected.

What we've learned in this book is that there is power in small numbers. You may not think that believing and doing something in your small way would amount to significant changes. But if this book has shown anything, it is the power of small numbers making a massive change when they come together. Ordinary Malaysians came together, unbeknownst to each other, to protest in Bersih's fourth rally, and that helped tip the scale and ushered the defeat of the longest-ruling coalition in the democratic world.

There is another reason to get involved too: If you don't, others will. And others may not believe the same things you do. In the United States, there is an organization called Run For Something that encourages progressives to run for office. The basic premise is that if progressives do not run, then conservatives will. When that happens, progressives are only left to complain. The bottom line is that someone will run and make policies that fit their beliefs anyway. So, it's best for you to get involved if you genuinely want a future you can call your own.

Progressives around the world are guilty of not participating directly. If you believe in a country that is progressive and open-minded, then it is about time we get involved and do something.

2. Quiet Anger is Good—Resist Firmly but Gently

If you met Peter Kallang in person, you wouldn't have guessed that he is an activist. How could a man so sweet and gentle lead the fight against the gargantuan forces of governments and corporations? The more I talked to him, the more I realized that it was precisely his gentleness that made his fight so effective.

In many southeast Asian countries that have a legacy of colonialism and feudalism, it is not natural for us to protest against authorities. It takes a lot for us to defy orders and rebel for a cause. Even after knowing the corruption scandals of former prime minister, Najib Razak, Malaysians still did not openly curse him. No one went up and yelled at him for siphoning people's money. That is not our style. But that does not mean we are without morals. We simply harbour a form of quiet anger in the way we resist.

Peter Kallang's method is the perfect representation of this. If you watch Peter Kallang's interviews, he never once used expressions or words that were deemed rude or aggressive. While he was frustrated with what went through, he never once crossed the line of personally attacking any of his opponents. Instead, he had to endure mistreatment and hurtful name-calling.

But he did build a blockade—piles of tree trunks stacked onto one another, stopping any vehicles or unauthorized personnel from going in. A blockade is a physical resistance that was not soft at all. It represented his firmness, his anger, but they were neither unreasonable nor violent. Peter Kallang and the blockade were the perfect representation of quiet anger. You ought to be courteous and gentle, but you should not be a pushover. You should use methods that are firm, but not violent.

Quiet anger was something harboured by the other characters in the book who were put in tough situations. Dr Serena Nik-Zainal was not happy with the double standards she saw at the research institute, and she refused to concede until the very end, against her lawyer's advice. But never once did she pursue an aggressive or violent or unethical path that crossed the line. Nor Salwani Muhammad's method of recording, storing, and retaining important evidence relating to audit tampering is another great representation of resisting firmly but gently. Fahmi Reza's anger was evident in his artwork, inspired by punk traditions, but never once did he apply any violent techniques to achieve his goal. In fact, he believed that going overboard would weaken his cause. You need anger, but also restraint.

Erica Chenoweth's paper of non-violence gives foundation to this technique. The reason why quiet anger works is because it makes it easier for others, especially fence-sitters, to buy into your cause. Appearing reasonable and measured, without losing your commitment to the cause, would also likely encourage your opponents to concede, like how the former Sarawak chief minister, Adenan Satem, did for Peter Kallang.

3. Do Even the Smallest Things with Integrity

One thing tourists always complain about when they come to Malaysia is how dirty our public toilets are. They could not understand why a nation of warm and polite people could have such dirty toilets. This is the same country where you find skyscrapers, buildings, and malls that astound from the outside. The reason for this contrast, I think, is the culture of how we treat the little things.

The best test for integrity is what you would do when no one was watching. Perhaps the best example of integrity is the Japanese culture of gift-wrapping. For most cultures, wrapping is merely a way of obscuring the main gift so that there is an element of surprise. Most people know that the recipient of the gift will likely spend only a few seconds on the wrapper before opening them. But the Japanese culture sees even the smallest part of gift-wrapping as important. The concept of Japanese wrapping, *tsutsumi*, is to see the wrapping as part of the gift, like giving a piece of the giver's heart. Even if the gift is merely a small confection, the manual and troublesome task of wrapping it with beauty and care, with a pleasurable unwrapping experience, is worthwhile. The details count. Like how the Japanese design toddler-friendly pavements even though toddlers are the least frequent users. Or how they pay attention to the curvature of a spoon so that you can drink the hot soup without burning your tongue.

That was what I found most fascinating about Nor Salwani Muhammad's story and how she handled the audit tampering case. As an auditor, she cared for the details of the reports and how she kept the secret documents, so that the evidence was complete. She did not do this with the possibility of a high-profile coverage (she abhorred the attention on her). Instead, she took the greatest risk imaginable simply because she performed the smallest things with integrity—a value expounded repeatedly in the department she spent her career.

Remember how Dr Serena Nik-Zainal got started with studying passenger mutations of cancer? 'I wasn't at all sure that it was going to work. I didn't really care . . . My aim wasn't to make it big—it was just to ask stupid questions and learn as much as possible.' Doing the small things, which some people regarded as a waste of time, with integrity.

It was also in how Dilpreet Kaur from GSPJ sorted her care packs for the flood victims. At the most desperate hour, she still cared about the hygiene of the tools given away, separating them into individual packages. The gravy in the food was also starchier than usual so that the victims do not spill when they eat. The team led by Amarraj Singh went to the darkest corners of a village to help an aged resident even though there were no cameras, and the team came back the next day with electrical items when the resident needed them.

In the evenings out on her own, Anne Ooi would be picking up rubbish in the alleyway of a shop lot. No fanfare, no visibility—armed only with integrity for the little things.

4. Follow Values, Not Leaders

There is a perception that southeast Asia prefers strongman rule—occasionally at the expense of democracy. The region is mired with examples of Marcos, Soekarno, Duterte, Mahathir, and Hun Sen, who ruled with an iron fist and displayed performative masculinity. It is tempting to vote in strongmen as leaders so they could magically solve our problems once and for all, like they promised. But what we've also learned is that this is rarely the case. More often than not, strongman rule leaves behind a system that is impoverished and corrupt, necessitating decades of reversal. Supporting leaders regardless of the ethical lines they've crossed is dangerous.

Leaders may change, but values as a nation must stay. The underlying message from the stories of this book is that values ultimately triumph over leaders and circumstances. The leaderless organization of GSPJ, guided only by the values of kindness, helped modern Malaysia's largest flood relief effort succeed. The values of anti-corruption and freedom of expression that Fahmi Reza held dearly enabled him to bring a nationwide consciousness of a massive corruption scandal by a former prime minister, who carried awesome and near-limitless power. The value of equality and justice prompted Dr Serena Nik-Zainal to protest the unequal treatment she experienced even though this required her to go against high-profile leaders with a strong reputation in the field.

Doing what is right is never easy; it often comes with a price. But if you are guided by values and not the people you serve, you are more likely to do what is right and not what is safe and popular. That was the consistent message by the characters in the stories. They did not think it was a big deal to do what they did—they followed their values long held in their hearts.

5. Run into Conflict

One reason polarization exists between races today is the lack of mutual understanding. In Malaysia, it is possible to grow up, from kindergarten to university, and right up to workplaces, to be surrounded only by people of your race. Learning about another race and seeking common ground could be uncomfortable and difficult. And in siloed Malaysia, it is technically possible to avoid them altogether.

Marcus Yam's life story of running into conflict, when most people run away from it, intrigued me. While it is undoubtedly horrifying in that moment of doing, Marcus Yam always talked about the beautiful humanity that he saw on the other side of conflict. He saw extreme altruism when Ukrainians stayed back to defend their village from Russian attacks; mothers in Gaza helping other children to get out of harm's way; the heroic acts of Iraqi bomb defusers who lived everyday like it was their last, defending their fellow countrymen from terrorist attacks.

Groundbreaking research by David Broockman and Joseph Kalla showed that deep, non-confrontational conversations between strangers could reduce identity-based prejudice. By talking about the prejudice they've faced and relating it with the struggle of others who are not like them, it took only ten minutes before decades-long prejudice got significantly reduced. And that reduced prejudice lasted for at least three months, showing that conflict done in an honest and sincere way is more effective than avoidance. Breaking the walls of prejudice starts by taking small acts of conflict.

In a world where algorithms confine us to our respective bubbles to a greater degree, running into conflict by understanding others who are not like us becomes one of the most valuable things to do.

6. Make Space for the Invisible Ones

A country's character is not defined by how many skyscrapers it has, but by how it treats its weakest members. After experiencing imprisonment, the late Nelson Mandela knew that a country's humanity is shown most evidently by looking at how they treat their worst prisoners. A country's constitution is measured by how it accords rights to protect the minorities, not how well it treats its majority.

Dr Serena Nik-Zainal's story was ultimately about making space for the invisible ones. When she first took her PhD, she was a thirty-something Asian mother studying something unknown among young, energetic twenty-something aspirants. When she finally rose up as one of the top cancer researchers in the world, she made it a point to provide the best work environment she knew, where everyone's opinions were valued, and no one was cast aside.

Making space for the invisible ones, typically the shy, introverted, soft-spoken ones who are easily overlooked, would mean that we get the best out of a group without succumbing only to the loudest. To Dr Serena, that may mean adapting and personalizing your approaches to cater to different people. Always think about those who escaped our gaze and give them the opportunity to shine. After all, if we missed the invisible, we wouldn't have known the courage of people like Nor Salwani.

7. Make Brave Art

At every turn of humanity, there is always a special place for art. In a commencement speech in 2012, Neil Gaiman urged graduates to embrace a life of making good art. He said:

'Husband runs off with a politician? Make good art. Leg crushed and then eaten by mutated boa constrictor? Make good art. IRS on your trail? Make good art. Cat exploded? Make good art. Somebody on the internet thinks what you do is stupid or evil or it's all been done before? Make good art. Probably things will work out somehow, and eventually time will take the sting away, but that doesn't matter. Do what only you do best. Make good art.'

There's a magical quality in art. They capture imagination like none other. No matter how many times the corruption of 1Malaysia Development Berhad was brought up, furnished with detailed numbers, it still could not capture a nation's heart like Fahmi Reza's Clown Face could. The same way the Tank versus Bread Biker did for Egypt that ignited the Arab Spring.

To make great art, you must reveal yourself and your innermost feelings about the world, to the world. That takes courage. To reveal your rebellious side that dislikes oppression, corruption, and racism, you need even more courage to make resistance art.

I am convinced that everyone has a creative side that is just waiting to be discovered. If you feel strongly for something, you need to make good art. And if you are a parent, you need to encourage your children to make good art. Make it unapologetically, and stand behind every artist who had the courage to express how they feel.

Acknowledgements

When I asked the subjects whether I could interview them for this book, their first reaction was, 'Are you sure you want to interview *me?*' There is an inherent challenge in writing a book about underdogs— they don't like talking about themselves. Shy, quiet, and away from the spotlight—all of them felt I was mistaken to feature them. Dr Serena Nik-Zainal said she was 'just a mom in a jumper who's trying to get through the day.' Anne Ooi refused to answer a single question about herself. Jagmeet Singh insisted that I talk to four other people at the gurdwara instead, who he thought did more than him. Marcus Yam never talked about himself for more than two sentences. Fahmi Reza took a long time to agree to be interviewed, and only did so if it served a useful public purpose. Peter Kallang asked me, in our fourth interview, if this book featured other people, because 'if it's just about me, it's going to be very boring—nobody's going to read it.'

I am thankful that they eventually agreed, trusted me, and opened their hearts. I am but a vessel to their magnificence. Any shortcomings are my own. I've become a better person after hearing their stories.

In the order of the chapters presented, I am thankful to Anne Ooi, Elaine Pedley, Peter Craig, Kevin Pedley, Ong Khoon Chuan, Dr Serena Nik-Zainal, Hidir Reduan, Emir Zainul, Fahmi Reza, Cheng Chean, Peter Kallang, Way Loon, John Tan, Jagmeet Singh, Jagdave Singh, Pavandeep Singh, Amarraj Singh, Dilpreet Kaur, Gurdwara Sahib Petaling Jaya, and Marcus Yam.

My special thanks to Nora Abu Bakar for opening the door of Penguin Random House SEA and taking a chance on me. This book would not have seen the light of the day had it not been for the marvellous eyes and hearts of the Penguin editorial and marketing team. Working with all of you has been the honour of my life.

This book would not have been possible without the generous support of The Fan Yew Teng Grant for Independent Writing 2023. I first read a book about the late Fan Yew Teng, called *The Sweet Rebel*, when I was a teenager. His spirit of defiance lives on these pages.

Initially I thought that writing a book was like writing a long essay. I was wrong. Many people had to endure reading my terrible early drafts. I'm thankful to Christine Helliwell, Edwin Goh, and Lily Chai for reading and providing invaluable reader feedback; Mervyn Lai for providing legal advice; Sandra C for keeping me sane. I'm also thankful for my parents who taught me the value of unbridled optimism and passion for my country. I'm also held steady by the love of family and friends. It's true that what people don't see behind every book is that the painful process of writing a book actually falls hardest on those closest to the writer. For this case, it was Ida Thien, who also provided the beautiful portraits at the start of every chapter (which arguably may be the main reason for buying this book). She was patient with my fluctuating emotions and gave me often painful, but necessary, feedback that made my final draft infinitely better than the first. Thank you for staying all the way.

Endnotes

Chapter 1

1. **Among the manuscripts was a 120-page small booklet . . .** Proudfoot, I. (2001). A "Chinese" Mousedeer Goes to Paris. Archipel, 61(1), 69–97. https://doi.org/10.3406/arch.2001.3613
2. **'It is an animal about the size of a cat.'** The Adventures of Mouse Deer (Malaysian, Indonesian Folktales). (n.d.). www.aaronshep. com. Retrieved October 26, 2020, from http://www.aaronshep. com/stories/R01.html
3. **It has wide eyes and a small stubby tail . . .** Quah Wai Kheong, C., Harris Satkunananthan, A., & Ismail Hamdan, S. (2019). Sang Kancil as Cultural Artefact: A Comparative Neo-Archetypal Study. *GEMA Online Journal of Language Studies*, 19(4), 243–257. https://doi.org/10.17576/gema-2019-1904-13
4. Story adapted from this translation: McKean, P. F. (1971). The Mouse-deer ("Kantjil") in Malayo-Indonesian Folklore: Alternative Analyses and the Significance of a Trickster Figure in South-East Asia. *Asian Folklore Studies*, 30(1), 71. https://doi. org/10.2307/1177765
5. **Revered author Benedict Anderson once talked about how cultural artefacts . . .** Anderson, B. (2016). *Imagined Communities Reflections on the Origin and Spread of Nationalism*. Paw Prints.

Chapter 2

1. **Death threat . . .** Kamal, S. M. (2011, June 23). Ambiga receives SMS death threat. *The Malaysian Insider*. https://web.archive.org/

web/20110624160125/http://www.themalaysianinsider.com/
malaysia/article/ambiga-receives-sms-death-threat/

2. **Ibrahim Ali's threats.** Sabri, A. R. (2011, June 20). Anything
   can happen on July 9, warns Perkasa. *MalaysiaKini*. https://www.
   malaysiakini.com/news/167389

3. **The then prime minister warned against chaos . . .** Anis, M. N.
   (n.d.). PM: July 9 rally organisers will be held responsible if chaos
   erupts (Updated). *The Star*. Retrieved February 13, 2023, from
   https://www.thestar.com.my/news/nation/2011/06/26/pm-
   july-9-rally-organisers-will-be-held-responsible-if-chaos-
   erupts-updated/

4. **The home minister called the rally 'illegal' . . .** Sipalan, J. (2011,
   July 6). Home minister: Bersih still illegal. *Malaysiakini*. https://
   www.malaysiakini.com/news/169094

5. **'I cannot stand rubbish . . .'** Chung, H. (2011, August 14). The
   face that launched a thousand protests. The Rocket. https://www.
   therocket.com.my/en/the-face-that-launched-a-thousand-protests/

6. **The oldest voter . . .** Watchdogs believe flaws to Malaysia voter list
   "tip of the iceberg." (2018, May 3). *Reuters*. https://www.reuters.
   com/article/us-malaysia-election-bersih-idUSKBN1I410T

7. **Mysterious power outages . . .** AFP. From dead voters to blackouts:
   Malaysia braces for "filthy" poll. *Bangkok Post*. Retrieved July 21,
   2022, from https://www.bangkokpost.com/world/1454769/from-
   dead-voters-to-blackouts-malaysia-braces-for-filthy-poll

8. **Operation Erase Bersih . . .** Associated Press in Kuala Lumpur (2011,
   July 9). Malaysia police detain hundreds at rally. *The Guardian*.
   https://www.theguardian.com/world/2011/jul/09/malaysia-
   opposition-protests-elections

9. **Anne spent the first hour finding a way into the protest . . .** Team,
   D. T. and C. U. (n.d.). BERSIH "Lady of Liberty", Annie Ooi
   Siew Lan, umur 65...amacam B– pondan? - I–u Semasa–– Semasa -
   Forum. CARI Infonet. Retrieved February 13, 2023, from http://b.
   cari.com.my/forum.php?mod=viewthread&tid=585301

10. **'Blood and bandage' . . .** Southgate, A., & Bracken, G. B. (2014).
    A Walking Tour Kuala Lumpur (2nd edition). In Google Books.
    Marshall Cavendish International Asia Pte Ltd. https://books.

google.com.my/books?id=Ex0dAwAAQBAJ&pg=PT48&redir_esc=y#v=onepage&q&f=false

11. **Account of ballooning crowd.** Razak, A. (2011, July 10). Fortress KL: How did Bersih 2.0 slip past? *Malaysiakini*. https://www.malaysiakini.com/news/169444

12. **Within two minutes of turning the corner towards the square . . .** Asia Times Online. Malaysia nips an hibiscus uprising. (2011, July 11). Web.archive.org. https://web.archive.org/web/20110711200613/http://atimes.com/atimes/Southeast_Asia/MG12Ae01.html

13. **It causes pain so great . . .** How Does Tear Gas Work? (n.d.). Www.youtube.com. Retrieved February 10, 2023, from https://www.youtube.com/watch?v=agXnXHfGc3k

14. **The gas stabs into your eyes, overflowing them with tears . . .** What does it feel like being tear gassed? (2019). Quora. https://www.quora.com/What-does-it-feel-like-being-tear-gassed

15. **No goggles, no masks, no protection, no salt . . .** The Malaysian Insider. "Lady of Liberty" at Bersih march draws online support (2011, July 12). Web.archive.org. https://web.archive.org/web/20110712213904/http:/www.themalaysianinsider.com/malaysia/article/lady-of-liberty-at-bersih-march-draws-online-support

16. **Iconic photo of Lady of Liberty by Hugo Teng.** https://www.therocket.com.my/en/the-face-that-launched-a-thousand-protests/ (Explicit permission has been obtained from Hugo Teng for use).

17. **Video tributes, poems, posters . . .** Koleksi Poster Kempen Politik. La–y Bersih - Aunty Anne. (2011, July 14). http://haha-politik.blogspot.com/2011/07/lady-bersih-aunty-anne.html

18. **Video on YouTube amassed forty-seven million views . . .** Tortoise–vs. Hare - Who Wins? (n.d.). YouTube. Retrieved February 13, 2023, from https://www.youtube.com/watch?v=m7NuVjpi72c

19. **Death of Baharudin Ahmad.** Sabri, A. R. (2011, July 10). 500 attend Bersih rally supporter's burial. *Malaysiakini*. https://www.malaysiakini.com/news/169480

20. **Zalina Abdullah's comment.** Anjung Setiawangsa. TABIK SPRING UNTUK AUNTIE BERSIH! http://anjungsetiawangsa. blogspot.com/2011/07/tabik-spring-untuk-auntie-bersih.html

21. **'Are you afraid of being handcuffed or put in jail?'** I've met Aun–y Bersih - Malaysia Lady of Liberty @ KLCC. Retrieved February 13, 2023, from https://www.tianchad.com/2012/09/ meet-aunty-bersih-malaysia-lady-of-liberty.html

22. **'Why are you making me wait?'** Aiman, A. (2018, October 18) At 72, Aunty Bersih still going strong. *Free Malaysia Today.* htts:// www.freemalaysiatoday.com/category/nation/2018/10/18/at-72- aunty-bersih-still-going-strong/

23. **'Walk proudly! Don't run like cowards!'** (2013, May 24) Auntie Bersih gives vigil-goers words of wisdom. YouTube. Retrieved February 13, 2023, from https://www.youtube.com/ watch?v=XuBsduqgLGo

24. **Poem for Aunty Bersih.** Lim Kit Siang. Aunty Bersih, Annie Ooi. Retrieved February 13, 2023, from https://blog.limkitsiang. com/2013/07/30/aunty-bersih-annie-ooi/

25. **Success rate of non-violence resistance.** Chenoweth, E., & Stephan, M. J. (2011). *Why Civil Resistance Works: The Strategic Logic of Nonviolent Conflict.* Columbia University Press. http://cup. columbia.edu/book/why-civil-resistance-works/9780231156820

26. **Peak Popular Participation and the 3.5 per cent rule.** Chenoweth, E. (2020). Questions, Answers, and Some Cautionary Updates Regarding the 3.5% Rule. Carr Center Discussion Paper Series, 2020-005. https://carrcenter.hks.harvard.edu/ publications/questions-answers-and-some-cautionary-updates- regarding-35-rule

27. **. . . only 50,000 people turned up** (and other Bersih protest participation numbers). Leong, C. et al (2020). Digital organizing of a global social movement: From connective to collective action. Information and Organization. Volume 30, Issue 4. December 2020, 100324. https://www.sciencedirect.com/science/article/pii/ S1471772720300488

Chapter 3

1. **Scientists only found out that genes are made of DNA in 1952** . . . Genomes.gov. Genetic Timeline. https://www.genome.gov/Pages/Education/GeneticTimeline.pdf

2. **Malaysian dream team to Sydney for open-heart surgery.** Dr Wathooth, R. (2021, June 27). Remembering the "Dream Team" by one of Malaysia's pioneering cardiothoracic surgeons. *New Straits Times.* https://www.nst.com.my/Lifestyle/sunday-vibes/2021/06/702656/remembering-dream-team-one-malaysias-pioneering-cardiothoracic

3. **Dr Rozali Wathooth's quote of Dr Nik-Zainal.** "TOKOH NEGARA MALAYSIA: Datuk Dr Nik Zainal Abidin Nik Abdul Rahman." (2014, April 3). *TOKOH NEGARA MALAYSIA.* Accessed February 17, 2023. http://penatokoh.blogspot.com/2014/04/datuk-dr-nik-zainal-abidin-nik-abdul.html

4. **Clean toilets.** Rahim, S. (2019, October 18). Dr Serena wins cancer research prize. *New Straits Times.* https://www.nst.com.my/news/exclusive/2019/10/531038/dr-serena-wins-cancer-research-prize

5. **Cancer dependent on computers and number crunchers.** McKie, Robin. (2010, May 29) "Genetics: The Number Crunchers Who Are Saving Lives." *The Guardian.* https://www.theguardian.com/theobserver/2010/may/30/dna-human-genome-project-sanger

6. **The first fifteen close-knit scientists who contributed** . . . "The Quest to Know Everything: 25 Years of the Sanger Institute." (2018, October 4). *Wellcome,* https://wellcome.org/news/quest-know-everything-25-years-sanger-institute

7. **Producing a couple of genomes every twenty-four hours** . . . McKie, R. (2010, May 30). The number crunchers who are saving lives. *The Guardian.* https://www.theguardian.com/theobserver/2010/may/30/dna-human-genome-project-sanger

8. **Most visitors who come to Sanger Institute...** (footnote). https://www.artcontact.co.uk/projects/wellcome-trust-you/

9. **Professor Leena Peltonen.** Prof. Leena Peltonen (Profile). Wellcome Sanger Institute. https://www.sanger.ac.uk/external_person/peltonen-leena/

10. **Beach analogy.** Cambridge Sci Soc (2020, November 9). DNA: Building blocks that made me a learner in perpetuity | Dr Serena Nik-Zainal. YouTube. https://www.youtube.com/watch?v=bWn0ien0aXI

11. **Joshua Barnfathers' career background.** Joshua Barnfather (Profile). *LinkedIn.* https://uk.linkedin.com/in/joshua-barnfather

12. **'[We] realize that the standard treatment doesn't quite fit me . . .'** Joshua Barnfather (Video). Facebook. https://m.facebook.com/watch/?v=1176296909195775&_rdr

13. **Chart of Joshua Barnfather's illness.** Momen, S. et al (2019). Dramatic response of metastatic cutaneous angiosarcoma to an immune checkpoint inhibitor in a patient with xeroderma pigmentosum: whole-genome sequencing aids treatment decision in end-stage disease. *Cold Spring Harbor Molecular Case Studies.* http://molecularcasestudies.cshlp.org/content/5/5/a004408.full.pdf

14. **'Joshua's former high school, Withersea High School...** (footnote). Read more: http://www.withernseahigh.org.uk/latest-news/this-month/1052-treatment-progressing-well-for-former-student-josh

15. **Pygmalion in the Classroom.** Rosenthal, R. and Jacobson, L. (1968, September). Pygmalion in the classroom. *Springer Link.* https://link.springer.com/article/10.1007/BF02322211

16. **Golem Effect.** Reynolds, D. (2007). Restraining Golem and Harnessing Pygmalion in the Classroom: A Laboratory Study of Managerial Expectations and Task Design. *Academy of Management Learning & Education.* https://web.archive.org/web/20160820092827/http://www.rhetcomp.gsu.edu/~gpullman/3080/articles/Golem%20and%20Pygmalion.pdf

17. **Mouse target experiment.** Mouse target. *Sendvid.* https://sendvid.com/23jxr8uj

18. **'What happens when we think that others expect us to fail?'** Nurmohamed, S. (2020, January 14). The Upside of Being an Underdog. *Harvard Business Review.* https://hbr.org/2020/01/the-upside-of-being-an-underdog

19. **Howard Schultz, Jermaine Cole, Aly Raisman.** Nurmohamed, S. (2020, August 24). The Underdog Effect: When Low Expectations Increase Performance. *Academy of Management Journal, Vol 63, No 4.* https://journals.aom.org/doi/abs/10.5465/amj.2017.0181

20. **'Even when the cost part is settled, many doctors still fear . . .'** Tan, Z.Y. (2019, July 18) Cutting Edge: Cancer and genome. *The Edge Malaysia.* https://www.theedgemarkets.com/article/cutting-edge-cancer-and-genome

21. **Bullying statistics in academia.** Keashly, L. (2019, April 27). Workplace Bullying, Mobbing and Harassment in Academe: Faculty Experience. *Part of the Handbooks of Workplace Bullying, Emotional Abuse and Harassment book series.* https://link.springer.com/referenceworkentry/10.1007/978-981-10-5154-8_13-1

22. **Bullying in academia is twice as high than other workplaces.** Else, H. (2018, November 28). Does science have a bullying problem? *Nature.* https://www.nature.com/articles/d41586-018-07532-5

23. **Tania Singer's case.** Kupferschmidt, K. (2018, August 8). She's the world's top empathy researcher. But colleagues say she bullied and intimidated them. *Science.* https://www.science.org/content/article/she-s-world-s-top-empathy-researcher-colleagues-say-she-bullied-and-intimidated-them

24. **'They're going to explode'.** Devlin, H. (2018, August 29). In the science lab, some bullies can thrive unchecked for decades. *The Guardian.* https://www.theguardian.com/science/2018/aug/29/science-lab-bullying-claims-at-odds-noble-ideals

25. **'Toed the line and stayed in the box'.** Liew, J. (2019, December 5). Award-Winning Malaysian Scientist Dr Serena Nik-Zainal Speaks Up About Breaking The Glass Ceiling. *Tatler.* https://www.tatlerasia.com/power-purpose/ideas-education/my-scientist-dr-serena-nik-zainal-dr-josef-steiner-cancer-research-prize

26. **'Bosses at leading UK science institute accused of bullying staff.'** Marsh, S. and Devlin, H. (2018, August 28). Bosses at leading UK science institute accused of bullying staff. *Guardian.* https://www.

theguardian.com/science/2018/aug/29/wellcome-sanger-institute-bosses-accused-bullying-staff

27. **Interview by Serena Nik-Zainal.** Nik-Zainal, S. (2018, September 25). The duty to speak up. *Nat Cell Biol, 2018 Sept; 20(9); 1006.* https://www.ncbi.nlm.nih.gov/pmc/articles/PMC6155444/

28. **300 academic staff bullied in the past year alone . . .** Devlin, H. and Marsh, S. (2018, September 28). Hundreds of academics at top UK universities accused of bullying. *Guardian.* https://www.theguardian.com/education/2018/sep/28/academics-uk-universities-accused-bullying-students-colleagues

29. **Interviewed 22 complainants and all 23 signed witnesses . . .** and **'THE REST OF US WERE RESTRICTED . . .'** Nik-Zainal, S. (@SerenaNikZainal) (2018, November 9). Twitter. https://twitter.com/SerenaNikZainal/status/1060616211019558912?s=20

30. **Nazneen Rahman's case.** Else, H. (2018, August 17). Top geneticist loses £3.5-million grant in first test of landmark bullying policy. *Nature.* https://www.nature.com/articles/d41586-018-06009-9

31. **Stellenbosch University wrote to the Sanger Institute . . .** Njilo, N. (2019, October 16). Stellenbosch University demands return of DNA samples—but UK lab hits back. *Times LIVE.* https://www.timeslive.co.za/news/south-africa/2019-10-16-stellenbosch-university-demands-return-of-dna-samples-but-uk-lab-hits-back/

32. **'It's great to see the silence around this being broken . . .'** Dr Gurdasani, D. (@dgurdasani1)(2019, October 19). *Twitter* https://twitter.com/dgurdasani1/status/1183657375833694208

33. **Building of the University of Bern.** Main building, Hoch schulstrasse 4, Universitat Bern. https://www.unibe.ch/university/portrait/history/history_and_architecture/main_building_hochschulstrasse_4/index_eng.html

34. **Josef Steiner Award.** Academic Department of Medical Genetics (2019, October 16). Award Ceremony of the Dr Josef Steiner Cancer Research prize. *University of Cambridge.* https://medgen.medschl.cam.ac.uk/blog/award-ceremony-of-the-dr-josef-steiner-cancer-research-prize/

35. **The Francis Crick Medal and Lecture 2022** (footnote). Read more: https://royalsociety.org/grants-schemes-awards/awards/francis-crick-lecture/

Chapter 4

1. Nor Salwani Muhammad did not accept the interview request for this book. This chapter relied extensively on publicly available information and witness accounts. My admiration for Nor Salwani remains.

2. **'How do I explain to my eleven-year-old son [audit]?'** Garg, A. (2016). How do I explain to my 11-year-old son the difference between an internal and an external audit? *Quora.* https://www.quora.com/How-do-I-explain-to-my-11-year-old-son-the-difference-between-an-internal-and-an-external-audit

3. **To audit the highly controversial 1MDB . . .** and **What would have taken five months . . .** Tay, C. (2019, December 18). 1MDB Audit Report Tampering Trial: Ambrin's thankless audit of 1MDB. *The Edge Weekly.* https://www.theedgemarkets.com/article/1mdb-audit-report-tampering-trial-ambrins-thankless-audit-1mdb

4. **Three of the Big Four accounting firms fired or terminated . . .** Wong, J.I. (2018, May 23). There's only one untainted "Big Four" accounting firm left to audit Malaysia's scandal-ridden wealth fund. *Quartz.* https://qz.com/1286534/pwc-is-the-last-big-four-accounting-firm-untainted-by-1mdb/

5. **KPMG took the mantle for two years after that . . .** Pua, T. (2021, May 11). Where's 1MDB suit against former auditor KPMG? *Malaysiakini.* https://www.malaysiakini.com/columns/574213

6. **Mohd Hazem felt pressured, and thus suggested for KPMG to be dropped . . .** Zainul, E. and Achariam, T. (2020, September 15). 1MDB ex-CEO: Najib pressured me to replace 1MDB auditor. *The Edge.* https://www.theedgemarkets.com/article/1mdb-exceo-najib-pressured-me-replace-1mdb-auditor

7. **Largest ever by the US Department of Justice.** The United States Department of Justice (2016, July 20). Attorney General Loretta E. Lynch Delivers Remarks at Press Conference Announcing Significant Kleptocracy Enforcement Action to Recover More Than $1 Billion Obtained from Corruption Involving Malaysian Sovereign Wealth Fund. https://www.justice.gov/opa/speech/attorney-general-loretta-e-lynch-delivers-remarks-press-conference-announcing-significant

8. **A week later, Deloitte resigned . . .** Yatim, H. (2021, March 3). Putrajaya settles with Deloitte for RM324m in relation to 1MDB scandal. *The Edge.* https://www.theedgemarkets.com/article/putrajaya-settles-deloitte-rm324m-relation-1mdb-scandal

9. **A special audit is an audit requested...** (footnote). https://www.theedgemarkets.com/article/1mdb-audit-report-only-special-audit-report-najib-asked-see-and-amend-it-was-presented-pac

10. **'[F]inancial statement for 1MDB was [given] only until March 2014 . . .'** Yatim, H. and Zainul. E. (2020, August 24). Ambrin: Watermark-bearing audit report would have been given to PAC if not for amendments sought by Najib. *The Edge.* https://www.theedgemarkets.com/article/ambrin-watermarkbearing-audit-report-would-have-been-given-pac-if-not-amendments-sought

11. **Constitutional right of Auditor General to receive documents.** Audit Act 1957 (Act 62), Laws of Malaysia. https://tcclaw.com.my/wp-content/uploads/2020/12/Audit-Act-1957.pdf

12. **Arul Kanda prevented auditors from photocopying documents.** Singh, S. (2019, October 14). 'I want to peel this like an onion . . . layer by layer'. *New Straits Times.* https://www.nst.com.my/news/crime-courts/2019/10/529922/i-want-peel-onionlayer-layer

13. **'I met [Arul] many times, but information never came . . .'** Reduan, H and Mohd, H. (2020, Jan 16). Day 9: Arul Kanda promised full information but only provided 60 pct, court hears. *Malaysiakini.* https://www.malaysiakini.com/news/507343

14. **In the history of special audits . . .** Ikram, I. and Achariam, T. (2021, October 20). 1MDB audit report the only special audit report Najib asked to see and amend before it was presented to PAC. *The Edge.* https://www.theedgemarkets.com/article/1mdb-audit-report-only-special-audit-report-najib-asked-see-and-amend-it-was-presented-pac

15. **Ali Hamsa told the civil service to not 'bite the hand that feeds you.'** KiniTV (2017, March 28). Ali Hamsa: Don't bite hand that feeds you because of lies. https://www.youtube.com/watch?v=vYTFVz14s3Y

16. **Pokemon Go ban.** Perbadanan Kemajuan Negeri Pahang (2016, August 10). Ali Hamsa: No notice on game for civil servants yet.

https://www.pknp.gov.my/index.php/akhbar/598-ali-hamsa-no-notice-on-game-for-civil-servants-yet

17. **Nor Salwani didn't have time to tell anyone her concerns . . .** and **Shafee: Are you so unethical . . .** Singh, S. (2019, November 21). Gutsy officer's audio recording becomes highlight of 1MDB audit report trial. *New Straits Times.* https://www.nst.com.my/news/crime-courts/2019/11/540823/gutsy-officers-audio-recording-becomes-highlight-1mdb-audit-report

18. **Talking points for coordination meeting.** Zainul, E. and Yatim, H. (2020, August 24). Najib told me 'talking points' will be provided for 1MDB audit report coordination meeting—Ali Hamsa. *The Edge.* https://www.theedgemarkets.com/article/najib-told-me-talking-points-will-be-provided-1mdb-audit-report-coordination-meeting-%E2%80%94-ali

19. **'So that's why I thought we can go through some areas of concern . . .'** Zainul, E. and Tay, C. (2019, November 29). 'Government very worried about audit report'. *The Edge.* https://www.theedgemarkets.com/article/government-very-worried-about-audit-report

20. **'Another version of the financial statement sent to the Finance Ministry . . ."** Reduan, H. and Mohd, H. (2020, January 13). Ali Hamsa called original 1MDB audit report content 'dangerous material evidence'. *Malaysiakini.* https://www.malaysiakini.com/news/506958

21. **"He was the prime minister, I had no reason to not believe him . . ."** Reduan, H. and Asyraf, F. (2019, November 27). Day 5: Audio recording of crucial meeting replayed. *Malaysiakini.* https://www.malaysiakini.com/news/501388 and https://www.theedgemarkets.com/article/ambrin-watermarkbearing-audit-report-would-have-been-given-pac-if-not-amendments-sought

22. **With a chubby baby face and a penchant for a lavish lifestyle . . .** Bloomberg (2022, February 16). Malaysia 1MDB scandal: jury hears Jho Low 'partied like there was no tomorrow', paid US$385,000 bar bill. *South China Morning Post.* https://www.scmp.com/news/asia/southeast-asia/article/3167240/malaysia-1mdb-scandal-jury-hears-jho-low-partied-there-was

23. **1MDB transferred up to US$1 billion to 1MDB PetroSaudi Ltd . . .** Yatim, H, Tay, C., and Shankar, A.C. (2019, November 19). What were removed from the 1MDB audit report. *The Edge.* https://www.theedgemarkets.com/article/what-were-removed-1mdb-audit-report

24. **"It was difficult, it was almost like an instruction."** Reduan, H. (2020, August 13). Ali Hamsa told me to keep my opinion out of 1MDB audit report. *Malaysiakini.* https://www.malaysiakini.com/news/538458

25. **To quell all kinds of refutation, Ali turned to Ambrin . . .** and **"Don't worry, you can speak freely . . ."** and **"In the end, there should not be two or three versions . . ."** Zainul, E. (2019, December 12). 1MDB Audit Report Tampering Trial: To Ali, Najib's interests were national interest. *The Edge.* https://www.theedgemarkets.com/article/1mdb-audit-report-tampering-trial-ali-najibs-interests-were-national-interest

26. **That means "people accept a hierarchical order in which everybody has a place . . ."** Malaysia. Hofstede Insights. https://www.hofstede-insights.com/country/malaysia/

27. **A year before the meeting, the Attorney General and his deputy prime minister was sacked . . .** The Associated Press (2015, July 28). Facing corruption scandal, Malaysian PM fires officials investigating him. *Al Jazeera America.* http://america.aljazeera.com/articles/2015/7/28/malaysias-najib-razak-sacks-attorney-general.html

28. **[The threats] may come from the previous [Najib] government...** Yatim, H., Aziz, A., and Zainul, E. (2019, September 20). Najib still powerful enough to create 'instability' in my livelihood, says witness. *The Edge.* https://www.theedgemarkets.com/article/najib-still-powerful-enough-create-instability-my-livelihood-says-witness

29. **Do not print the 1MDB Audit Report...** Reduan, H. and Mohd, H. (2020, Jan 13). Day 7: Recording of Ali Hamsa's concern about 1MDB audit report played in court. *Malaysiakini.* https://www.malaysiakini.com/news/506892

30. . . . 'resolute and steady.' Interview with journalist, Hidir Reduan, who covered the case for MalaysiaKini.

31. In a corruption trial against former prime minister's wife... (footnote). https://www.theedgemarkets.com/article/rosmah-tells-sri-ram-not-raise-his-voice-her

32. "At first I'm inside the meeting room . . ." Lim, I. (2019, November 21). The pencil case story: How meeting to alter 1MDB audit report was recorded without anyone knowing. *The Malay Mail Online.* https://www.malaymail.com/news/malaysia/2019/11/21/how-the-meeting-to-alter-1mdb-audit-report-was-recorded-without-anyone-know/1812075 and Mohd, H. and Reduan, H. (2019, November 21). Salwani—The person who saved the original 1MDB audit report. *Malaysiakini.* https://m.malaysiakini.com/news/500730 and Bernama (2019, November 22). 'I slipped voice recorder into pencil case', witness tells court. *The Borneo Post.* https://www.theborneopost.com/2019/11/22/i-slipped-voice-recorder-into-pencil-case-witness-tells-court/

33. "After I switched off the recording device..." Reduan, H. (2020, October 13). 11 more prosecution witnesses for Najib-Arul Kanda 1MDB audit report trial. *Malaysiakini.* https://www.malaysiakini.com/news/546397

34. After learning about the ins and outs, Madinah would conclude... Achariam, T. and Palani, T. (2022, March 30). Former auditor-general Madinah says she was 'shocked' on discovering 1MDB audit report was tampered with. *The Edge.* https://www.theedgemarkets.com/article/former-auditorgeneral-madinah-says-she-was-shocked-discovering-1mdb-audit-report-was

35. Salwani Act. Beza antara "Saya yang menurut perintah" dengan "Saya yang menjalankan amanah". Reddit. https://www.reddit.com/r/malaysia/comments/dzvgaa/beza_di_antara_saya_yang_menurut_perintah_dengan/

36. Extraverted qualities give 25% higher chance of getting a job. Rentfrow, J,. and De Vries, R. (2016, January 16). A Winning Personality. *The Sutton Trust.* https://www.suttontrust.com/

our-research/a-winning-personality-confidence-aspirations-social-mobility/

37. **65% senior executive see quietness as a barrier.** Featherstone, E. (2018, February 23). How extroverts are taking the top jobs— and what introverts can do about it. *The Guardian.* https://www.theguardian.com/business-to-business/2018/feb/23/how-extroverts-are-taking-the-top-jobs-and-what-introverts-can-do-about-it

38. **Or you could even take a pill called Paxil . . .** Shah, R. (2021, January 20). Extrovert Leaders: Do They Have an Unfair Advantage? *Shortform.* https://www.shortform.com/blog/extrovert-leaders/

39. **Princeton study on 100 milliseconds to decide . . .** Boutin, C. (2006, August 22). Snap judgments decide a face's character, psychologist finds. *Princeton University.* https://www.princeton.edu/news/2006/08/22/snap-judgments-decide-faces-character-psychologist-finds

40. **Halo over their heads.** Perera, A. (2021, March 22). Why the Halo Effect Affects How We Perceive Others. *Simply Psychology.* https://www.simplypsychology.org/halo-effect.html

41. **Sharply dressed in expensive clothes and well-groomed with a combed-back white hair . . .** Bernama (2019, June 21). Counsel tells court Shafee has three wives, won't flee. *Malaysiakini.* https://www.malaysiakini.com/news/480640

42. **He would accept interviews by newspapers to talk about his achievements . . .** Anbalagan, V. (2015, July 24). Shafee wins appeal against professional misconduct. *Malaysian Bar.* https://www.malaysianbar.org.my/article/news/legal-and-general-news/legal-news/shafee-wins-appeal-against-professional-misconduct

43. **After winning a controversial case against Anwar Ibrahim . . .** Yatim, H. (2015, February 17). Ex-AG frowns at Shafee's self-promotion. *Malaysiakini.* https://www.malaysiakini.com/news/289550

44. **"I was working together with the current senior officials . . ."** Zainul, E. and Achariam, T. (2021, February 23). Nor Salwani: I was nominated for Datukship even before I testified against

Najib. *The Edge.* https://www.theedgemarkets.com/article/nor-salwani-i-was-nominated-datukship-even-i-testified-against-najib

45. **Middle manager research by Quy Huy.** Huy, Q. (2001, September). In Praise of Middle Managers. *Harvard Business Review.* https://hbr.org/2001/09/in-praise-of-middle-managers

Chapter 5

1. This chapter substantially benefited from the only known biography of Fahmi Reza, entitled *Anatomy of a Graphic Designer*, written by Vinod J. Nair.

2. **Middle fingered caricature of the former prime minister Mahathir Mohamad.** Malaysiakini (2016, June 4). Mahathir speechless over middle finger-flauntiictatorr diktator' likeness. *Malaysiakini.* https://www.malaysiakini.com/news/344108

3. **To which Fahmi Reza replied...** (foonote). https://twitter.com/kuasasiswa/status/1384885088840822785

4. **At that time, the Malaysian government under Mahathir Mohamad was pushing for more opportunities . . .** Lee, H.A. (2021, November 23). The New Economic Policy Beyond Fifty: Assessing its Strengths and Weaknesses to Chart a Cohesive Malaysian Society. *Institute for Democracy and Economic Affairs.* https://www.ideas.org.my/publications-item/policy-paper-no-73-the-new-economic-policy-beyond-fifty-assessing-its-strengths-and-weaknesses-to-chart-a-cohesive-malaysian-society/

5. **Ransom note in punk style.** Andersen, K. Ransom Note by gryren on DeviantArt. Pinterest. https://www.pinterest.com/pin/383087512045235172/

6. **The 600-page report concluded that there were "extensive and consistent abuse . . ."** Human Rights Watch (2014, April 1). "No Answers, No Apology". *Human Rights Watch.* https://www.hrw.org/report/2014/04/01/no-answers-no-apology/police-abuses-and-accountability-malaysia#_ftn18

7. **And then the policemen, one in grey and another in white . . .** and **On one occasion, he even brought up the 2004 police beating . . .** Reza, F. (2016, February 3). Kenapa aku berani? Sebab

ini bukan 1st time . . . Twitter. https://twitter.com/kuasasiswa/
status/694732803456389120/photo/1

8. **Below is the 5-minute-and-35-second recording . . .**
OccupyDataran (2012, April 24). Fahmi Reza & Umar Azmi
ditangkap di Occupy Dataran, 22 Apr 2012, 8.00am. YouTube.
https://www.youtube.com/watch?v=RePEkMd9QVo (edited for
readability)

9. **DBKL and the police were ordered to pay Fahmi compensation**
. . . Kumar, K. (2015, October 2). Fahmi Reza to donate RM38k
from court win to activism fund. *The Malay Mail Online.* https://
www.malaymail.com/news/malaysia/2015/10/02/fahmi-reza-to-
donate-rm38k-from-court-win-to-activism-fund/980321#sthash.
Fs4Ervmz.dpuf

10. **He posted this on his social media after the verdict . . .** Wee,
H.T. (2015, October 2). Fahmi Reza: Vindicated by the Court
of Appeal. *weehingthong.* https://weehingthong.org/2015/10/02/
fahmi-reza-vindicated-by-the-court-of-appealhttpswordpress-
compost27055337new/

11. **For their later life, they have decided to dedicate their lives
to environmental causes.** Wasserman, J. (2002, November
4). California Coast Gets Intrepid Internet Watchdog. *The
Washington Post.* https://www.washingtonpost.com/archive/
politics/2002/11/04/california-coast-gets-intrepid-internet-
watchdog/41997c76-9243-4259-b69b-065df3fb9734/

12. **The Adelman Family Homepage website.** The Adelman Family
Homepage. https://www.adelman.com

13. **All these photos would be uploaded to a website called . . .**
Barbra Streisand Sues to Suppress Free Speech Protection for
Widely Acclaimed Website: www.Californiacoastline.org https://
www.californiacoastline.org/streisand/pressrelease-lawsuit.pdf

14. **Website visit ballooned to 420,000 per month.** Parkinson, J.
(2014, July 31). The perils of the Streisand Effect. *BBC News.*
https://www.bbc.com/news/magazine-28562156

15. **'Largest kleptocracy case to date'.** FBI (2016, July 20).
International Corruption. US Seeks to Recover $1 Billion in Largest

Kleptocracy Case to Date. *FBI.* https://www.fbi.gov/news/stories/
us-seeks-to-recover-1-billion-in-largest-kleptocracy-case-to-date

16. **The scandal involved billions of dollars . . .** Chen, H., Ponniah,
K., and Lin, M.M. (2019, August 9). 1MDB: The playboys, PMs
and party-goers around a global financial scandal. *BBC News.*
https://www.bbc.com/news/world-asia-46341603

17. **'A dark era of repression'.** Agence Francce-Presse (2015, July 6).
Malaysian taskforce investigates allegations $700m paid to PM
Najib. *The Guardian.* https://www.theguardian.com/world/2015/
jul/06/malaysian-task-force-investigates-allegations-700m-paid-
to-pm-najib

18. **'Individual who defamed the portrait of the country's leader
is facing jail and/or fine.'** Amnesty International (2016, March
11). Malaysia: End unprecedented crackdown on hundreds of
critics. *Amnesty International.* https://www.amnesty.org/en/latest/
press-release/2016/03/malaysia-end-unprecedented-crackdown-
on-hundreds-of-critics-through-sedition-act/

19. **So, he created a parody poster of it using the Malaysian
Communications and Multimedia Commission (MCMC) . . .**
FMT Reporters (2016, February 5). Penjara 1 tahun, denda RM50k
menanti individu aib gambar pemimpin. *Free Malaysia Today.* https://
www.freemalaysiatoday.com/category/bahasa/2016/02/05/
penjara-1-tahun-denda-rm50k-menanti-individu-aib-gambar-pe
mimpin/?fbclid=IwAR3fHD8YftMelQc2Jil72MyXKNhghKWt8
QrCJLO0k3r3uCxISTY80Xi5xA4

20. **'I designed the warning poster as a piece of political satire . . .'**
Reza, F (2016, February 7). AMARAN: Henti Sebar Gambar . . .
Facebook. https://www.facebook.com/100000763298189/posts/
957285087640259/?d=n and The Malaysian Insider (2016,
February 8). MCMC not amused by artist Fahmi's latest parody.
Yahoo! News. https://sg.news.yahoo.com/mcmc-not-amused-artist-
fahmi-105700495.html

21. **BBC went first . . .** BBC Trending (2016, February 3). PM left red
nosed by censorship protest. *BBC News.* https://www.bbc.com/
news/blogs-trending-35486530

22. **His art had been, and always will be, only for social good.**
and **Sepatah Kata.** Reza, F. (2018, July 3). Nope. Dan sebagai
seorang freelance . . . Twitter. https://twitter.com/kuasasiswa/
status/1014019200182972417

Chapter 6

1. **The human-turned-crocodile who protected the river . . .** Baun,
L. (2020, December 13). Kenyah Folklore : Crocodile and Tiger.
YouTube. https://www.youtube.com/watch?v=td17zJwQIxc
2. **The assembly of animals, led by the king of the jungle . . .** Borneo
Post Online. (2014, July 22). Setting foot on 'Rock of Ages' at last.
Borneo Post Online. https://www.theborneopost.com/2014/07/22/
setting-foot-on-rock-of-ages-at-last/
3. **The white beast who turned into a beautiful woman . . .**
Dayak Pride (2016, June 10). Mysterious Kayan Hunter &
Beads Folklore—Teba'eng Inu. *Dayak Pride.* https://dayakpride.
wordpress.com/2016/06/10/mysterious-kayan-hunter-origin-of-
beads-folkfore-tebaeng-inu/
4. **Borneo's biodiversity concentration of 700 species for every
fifteen hectares . . .** Carrington, D. (2018, March 12). What is
biodiversity and why does it matter to us? *The Guardian.* https://
www.theguardian.com/news/2018/mar/12/what-is-biodiversity-
and-why-does-it-matter-to-us
5. **Orangutan is the smartest ape.** Solly, M. (2018, November
15). Orangutans Are the Only Non-Human Primates Capable
of 'Talking' About the Past. *Smithsonian Magazine.* https://www.
smithsonianmag.com/smart-news/orangutans-are-only-non-
human-primates-capable-talking-about-past-180970827/
6. **Borneo's 15,000-plant status ranked it the highest . . .** Facts
and Details. Borneo. https://factsanddetails.com/indonesia/
Minorities_and_Regions/sub6_3f/entry-6692.html#chapter-6
7. **'Probably the biggest environmental crime of our time'** Worrall,
S. (2015, January 10). Can Borneo's Tribes Survive 'Biggest
Environmental Crime of Our Times'? *National Geographic.* https://

www.nationalgeographic.com/culture/article/150111-borneo-rainforest-environment-conservation-ngbooktalk

8. **A February 2022 edition of *Nature Plants*...** (footnote). https://phys.org/news/2022-01-ancient-trees-deemed-vital-forest.html

9. **'Given substandard houses and infertile farmland' . . . 'floating houses'.** Gan, P.L. (2013, March 1). Megadam Project Galvanises Native Opposition in Malaysia. *National Geographic.* https://www.nationalgeographic.com/science/article/130227-malaysia-score-megadam-project and Borneo Post Online (2012, July 30). Uma Jawe residents ready to swap 'jelatongs' for longhouse. *Borneo Post Online.* http://www.theborneopost.com/2012/07/30/uma-jawe-residents-ready-to-swap-jelatongs-for-longhouse/#ixzz228uNHZOK

10. **. . . police shot a few bullets in the air as a sign of intimidation.** Papau, D. (2013, October 3). Police arrest a Penan near Murum dam. *Malaysiakini.* https://www.malaysiakini.com/news/242874

11. **He thought about the Swiss activist, Bruno Manser . . .** Human Rights Watch (1992). Defending the Earth: Abuses of Human Rights and the Environment. https://books.google.com.my/books?id=EYU5yqinsYMC&pg=PA62&redir_esc=y#v=onepage&q=Bruno%20Manser%20persona%20non%20grata&f=false

12. **Global Witness found that more than 700 environemntalists were murdered since 2001 . . .** Wallace, S. (2014, February). Why Do Environmentalists Keep Getting Killed Around the World? *Smithsonian Magazine.* https://www.smithsonianmag.com/science-nature/why-do-environmentalists-keep-getting-killed-around-world-180949446/

13. **Instead of obtaining the free, prior, and informed consent . . .** United Nations Declaration on the Rights of Indigenous People (2008). Article 32(2) of UNDRIP: States shall consult and cooperate in good faith with the indigenous peoples concerned through their own representative institutions in order to obtain their free and informed consent prior to the approval of any project

affecting their lands or territories and other resources, particularly in connection with the development, utilization or exploitation of mineral, water or other resources. Read: https://www.un.org/esa/socdev/unpfii/documents/DRIPS_en.pdf

14. **There was a townhall meeting . . .** Borneo Post Online (2015, May 17). Aye to Baram Dam Finally. *Sarawak Government.* https://sarawak.gov.my/web/home/news_view/119/5355

15. **In the months before, government-appointed consultants told villagers . . .** Lee, T. et al (2014, August). No Consent to Proceed: Indigenous Peoples' Rights Violations At The Proposed Baram Dam in Sarawak. *SAVE Rivers Network.* https://www.forestpeoples.org/sites/default/files/publication/2014/08/noconsenttoproceedbaramreport2014-1.pdf

16. **They also asked the villagers to fill the form with pencils . . .** Word, J. (2013, July 17). Coercion and Lies Along the Banks of the Baram. *The Borneo Project.* https://borneoproject.org/coercion-and-lies-along-the-banks-of-the-baram/

17. **'We, the leaders of the Orang Ulu people in Baram . . .'** Borneo Post Online (2014, May 22). Community leaders want action taken against SAVE Rivers. *Borneo Post Online.* https://www.theborneopost.com/2014/05/22/community-leaders-want-action-taken-against-save-rivers/

18. **We have worked so hard to promote the benefits of Baram [D]am . . .** Borneo Post Online (2014, September 4). Penghulu wants Baram HEP dam project to proceed. *Borneo Post Online.* https://www.theborneopost.com/2014/09/04/penghulu-wants-baram-hep-dam-project-to-proceed/

19. **Peter tried to laugh off the simmering despair . . .** Lau, C. (2016, July 17). Denounced by relatives, ex-engineer battles on for indigenous S'wakians. *Malaysiakini.* https://www.malaysiakini.com/news/348820

20. **'We have been victimized by the Bakun Dam!'** 草民电影 (2021, September 14). Bakun Dam 最大水坝 巴贡水坝 | 东马 Sarawak | 纪录片Documentary | 周泽南 Leerang Bato | Episode 3/3 CC Subtitle 字幕. YouTube. https://www.youtube.com/watch?v=blzwm_jDHuA

21. **'A cultural genocide'.** The Borneo Project (2016). Broken Promises: Displaced by Dams. Vimeo. https://vimeo.com/130516168? embedded=true&source=vimeo_logo&owner=29471553# at=144

22. **"The chief minister should just come here and bomb us . . ."** KiniTV (2016, April 21). Documentary: The dams damning Sarawak. YouTube. https://www.youtube.com/watch?v=HENYw YHD8Ys

23. **In his 1974 classic book . . .** Granovetter, M. (1974). Getting a Job: A Study of Contacts and Careers. *University of Chicago Press.* https://press.uchicago.edu/ucp/books/book/chicago/G/bo363 6056.html

24. **In another 1973 paper called 'The Strength of Weak Ties' . . .** Granovetter, M.S. (1973, May). The Strength of Weak Ties. *American Journal of Sociology Vol 78, No.6* https://www.jstor.org/ stable/2776392

25. **Through the multi-layered network of weak ties, Peter and a village headman . . .** The Borneo Project (2012, December 14). Victory for Sarawak Dams Campaign: Let's Keep up the Pressure! *The Borneo Project.* https://borneoproject.org/victory-for-sarawak-dams-campaign-help-us-to-keep-up-the-pressure-for-them-to-leave-immediately/

26. **Christine Milne.** Burling, A. (2012, December 5). Leader of Australian Greens call on Hydro Tas to get out of Sarawak. *YouTube.* https://www.youtube.com/watch?v=enip5030x2s

27. **Bob Brown.** Burling, A. (2012, December 2). Bob Brown meets Save Sarawak Rivers Tour. *YouTube.* https://www.youtube.com/ watch?v=SEPIC7ilU3Y

28. **Hydro Tasmania's annual report.** This annual report has since been taken down, as shown here: https://www.hydro.com.au/ annual-reports/2010/contents/people/page04.html. See Sarawak Report instead: Sarawak Report (2012, May 17). What Is Damn Well Going On?!—Australian Greens Query Hydro-Tasmania's Sarawak Projects. *Sarawak Report.* https://www.sarawakreport. org/2012/05/what-is-damn-well-going-on-australian-greens-query-hydro-tasmanias-sarawak-projects/

29. **300-megawatt coal-fired plant at Sabah's 'Eden'.** Pinkowski, J. (2011, February 22). Borneo Says No to Dirty Energy. *TIME*. http://content.time.com/time/health/article/0,8599,2052627,00.html

30. **The research paper found that the electricity that will be produced right up to Bakun Dam . . .** Shirley, R. and Kammen, D. (2015). Energy planning and development in Malaysian Borneo: Assessing the benefits of distributed technologies versus large scale energy mega-projects. *Energy Strategy Reviews 8 (2015) 15—29* https://www.sciencedirect.com/science/article/abs/pii/S2 211467X15000292

31. **Not even China during the peak of its industrialisation.** and **Rebekah Shirley suggested that 'micro-hydro and solar . . .'** The Borneo Project (2016). Development without Destruction. *The Borneo Project.* https://vimeo.com/159726367?embedded= true&source=vimeo_logo&owner=29471553

32. **In an Oxford study by Dr Atif Ansar et al . . .** (footnote). https://www.sciencedirect.com/science/article/abs/pii/S030142151 3010926

33. **Protest in front of the International Hydropower Conference.** Sarawak Report (2013, May 22). Protestors Make Their Voice Heard At Hydro-Power Conference. *Sarawak Report.* https://www.sarawakreport.org/2013/05/protestors-make-their-voice-heard-at-hydro-power-conference/

34. **SEB appointed NorPower . . .** (footnote). https://www.theedge markets.com/article/save-rivers-swedish-power-tech-company-agrees-review-business-malaysia

35. **Peter was referred by Jonas Ådnøy Holmqvist . . .** (footnote). https://www.sarawakreport.org/2014/05/22118/)

36. **They gathered in front of the banner for photos . . .** Mahadi, N. (2012, April 23). Ritual held to seek blessings for Baram dam. *Borneo Post Online.* https://www.theborneopost.com/2012/04/23/ritual-held-to-seek-blessings-for-baram-dam/

37. **In the Orang Ulu tradition...** (footnote). https://www.sarawakreport.org/2014/01/sarawak-energy-reported-for-bribing-natives-expose/

38. **Before the authorities turned away and left . . .** The Malaysian Insider (2014, October 25). Sarawak's Baram Dam protestors survive one year of blockading. *Yahoo! News.* https://malaysia. news.yahoo.com/sarawak-baram-dam-protestors-survive-one-blockading-025434325.html

39. **'I called all my relatives, my children, my grandchildren . . .'** Ujang, A. and Bernama (2016, March 15). Adenan recounts close shave with death and God's will. *Malaysiakini.* https://www. malaysiakini.com/news/333874

40. **'Put fear of God into the people who are dishonest.'** Yu, J. (2014, November 17). Adenan Satem warns Sarawak's timber industry. *The Star.* https://www.thestar.com.my/News/Nation/2014/11/17/ adenan-satem-tells-off-sarawak-logging-firms-on-corruption/

41. **The gazette that earmarked the customary land . . .** (footnote). https://www.malaysiakini.com/news/334694

42. **We see the stories of Bakun before and after the Bakun Dam . . .** 草民电影 (2021, September 14). Bakun Dam 最大水坝 巴贡水坝 | 东马 Sarawak | 纪录片 Documentary | 周泽南 Leerang Bato | Episode 3/3 CC Subtitle 字幕. *YouTube.* https://www. youtube.com/watch?v=blzwm_jDHuA

43. **'Like my friend, [People's Justice Party's political secretary] Bill Kayong . . .'** Seacology (2020). Peter Kallang—2019 Seacology Prize winner. *Vimeo.* https://vimeo.com/364366874

44. **'It's everyone's job to imagine the world we want to live in . . .'** Butler, R.A. (2021, June 9). 'Listening to communities must go beyond ticking compliance boxes,' says Peter Kallang, a Kenyah leader. *Mongabay.* https://news.mongabay.com/2021/06/listening-to-communities-must-go-beyond-ticking-compliance-boxes-says-peter-kallang-a-kenyah-leader/

Chapter 7

1. **Developments . . . were aggressive.** Idris, A.A. (2022, January 9). How poor town planning led to Taman Sri Muda's deadly floods. *The Vibes.* https://www.thevibes.com/articles/news/51594/how-poor-town-planning-led-to-taman-sri-mudas-deadly-floods

2. **Residents estimate . . . three times.** Ariff, I. and Ramachandran, J. (2022, January 1). How Taman Sri Muda 'drowned' in other people's water. *Free Malaysia Today.* https://www.freemalaysiatoday.com/category/nation/2022/01/01/how-taman-sri-muda-drowned-in-other-peoples-water/

3. **These are the ingredients to make a good cup of Punjabi cha . . .** (footnote). https://www.foodnetwork.ca/recipe/punjabi-cha-not-chai/

4. **Gurmat Parchar Sammelan is one of the largest . . .** (footnote). https://asiasamachar.com/2015/12/19/khalsa-land-set-to-host-malaysias-largest-gurmat-camp/

5. **There are approximately 80,000 Sikhs . . .** (footnote). https://www.taylorfrancis.com/chapters/mono/10.4324/9781315272214-9/sikhs-malaysia-largest-sikh-population-asia-swarn-singh-kahlon

6. **'It was a harrowing time . . .'** Bernama (2021, December 21). Thinking only of death while trapped for hours in flood—victim. *Malaysiakini.* https://www.malaysiakini.com/news/603885

7. **Megala Murthi, a thirty-something resident of Taman Sri Muda . . .** Mohanakrishnan, A. (2021, December 20). [VIDEO] 'We screamed for help, but no one from police station next door came'. *The Vibes.* https://www.thevibes.com/articles/news/50112/we-screamed-for-help-but-no-one-from-police-station-next-door-came-to-our-aid

8. **'Disaster of epic proportions'.** Azmi, H. (2021, December 20). Malaysian PM Ismail Sabri Yaakob's government under fire over slow response to worst floods in recent memory. *South China Morning Post.* https://www.scmp.com/week-asia/health-environment/article/3160453/malaysian-pm-ismail-sabri-yaakobs-government-under

9. **Faizal Azumu's launch ceremony.** Ramachandran, J. (2021, December 20). Netizens tick off Faizal for standing on ceremony. *Free Malaysia Today.* https://www.freemalaysiatoday.com/category/nation/2021/12/20/netizens-scold-faizal-for-standing-on-ceremony/

10. **Rina Harun's ceremony.** Hassan, H. (2021, December 21). Malaysians Slam Rina Harun for Allegedly Organising a Grand Ceremony For Flood Relief. *World of Buzz.* https://worldofbuzz. com/malaysians-slam-rina-harun-for-allegedly-organising-a-grand-ceremony-for-flood-relief/

11. **Ministers who arrived at the scene were booed . . .** Zunar Cartoonist (@zunarkartunis). Nah, ambik kau! Twitter. https://twitter.com/zunarkartunis/status/1473297725798031362

12. **The then finance minister was seen waving from a truck . . .** Jalal Misai (jllmisai). Pesta 4x4 oleh . . . Twitter. https://twitter.com/jllmisai/status/14725757910072975 36

13. **At the time of writing, the video on Twitter received only 176 retweets . . .** Ismail Sabri (@IsmailSabri60). Ramai terkesan dengan banjir kali ini . . . Twitter. https://twitter.com/IsmailSabri60/status/1472582739618529281

14. **Around 136,030 people were affected . . .** and **estimated loss of lives and money.** The Star (2022, January 21). PM: Flood warnings ignored. *The Star.* https://www.thestar.com.my/news/nation/2022/01/21/pm-flood-warnings-ignored and Aiman, A. (2021, December 24). Flood losses 'could amount to RM20 billion'. *Free Malaysia Today.* https://www.freemalaysiatoday. com/category/nation/2021/12/24/flood-losses-could-amount-to-rm20-billion/

15. **Historic, cultural, and sentimental value of items . . .** Rahman, S. (2022, March 16). 2022/26 "Malaysia's Floods of December 2021: Can Future Disasters be Avoided?". *ISEAS Perspective.* https:// www.iseas.edu.sg/articles-commentaries/iseas-perspective/2022-26-malaysias-floods-of-december-2021-can-future-disasters-be-avoided-by-serina-rahman/

16. **'Sleep log' and visiting a sleep lab.** Bryant, A. (2009, May 23). For This Guru, No Question Is Too Big. *The New York Times.* https://www.nytimes.com/2009/05/24/business/24collins.html?_ r=1&pagewanted=all

17. **Formula of Level Five Leader.** Collins, J. (2001, October 16). Good to Great: Why Some Companies Make the Leap . . . And Others Don't. *Random House Business Books.*

18. **PLEASE DON'T JUST FOCUS [ON] SELANGOR . . .**
Twitter user [limited viewing] https://twitter.com/min_dy0/
status/1472868053310328834

Chapter 8

1. All *Los Angeles Times* photos were used with permission, with Marcus
Yam's photos credited to him. All such photos are assumed to carry
the following copyright: **Copyright @ 2021 Los Angeles Times.**

2. **For a long time, Afghanistan was considered the worst place . . .**
Reuters (2009, November 19). UNICEF Names Afghanistan 'Worst
Place To Be Born'. *RadioFreeEurope.* https://www.rferl.org/a/
UNICEF_Names_Afghanistan_Worst_Place_To_Be_Born/
1882881.html

3. **Music was deemed to have a 'corrupting influence' . . .** Zohra
Music. https://www.zohra-music.org/

4. **A suicide bomber infiltrated the concert . . .** Nordland, R. (2015,
December 30). After Taliban Attack in Kabul, a Music Teacher
Keeps Playing. *The New York Times.* https://www.nytimes.
com/2015/12/31/world/asia/after-taliban-attack-in-kabul-a-
music-teacher-keeps-playing.html

5. **The Taliban, who claimed responsibility for the bombing
. . .** Rasmussen, S.E. (2015, May 25). He was the saviour of Afghan
music. Then a Taliban bomb took his hearing. *The Guardian.*
https://www.theguardian.com/world/2015/may/25/he-was-the-
saviour-of-afghan-music-then-a-taliban-bomb-took-his-hearing

6. **"[W]e realized the Taliban knew about us . . ."** and **"[The
Talibans] can send bombers . . ."** and **"When I play music
[here], it makes me feel safe."** and **Music was one of the first
things the Taliban came to control.** CNA Insider (2022, October
15). Music Is Bann'd In Taliban's Afghanistan But These Women
Play On | Keeping The–Music Alive - Part 1. YouTube. https://
www.youtube.com/watch?v=BWixNX3jetA

7. **"The initial idea was to form a pop group of four to five girls . . ."**
Los Angeles Times (2021, December 9). For Afghans, a bittersweet
escape from a music school gone silent. YouTube. https://www.
youtube.com/watch?v=uJReLCvSLO8

8. **"We can't build a democratic society in Afghanistan . . ."** Nelson, S.S. (2017, January 31). All-Female Orchestra From Afghanistan Is A Force For Change. *NPR.* https://www.npr.org/sections/goatsandsoda/2017/01/31/512592727/all-female-orchestra-from-afghanistan-is-a-force-for-change

9. **They used Twitter, through their spokesperson Zabihullah Mujahid . . .** Brooking, E.T. (2021, August 26). Before the Taliban took Afghanistan, it took the internet. *Atlantic Council.* https://www.atlanticcouncil.org/blogs/new-atlanticist/before-the-taliban-took-afghanistan-it-took-the-internet/

10. **The Taliban's op-ed on *The New York Times.*** Haqqani, S. (2020, February 20). What We, the Taliban, Want. *The New York Times.* https://www.nytimes.com/2020/02/20/opinion/taliban-afghanistan-war-haqqani.html

11. **. . . brokered ceasefire with the Afghan government . . .** BBC News (2018, June 9). Afghan Taliban agree three-day ceasefire— their first. *BBC News.* https://www.bbc.com/news/world-asia-44423032

12. **Peace settlement with the United States.** Thomas, C. (2022, December 1). Afghanistan: Background and U.S. Policy in Brief. *Congressional Research Service.* https://fas.org/sgp/crs/row/R45122.pdf

13. **The renewed international standing was meant to distract and make people forget . . .** Bearak, B. (2001, March 4). Over World Protests, Taliban Are Destroying Ancient Buddhas. *The New York Times.* https://www.nytimes.com/2001/03/04/world/over-world-protests-taliban-are-destroying-ancient-buddhas.html

14. **"We don't know whether the Taliban are coming or not . . ."** and **Marcus Yam 5 (photo)** (adapted by author) Bulos, N. and Yam, M. (2021, December 8). The bittersweet escape for Afghans from a music school gone silent. *Los Angeles Times.* https://www.latimes.com/projects/afghan-music-institute-students-evacuated-taliban/

15. **Bombing of Sayed al-Shuhada.** Wikipedia. 2021 Kabul school bombing. https://en.wikipedia.org/wiki/2021_Kabul_school_bombing

16. **Marcus Yam's awards.** Marcus Yam (Profile). Los Angeles Times. https://www.latimes.com/people/marcus-yam#:~:text=Marcus

%20Yam%20is%20a%20roving,of%20conflict%2C%20 struggle%20and%20intimacy.

17. **Beirut explosion in 2020.** Wikipedia. 2020 Beirut explosion. https://en.wikipedia.org/wiki/2020_Beirut_explosion# Investigation

18. **That was until the province of Zaranj fell . . .** Nossiter, A., Shah, T., and Abed, F. (2021, August 6). Taliban Seize Afghan Provincial Capital Just Weeks Before Final U.S. Withdrawal. *The New York Times.* https://www.nytimes.com/2021/08/06/world/asia/taliban-afghanistan-capital-zaranj.html

19. **'Men and women tugged at my shirt . . .'** and **Marcus Yam 1 (photo)** and **'An elderly man in a bloodstained sports jacket . . .'** and **Marcus Yam 2 (photo)** and **Marcus Yam 3 (photo)** and **Marcus Yam 4 (photo)** Yam, M. (2021, December 31). A Times journalist's diary inside the fall of Afghanistan. *Los Angeles Times.* https://www.latimes.com/projects/afghanistan-photo-diary/

20. **'Afghanistan is dead. I am dead . . .'** Yam, M. and King, L. (2021, August 15). A falling capital's final hours: Fear, havoc and gridlock—then eerie silence. *The New York Times.* https://www. latimes.com/world-nation/story/2021-08-15/a-falling-capitals-final-hours-fear-chaos-and-gridlock-then-eerie-silence

21. **A few hung on to the wings of aircrafts . . .** Harding, L. and Doherty, B. (2021, August 16). Kabul airport: footage appears to show Afghans falling from plane after takeoff. *The Guardian.* https://www.theguardian.com/world/2021/aug/16/kabul-airport-chaos-and-panic-as-afghans-and-foreigners-attempt-to-flee-the-capital

22. **'Bloodthirsty statements'.** Wright, G. (2021, August 17). Afghanistan: Mysterious Taliban spokesman finally shows his face. *BBC News.* https://www.bbc.com/news/world-asia-58250607

23. **Independent journalism, prevent base of terrorism . . .** and **'Once again I would like to assure the media . . .'** Al Jazeera English (2021, August 17). Transcript of Taliban's first news conference in Kabul. *Al Jazeera English.* https://www.aljazeera.com/news/2021/8/17/transcript-of-talibans-first-press-conference-in-kabul

24. **'I moved out of the direct line of where the rifles ...'** Los Angeles Times Events (2021, November 11). Nov. 10: Ask a Reporter with foreign correspondent Marcus Yam. YouTube. https://www. youtube.com/watch?v=Hu2UfQI45ls

25. **In a Zoom call with the newsroom that same night...** (footnote). https://www.latimes.com/world-nation/story/2022-05-09/times-photographer-marcus-yam-wins-pulitzer-prize

26. **Unlike Marcus, Nemat Naqdi did not get his glasses back.** Bulos, N. and Yam, M. (2021, September 8). Taliban beats protestors and arrests journalists at women's rally in Kabul. *Los Angeles Times.* https://www.latimes.com/world-nation/story/2021-09-08/women-protest-against-taliban-responds-with-force

27. **Forty-year-old Zamairi Ahmadi, an aid worker ...** BBC News (2021, September 18). Afghanistan: US admits Kabul drone strike killed civilians. *BBC News.* https://www.bbc.com/news/world-us-canada-58604655

28. **A loud bang hit the neighbourhood, shaking houses.** Tribune News Service (2021, August 31). Afghan family says 7 children were killed in Kabul drone strike; US investigating. *South China Morning Post.* https://www.scmp.com/news/world/russia-central-asia/article/3146998/afghan-family-says-7-children-were-killed-kabul

29. **'Next time you don't try to kill a civilians.'** Yam, M. (@yamphoto). I met Emal Ahmadi . . . Twitter. https://twitter.com/yamphoto/status/1438971506118307843

30. **Taliban breaking promise about women and university.** Guardian staff and agencies (2022, December 23). Taliban minister defends closing universities to women as global backlash grows. *The Guardian.* https://www.theguardian.com/world/2022/dec/23/taliban-minister-defends-closing-universities-to-women-as-global-backlash-grows

31. **Teenage girls banned from secondary school.** Wintour, P. (2022, March 27). Taliban reversal on girls' education derails US plan for diplomatic recognition. *The Guardian.* https://www.theguardian.com/world/2022/mar/27/taliban-bar-girls-education-us-plan-diplomatic-recognition

32. **Women banned from seeing male doctors.** Sharma, I. (2023, January 12). Taliban Terror: Afghan Women Banned From Seeing Male Doctors, Athletes Barred From Playing. *India Times.* https://www.indiatimes.com/trending/social-relevance/afghan-women-banned-from-seeing-male-doctors-beauty-salons-to-shut-down-590044.html

33. **'Defeat the beast with the beauty of music.'** CNA Insider (2022, October 15). Afghan Music Lives On With All-Female Orchestra In Refuge | Keeping –he Music Alive - Part 2/2. YouTube. https://www.youtube.com/watch?v=4wK0ptrpnUs

34. **Saudi Arabia and Kenya winning more.** Reiche, D. (2016). Success and Failure of Countries at the Olympic Games. *Routledge.* https://www.routledge.com/Success-and-Failure-of-Countries-at-the-Olympic-Games/Reiche/p/book/9781138797215

35. **42–100 per cent medals from three sports.** Houlihan, B. and Zheng, J. (2013). The Olympics and Elite Sport Policy: Where Will It All End? *The International Journal of the History of Sport Vol 30.* https://www.tandfonline.com/doi/abs/10.1080/09523367.2013.765726

36. **South Korea's reign in women's archery.** Olympics (2021, March 31). Republic of Korea's archers extend their Olympic reign. *Olympics.* https://olympics.com/en/news/south-korean-archers-extend-their-olympic-reign

37. **'Before hard work comes play . . .'** Duckworth, A. (2017). Grit: The Power of Passion and Perseverance. *Vermilion.*

38. **'I was a natural busybody . . .'** Hendersen, K. Seizing the Moment. *At Buffalo.* https://www.buffalo.edu/alumni/at-buffalo.host.html/content/shared/www/alumni/stories/alumni-stories/opportunity-knocks/seizing-the-moment.detail.html

39. **That allowed him to hunt stories to its fullest . . .** Pignataro, T.J. (2013, July 16). Composite Sketch of Serial Arson Suspect Released. *Buffalo News.* https://buffalonews.com/news/composite-sketch-of-serial-arson-suspect-released/article_c93dd81e-bc55-51ec-839f-4a24c1382640.html

40. **The Battle of Mosul in Iraq was the single largest battle of that decade.** Watson, B. What the Largest Battle of the Decade Says

About the Future of War. *Defense One*. https://www.defenseone. com/feature/mosul-largest-battle-decade-future-of-war/

41. **ISIS's past track record in Iraq.** Yan, H. and Muaddi, N. (2021, March 9). Why the battle for Mosul matters in the fight against ISIS. *CNN*. http://edition.cnn.com/2016/10/17/middleeast/battle-for-mosul/

42. **'Goes against every instinct we have'.** Widyatmadja, G. and Lisenby, A. (2022, March 19). A photojournalist in Ukraine heads toward deadly conflict to humanize war. *NPR*. https://www.npr.org/sections/pictureshow/2022/03/19/1087533721/marcus-yam-ukraine-photos

43. **'Raw and urgent images of the US departure from Afghanistan . . .'** The Pulitzer Prizes. Marcus Yam of the Los Angeles Times. https://www.pulitzer.org/winners/marcus-yam-los-angeles-times

44. **'My gosh, a Puliltzer Prize . . .'** Yam, M. (@yamphoto) and Los Angeles Times (@latimesphotos). Instagram. https://www.instagram.com/p/CdxDHTwur3S/

45. **Epilogue: Sorrow and Defiance** or **Marcus Yam Photo 6 (photo).** Yam, M. Sorrow and Defiance. https://www.marcusyam.com/sorrow-and-defiance/cnuh3foruzhxdw2ibex9l8q4vfy7zy

46. **Epilogue: Afghan soldier looking out the window** or **Marcus Yam Photo 7 (photo).** Yam, M. Singles. https://www.marcusyam.com/singles/tbo08zarjj1rlp1iqj5dkm0zsj04b0

47. **Epilogue: Death from Above** or **Marcus Yam Photo 8 (photo).** Yam, M. Death From Above. https://www.marcusyam.com/death-from-above/3gje8r28wwy9tdect3uhjfo7hvlaos

48. **Epilogue: California Burning** or **Marcus Yam Photo 9 (photo).** Yam, M. California Burning. https://www.marcusyam.com/california-burning/irj5nyfbqfoj2jzzhovk1scwbpib9m

49. **Epilogue: "Dear Marcus Yam, I stood a few feet from you . . ."** or **Marcus Yam Photo 10 (photo).** Yam, M. Brief But Spectacular. *PBS News Hour*. https://www.pbs.org/newshour/brief/307459/marcus-yam

50. **Epilogue: Great March of Return** or **Marcus Yam Photo 11 (photo).** Yam, M. Great March Of Return. https://www.marcusyam.com/great-march-of-return/dvoho9b8p6tqqb5lbkr1juxjpodge4

and https://www.marcusyam.com/great-march-of-return/4bunb1
9gsiphu3viak4cu0zvdbvm0h

51. **Epilogue: Oso Landslide** or **Marcus Yam Photo 12 (photo).** Yam,
M. Shades of Hollywood. https://www.marcusyam.com/oso-land
slide/pocr15mq3n14mxobupysa3fz3argy5 and https://www.mar
cusyam.com/oso-landslide/od0yinw5xjckmsr3kz42wmbgqu1zi8'